MW00974593

Н. ЧЕРКАСОВ

Записки

СОВЕТСКОГО

АКТЕРА

N. CHERKASOV

Notes
OF A SOVIET
ACTOR

University Press of the Pacific
Honolulu, Hawaii

Notes of a Soviet Actor

by
N. Cherkasov

ISBN: 1-4102-1451-6

Copyright © 2004 by University Press of the Pacific

Reprinted from the original edition

University Press of the Pacific
Honolulu, Hawaii
http://www.universitypressofthepacific.com

All rights reserved, including the right to reproduce
this book, or portions thereof, in any form.

CONTENTS

THE BEGINNING

Every actor comes to the theatre in his own way. My acting career started in the early years of Soviet rule, after the October Revolution had thrown the gates of the theatre wide open to the masses. And since at that time my adolescent interests lay mostly in music, it is only natural that I began with the opera.

Music had been my love since childhood. I first heard it in my own home. In those days we lived in a big, sombre house in one of the most densely populated districts of St. Petersburg. Father was master of the St. Petersburg-Baltic Station, and our living quarters were provided by the railway administration. In the evenings and on Sundays Mother often played the piano—she loved music and was quite an accomplished pianiste. Father, too, was fond of music; he encouraged us in every possible way and later, when I was old enough, he often took me to the opera and symphony concerts.

I was still a lad when I first heard Feodor Chaliapin, and his portrayal in Moussorgsky's opera *Boris Godunov* left an indelible impression. I was little prepared for what I was to see and hear. Chaliapin's performance, from the coronation scene on, awakened in me a feeling of joy and unbounded enthusiasm. The scene in which Tsar Boris questions Shuisky about the death of Tsarevich Dmitri and the hallucination episode held me spellbound. Chaliapin's monologue in the death scene stunned me. Never shall I forget the way in which he spoke his lines, his horrified "What is that in the corner?" at the beginning of the hallucination scene and his deeply tragic cry "Wait, I am still tsar!"

I saw Chaliapin in that role many times after that, oftener than not from the wings, and I gradually came to grasp the finer points of his recitative art. It was as Boris that he excelled, for his monologues gave him ample opportunity to display his talent not only as a singer, but also as a tragedian. Those later impressions, instructive and thrilling as they were, could not erase the first. Rereading Pushkin's tragedy, I realized that there was only one way of faithfully interpreting the great poet's masterpiece, and that was through Moussorgsky's music and Chaliapin's intonations.

At that time my interest in art was restricted to the Narodny Opera House, where Chaliapin was appearing on the eve of the Revolution, the summer symphony concerts at the Pavlovsky Railway Station, the concerts by Count Sheremetiev's private orchestra and the philharmonic matinées. I was not at all attracted to the drama, and the first plays I saw at the Alexandrinsky Theatre made no impression; in fact, they left me cool. I thought then it was only musicians and opera singers who worked hard to achieve perfection and that it was simple and easy for anyone, even a beginner, to play in drama. In short, the interest that art had awakened in me was drawing me more and more to music.

Here Nature herself had a hand. I had a good ear for music, an excellent sense of rhythm and a fine memory. I could sit down at the piano and pick up any tune I had heard and liked, and I delighted in putting into notes the music that was surging in me. I could read music even before I had learned to spell, and by the time I was sixteen I could play piano duets, including Chaikovsky's "Sixth Symphony."

After the Great October Socialist Revolution the common people filled the theatres, museums, concert halls and palaces. In the past, visits to the opera house and concert halls were a holiday treat for me. Now, as I went there oftener, I grew increasingly fonder of art, particularly music. In those stormy revolutionary days, music rang everywhere—even in that once "unshakable" citadel of autocracy, the Winter Palace, in its Gerbovy and Georgievsky halls, where the first public concerts by the former court orchestra, renamed the First Communal Orchestra, were given as early as the spring of 1918. It was not hard to get tickets for those concerts, particularly for school pupils who were admitted free of charge. Here, in palatial surroundings, I delighted in Beethoven and Chaikovsky. Even St. Petersburg's premier theatre, the famed Mariinsky, threw open its doors to all.

Before the Revolution, it was perhaps the most exclusive theatre in the capital. It was owned by and catered to the élite; most of its tickets were distributed among season-ticket holders, and almost hereditary at that. For the ordinary man, there were two performances a week at most. One could never get a good seat: they were either distributed among friends or grabbed by spivs who resold them at a profit. It was quite an event to get inside the theatre and one had to queue up at the box-office at about midnight to procure a gallery ticket for the next evening.

My parents once took me to the Mariinsky Theatre to see Glinka's *Ruslan and Lyudmila*. From our seats we had a good view of the theatre's beautiful plafond with its huge crystal chandelier, but could see only part of the stage. And in spite of this I was deeply impressed by the wonders of what I saw and heard that evening—the Mariinsky orchestra, singers, chorus and ballet, scenery and costumes, and fairy-like effects—from Ruslan's battle with The Head to multicolour fountains. On another occasion I saw Borodin's *Prince Igor*, one of the theatre's masterpieces, distinguished by the splendid singing of the soloists, beautiful sets, the unforgettable Polovtsian dances and the perfect harmony of the chorus. Later I saw the theatre's famed ballet company, first in *The Sleeping Beauty* and then in *The Swan Lake*. I loved the music of the latter and could play it almost by heart.

Enthralled as I was by music, I was fascinated by other peculiarities inherent in the theatre. I could hear a melody in the discordant sounds that filled the auditorium as the musicians sat down to tune up their instruments, or guess the time of the day in the opening scene just from the colour of the footlights. Technical effects stimulated my inquisitiveness and added to the wealth and variety of the impressions I got from the opera and ballet.

The Mariinsky Theatre—its architectural form and the blue auditorium with velvet curtains and hangings, its orchestra and stage—seemed a fountain of art accessible to only the chosen few. After the October Revolution the doors of this temple of art were thrown open to all.

The school I was attending was reorganized into a trade school and we were given free tickets for special shows at the Mariinsky Theatre. Before the performance, A. V. Lunacharsky, then People's Commissar of Education of the Russian Soviet Federative Socialist Republic, usually made a speech, telling his young spectators that the Soviet government had set itself the task of making art accessible to all working people and that, hard times notwithstanding, old theatres would be preserved. The new audiences filling their auditoriums would stimulate them to new achievement. Then he would explain the substance of the opera and describe its characters. Chaliapin, who had returned to the Mariinsky after a brief engagement at another theatre, sang in most operas, and that alone was enough to give the presentation a festive air.

Briefly, the famous theatre was no longer exclusive and I became one of its habitués. I was there at least once a week and saw some of the operas for which it was difficult to get tickets even in those days, for instance, Chaliapin's jubilee performance in Rubinstein's *The Demon* early in the spring of 1919.

I had heard *The Demon* six or seven times with some first-class singers in the cast and knew it very well, but what Chaliapin achieved in the title role surpassed all expectation. His performance was the grandest, most powerful and striking I had ever seen.

The famous bass was superb in the role of the infatuated Demon. He succeeded in moulding a picture of a majestic and at the same time ephemeral being: he would suddenly appear as if from nowhere, just as suddenly grow to full stature and then no less suddenly vanish from sight. He achieved this effect by draping himself in a long cloak of purple-grey muslin thrown loosely over his chain mail. It was in this opera that I really saw and understood the greatness of this singer, his genius in creating a thrilling character.

Many years later, on my way to the Far East where I was to make personal appearances at various army units, I heard Chaliapin's recording of the Demon's aria just as the train was skirting Lake Baikal. The words—"Sailing in the air without rudder or mast", and the view of the lake brought forth memories. The grandeur of the Baikal and the magnificence of Chaliapin's voice seemed to blend naturally to make an organic whole.

Perhaps one of the reasons why I remember Chaliapin's jubilee performance so well is that it was some two weeks later that I made my stage début—at the Mariinsky.

I had met a friend who was a supernumerary there, and he had told me that there were jobs of this type at the theatre. I was thrilled at the very thought that here was a chance to get into my favourite theatre, and applied to the man in charge of the supers.

This person, Yermakov, was very useful in the theatre, and quite a specialist in his field. Almost illiterate and without any musical education, he knew the scores of all the operas and ballets produced by the Mariinsky Theatre, could describe off-hand the mises-en-scène of various mass scenes, stage processions just as the régisseur planned them, and faultlessly direct the supers. It was he who chose them, and they were known as "Yermakov's boys and girls."

I was immediately engaged, probably because of my height, and was told to report on the morrow, this time by the stage entrance. I was cast in a dramatization of "The Internationale" and then, at the discretion of the régisseur, in several scenes in *Boris Godunov*.

It was a special performance, staged for the first recruits of the newly-established General Military Training Organization, and the theatre was packed with young people.

The audience was first addressed by the War Commissar and then by Lunacharsky. In the meantime I took up my place on a dais in the centre of the stage, dressed in a shirt with sleeves rolled up and a blue apron, and with a big hammer in hand. My thinnish arms were painted up to look strong and sinewy. Facing me was another super, dressed as a peasant and holding a sickle. We were told how to stand, how to grasp each other's hand, how to hold the hammer and the sickle in our free hands. On either side of us were the other participants—on one, armed defenders of the Revolution, Red Guardsmen with rifles and sailors with cartridge-belts over their shoulders; on the other, peaceful workers, representatives of various nationalities, some of them with scythes and rakes. In front, there were children holding little flags.

There was an outburst of applause, and Lunacharsky walked off the proscenium.

The mighty strains of "The Internationale," sung by the chorus to orchestral accompaniment, reverberated in the auditorium. Stage lights went on, and the curtain rose, revealing a dramatic scene symbolizing the unity of workers and peasants. A powerful spotlight illuminated the sculptured emblem of the R.S.F.S.R. in the rear of the stage. The last refrain was drowned in applause.

There was a short intermission, and I rushed to change for the second scene of the prologue to *Boris Godunov*.

Garbed in the long and heavy boyar costume, embroidered with gold and adorned with multicolour gems, and sporting a short beard hastily pasted on my chin by the make-up artist, I waited for the signal to go on to the stage.

The first scene was drawing to a close.

I watched enchanted. Then the curtain came down, the drop scenery went up, the dais near by was being moved on to the stage. Suddenly I received a sharp blow on the shoulder.

"Hey, newcomer, get out of the way," an elderly red-bearded carpenter shouted as stage hands scurried to and fro, changing props and settings, getting the stage ready for the second scene. Confused by the hustle and bustle, I lost all sense of direction, and it was some time before I stepped aside.

The orchestra finally struck up and the curtain rose for the coronation scene.

As one of the tallest, I was placed in the first pair of the boyars following Boris Godunov in the procession. My partner, dressed and bearded exactly as I, was a well-built youth, Yevgeni Mravinsky, later one of my closest friends. At that time he was in his last year at school and played bit roles at the Mariinsky Theatre. A few years later he became conductor at the same theatre and then chief conductor of the Leningrad Philharmonic.

We were waiting for the signal to walk on to a broad dais covered with red cloth. Before us, huddled closely together, were boyar children, the *ryndas** with their golden axes, and the *streltsi.***

"Follow Chaliapin a step away straight up the dais," the régisseur told me.

The man was Isai Dvorishchin, and Chaliapin, whose operas he always directed, had great faith in him.

"Only don't rush Chaliapin," he continued. "Keep a little bit behind and walk in step with your partner. After this scene, change into another costume. You'll be a bailiff in the tavern scene. I'll explain the mise-en-scène during the intermission."

* Tsar's body-guards.
** Muscovite standing army in the 14th-17th centuries.

We could hear Prince Shuisky addressing the people, and at that moment Chaliapin, resplendent in his tsar's regalia, glided on to the stage.

The chorus greeted Boris Godunov with "Glory." The coronation procession was on. Chaliapin took his place before us and walked on to the dais amidst thunderous applause from the audience. Keeping in step with Mravinsky, I followed him. This was the first time I saw the auditorium from the stage. I took up my place next to Chaliapin. It was a thrilling experience—taking part in the ceremonial scene that I knew so well and had so often applauded with all my youthful fervour.

With a sweeping gesture Chaliapin placed his right hand on the heart. I had seen this gesture so often and knew it so well that I did not have to see it to picture how the gems of his rings sparkled in the stage light. Then in a voice filled with emotion and sorrow he sang the first words of his aria:

> My soul's afire.
> My heart, despite myself,
> Is cruelly troubled
> With ominous foreboding.

Blinking from the lights, I saw the familiar auditorium as if in a mist. Far down the central aisle, as it seemed to me, I saw something white fluttering like a little flag or a handkerchief. I strained my eyes and saw that this little "flag" was really quite near, that it was the starched dicky of the conductor.

Chaliapin was finishing his speech to the people, and was moving abruptly yet majestically to the Arkhangelsky Cathedral in the left corner of the stage. The church bells were tolling and the chorus was singing a hymn when Tsar Boris emerged from the cathedral at the head of the procession. The curtain fell and rose several times before it finally came down.

I rushed to the supers' dressing-room on the third floor to prepare myself for the tavern scene. After that I played in the Polish act and finally in the death scene. On the whole, my début passed off without a hitch and I was told to return on the morrow, for the day rehearsal this time.

The unforgettable 1919! This was the time of the heroic defence of Red Petrograd, which had so deeply impressed itself on the younger generation whose life was then only beginning.

There were difficulties at every step. The Revolution was felt everywhere and in everything, and constantly set us new, unexpected tasks. Life was hard. We lived through the winter in an almost unheated house; the walls were often covered with rime. We never had enough to eat, and in spring we learned what famine was. I felt very weak, always hungry, but despite it extremely buoyant: firstly, because like everybody else I was swept by revolutionary enthusiasm; secondly, because my youthful dream had come true and I was on the stage; and thirdly, because—and that went for all of my generation—there were wonderful prospects ahead.

We lived through some anxious days in May and June 1919. The front line was just outside Petrograd's walls. In the day it was graduation exams at the trade school, in the evening the Mariinsky Theatre. Most of the performances were for the fighters going to the front, for the newly-mobilized Baltic sailors, for the delegates attending poor peasants' conferences and congresses. No sooner had I graduated than I was mobilized by the General Military Training Organization and sent to build defences immediately behind the front lines. There were many other youths of my age, and we dug trenches, filled bags with sand and erected parapets, and did it all enthusiastically. Mine was but a very insignificant contribution to the city's defence, but I was nevertheless proud of it.

Demobilized after the rout of the Whiteguards (since I had been called up before time and was not yet sixteen), I followed my school friends' advice and applied for admission to the Military Medical Academy although, I must say, I was not over-eager to become a doctor. At the same time I wanted to strengthen my ties with the theatre and enrolled for the short-term pantomime course that had been organized at the Mariinsky. We were taught plastic movements and pantomime, rhythmics, expressive gestures and dances—especially the dances from *Eugene Onegin, The Queen of Spades* and other operas of the Mariinsky repertoire.

The course was quite easy and did not take up much time. That gave me ample opportunity to do other things. I played piano at youth dances and did extra roles at the Bolshoi Drama Theatre. It was hard for the family to make ends meet and I took every chance to earn some money.

The Bolshoi Drama Theatre was the first theatre established in Petrograd after the Revolution and was very popular with young people. It was set up on the initiative of Maxim Gorky, and Chaliapin had a hand in its organization. We were genuinely thrilled by the romantic characters at its première—Schiller's *Don Carlos*, one of the most popular plays at that time.

The atmosphere at the Bolshoi Drama Theatre was radically different from that at the Mariinsky, and I sensed it the very first time I went there. There was still an undercurrent of bureaucracy in the Mariinsky management, and the vestiges of the past, particularly its caste character, were keenly felt. We, the young actors, always had the feeling that we were outsiders, unnoticed and avoided. At the Bolshoi Drama Theatre, on the other hand, I at once knew I was one of the family, a member of a closely-knit collective, though I was doing only minor roles. There was comradery because we were all convinced that it was necessary to stage heroic plays, because we put our faith in Gorky's words that the modern theatre should present a hero in the full sense of the word. This faith was our motive force and was reflected in all our activity.

In the summer of 1919 I took part in two new plays—*The Destroyer of Jerusalem* by the Finnish playwright Arvid Järnefelt and *Danton* by Maria Levberg. In the first I appeared in a mass scene and in two episodes with Yuri Yuriev who played the title role. In *Danton* I was engaged in mass scenes and did a pantomime bit as a citizen of revolutionary Paris. The régisseur and his assistants thoroughly acquainted us with our little roles and even allowed us to attend rehearsals in which we were not engaged. Thus, I saw Schiller's *Robbers* and watched régisseur Boris Sushkevich and the leading players, Vladimir Maximov and Nikolai Monakhov. I was becoming used to dramatic

The "Pat, Pataschon and Charlie Chaplin"
number from the film *Concert No. 1*. 1938

As Don Quixote. 1926

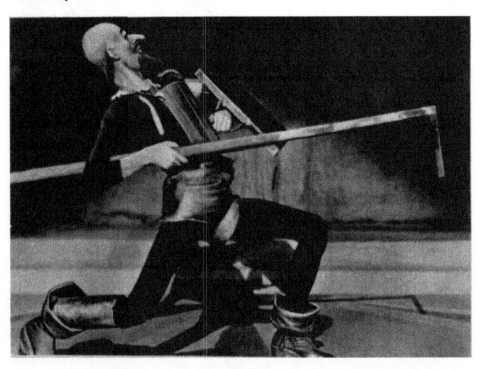

art. In those days romantic plays dealing with the conflict of passions and exalting and idealizing the hero were more popular with the younger generation than minor psychological dramas about everyday life. I liked them too. But even at the Bolshoi Drama Theatre I continued to dream of an opera career, for to me opera was art with a capital A, since I considered music the most important of all arts.

That is why I was so impatient for the pantomime contest at the Mariinsky Theatre which I thought would decide my future. I passed the various exercises successfully and on July 23, 1919, signed my first stage contract.

The atmosphere at the Mariinsky was one of full-blooded, brisk creative activity. Despite all difficulties it proved worthy of the tasks it had been set, popularizing Russian classical music and improving the quality of its performances.

The Revolution was exerting a vast influence on the theatre, and this could be seen in its productions. Very often the theatre was the venue of congresses and conferences which were usually rounded out by concerts and pageants on revolutionary themes. There were no admission fees for the shows, and the tickets were distributed among workers, students and school children. Most of the shows were for the Red Army and Navy. Petrograd continued to lead a front-line existence and that laid its imprint on the activity of its premier theatre too: it had close ties with the army, made concert tours of various units, gave special performances for soldiers and sailors, and the entire company were supplied with Red Army rations by the Political Department of the Seventh Army then defending the city.

The old Mariinsky Theatre would never have been able to stand the pace of revolutionary life, its conditions and demands. At the time I joined it there were only about 50 per cent of old members left; the rest were new, and that gave the theatre the necessary stimulus. The theatre had been on the down grade the season before: its repertoire had dwindled down considerably. Now it was growing, and in the spring of 1920 there were 27 operas on its list, among them all the best-known classics of the Russian musical genius—the works of Glinka, Dargomizhsky, Serov, Moussorgsky, Borodin, Chaikovsky and

Rimsky-Korsakov. The theatre itself was renamed the Academic Opera and Ballet Theatre.

Engaged by the theatre, I set about the little tasks entrusted to me with all the fervour of youth.

Performances usually started at 6.30 p.m., sometimes even at six. Because it was necessary to economize on power, tram services terminated at about the same time and life in the streets soon came to a standstill.

When I was not engaged in rehearsals I would come to the theatre about an hour and a half before the show. Crossing the theatre's threshold, I would run up jauntily to the pantomimers' dressing-room on the third floor. The theatre was heated very seldom and all too little, and it was so cold in our dressing-room that water in a glass would freeze.

Warming myself with hot carrot tea, I would start preparing for the performance, dressing and making up with the greatest care even when my appearance was only in a mass scene. I had five or six bits to do every evening, depending on the opera, and each time I had to don a new costume and a new make-up. I played in every opera of the repertoire, knew them by heart and loved their music. It was this interest in music that guided my activities in the opera house.

The shows ended shortly after 10 p.m. and sometimes even earlier. In very particular cases, special trams were placed at the service of the audience and an announcement to this effect would usually be made during an intermission. Like everyone else, I always tried to avail myself of the opportunity of riding home, but most of the times I had to remain at the theatre for some reason, and then, armed with a curfew pass that allowed me to be out in the streets after 11 p.m. and proud that it was given me because I was doing a socially useful job, I would walk home. Never shall I forget those walks in the streets deserted but for military patrols that checked on the passes, nor the spring and summer of 1919 when the front line passed in the city's outskirts and appeals to the Petrograd workers to stem the White-guard advance on their city, orders on the mobilization of the Communists for the front and Civil War reports signed by V. I. Lenin were posted in the streets and even in our theatre.

I was proud that I was contributing, even though little, to the cause of the Revolution by taking part in stirring theatre performances, allegoric plays, and especially in the mass pageants in the city's squares on May Day and November 7.

On the third anniversary of the October Revolution, in 1920, I was engaged in the pageant "The Capture of the Winter Palace," staged in Palace Square. The role was that of a tsarist minister—a treacherous and cowardly bureaucratic official. I had a court uniform on and a cocked hat, and my appearance was greeted with hoots and jeers that sounded sweeter than applause.

I was kept very busy at the theatre, but it always gave me leave to take part in these pageants, and I shall ever remember them for their scope and the revolutionary enthusiasm they stimulated in the people.

However, to go back to the theatre—my first and true love. I was interested in every aspect of its complex mechanism and particularly in stage techniques. I took every opportunity to see how the trapdoor operated, how magic flights were staged and how the panoramic scenery in *The Sleeping Beauty* was moved.

I was interested even more in the chorus. And I never missed an opportunity to hear such choral masterpieces as the women's song in the last act of *The Maid of Pskov*, the villagers' chorus from *Prince Igor* or the *streltsi*'s song from *Khovanshchina*. The latter was invariably encored.

But what I was most interested in was the first-class orchestra, and I attended all the rehearsals I could. My friend Mravinsky and I had our favourite seats too—in the lower box immediately above the drummer—from which we had an excellent view of the orchestra and its conductor. With time I learned to understand his gestures and could guess correctly why he stopped the orchestra. I might add that I probably suffered even more than the musicians themselves when things went wrong, as they are apt to do during rehearsals. The musicians waged a bitter, but vain struggle against the cold; the theatre was heated very rarely and very little, the temperature on the stage and in the auditorium was seldom above 40° F., and because of that the sounds produced by wooden and brass instruments were sharp to the point of jarring on the ear.

I strove from the very first to find my place in this large theatre group that was working so hard in the extremely difficult conditions caused by nation-wide devastation.

The roles I was given in those days were insignificant, but I played each and every one of them to the best of my ability. In Rimsky-Korsakov's *Sadko* I was a "seaweed" in the underseas kingdom scene and I twisted and twined as if swaying in water. I doubt very much that anyone in the audience saw me in this mass scene, but that did not disturb me. The praise of my colleagues—the pantomimers, choristers and assistant régisseurs—was ample reward. In bigger character roles I worked with even greater zeal, gradually moulding myself into an actor.

In the opera *Tale of the Tsar Sultan* I was given a small pantomime role, that of a scribe looking after a tame squirrel that sat in a little crystal house, cracking nuts and whistling all day long. I perfected my movements to fit the rhythm of the music and had myself made up to look as near as possible like the scribe envisaged by Rimsky-Korsakov, complete with a goose pen in his ear.

In *Khovanshchina* I played Prince Ivan Khovansky's assassin. The role was dramatic and expressive, and although it lasted less than a minute it was quite important, since the episode marked one of the turning points of the drama. Prince Khovansky, splendidly played by Vasily Sharonov, is invited to a council in Tsarina Sophia's chambers. At first he refuses the unexpected invitation, but soon gives in to flattery and orders his best attire to be brought in. As he starts out, I appear at the door, pause for a fraction of a second and then plunge a dagger into his heart. The Prince falls dead. Such parts taught me to act with precision, to move and gesticulate with plastic expressiveness and in time with the music.

It was while I was playing my first episodical roles that Dvorishchin noticed me. It was he who had directed me in my début. He rose from a chorister to become one of the most gifted régisseurs in the theatre and was utterly devoted to the stage. A favourite with Chaliapin, he exerted a considerable influence on the famous singer and at his request supervised all the operas in which he appeared and particularly the scenes in which Chaliapin was engaged. It was also at Chaliapin's request that Dvorishchin played Misail in the tavern scene in *Boris Godunov* when the former sang the role of Varlaam, and I must say that Dvorishchin played that little role to perfection. Sympathetic and very attentive to young actors, Dvorishchin did much to help them in their work.

That season I was often cast in ballet, at first in mass scenes and then in pantomime episodes. One of my first appearances was in Glazunov's *Raymonda*.

In the early years of the Revolution the famous composer himself conducted the orchestra, and that made his ballet doubly fascinating. The audience loved to see him behind the conductor's stand. The musicians used to greet him by striking the sounding boards of their instruments with the bow, the excitement spread to the auditorium and grew into ovation. An uninitiated theatre-goer, unaware that the auditorium was applauding a famous composer, would have been justified in expecting something out of the ordinary in the art of conducting. But Glazunov conducted somewhat sluggishly. Now and then he would look at a musician and nod approvingly. There was nothing extraordinary in the way he conducted *Raymonda,* and yet there was something exciting in it all: wasn't it the author, the beloved and venerable composer himself who was conducting! And everybody—in the auditorium, on the stage and in the orchestra pit—was happy to see and honour him as a composer and as the author of the ballet, and that was enough to make his appearance a success.

After *Raymonda* in which I played a knight, I was given more ballet roles. How happy I was when I was cast in two bigger parts! True, they were still episodic, but I rehearsed them as if they were star roles. I was a drum major in Stravinsky's *Petrushka* and Knight of the Day in his *Fire-Bird*.

In those days ideology was an unknown quantity to me and, what is more, the modest roles I was playing offered me little opportunity of judging ideologies. I looked upon each ballet role as another step forward in my career. In *Fire-Bird* I was occupied for a whole scene: as Knight of the Day I killed the Knight of the Night, and that marked an important event in the narrative. The role of the Knight of the Night was played by my inseparable friend Mravinsky, and we were happy that we had been noticed and given a chance, and did our very best to justify the régisseur's choice.

In Grieg's *Solvejg*—my last ballet before leaving the theatre—I had a small but important pantomime role of a violinist. Standing in the proscenium with a dummy instrument in hand, I synchronized my movements with the violinist in the orchestra and achieved the necessary effect. Such roles taught me to achieve precision and expressiveness of movement and gesture in their correlation with music.

The two men I tried to copy were Ivan Yershov and particularly Chaliapin. I spent every moment I could spare watching them from the wings. Both were past masters at expressiveness—their laconic gestures were superb. I shall never forget Yershov in *Ruslan and Lyudmila* in which as Finn he created a majestic character. Neither shall I forget Chaliapin's monumental figure as the Varangian Guest in *Sadko*, a small role with just one aria. Leaning on a heavy sword, he towered above the others like a sculpture of grey granite, coming to life only at the beginning of the song when he swept his right arm back to the rhythm of the music. "Oh, waves that smash the tow'ring rocks and whirl and ebb with foam," he sang. At the words "whirl and ebb" he would lower his hand slowly to the hilt and remain motionless. The power of his gesture in this brief sequence was extraordinary.

Yershov's portrayal of weak-minded Grishka Kuterma in Rimsky-Korsakov's *The Tale of the Invisible City of Kitezh* held audiences spellbound. It was his masterpiece, and he made the most of every little detail, greatly assisted by the guttural timbre of his voice.

I had ample opportunity of watching Chaliapin, especially in the scenes in which I myself was engaged. In those days the bass appeared oftener than before the Revolution, sometimes as much as twelve times a month. Thus the opportunity of seeing him presented itself frequently enough. Soon after I joined the Mariinsky as a super, I was cast as a soldier in *Judith*, right-flanking the first file of the Assyrian forces parading in front of Holofernes's tent. Chaliapin (Holofernes), majestic and terrible in his pent-up wrath, was so natural that the first

22

time I approached him it gave me the shivers. In the next act, in which I played a body-guard, Chaliapin gave such a vivid performance as a man overcome by passion—without once losing his majestic bearing—that I trembled when he fell exhausted at Judith's feet. Controlling a gripping fear, I helped the other body-guards to carry him to a bed in the rear of the stage, and was surprised to hear Chaliapin softly whisper: "Thank you, comrades, thank you."

Chaliapin then was at the height of his career, and his art knew no equal. I liked him most in tragic roles which revealed him as a master in conveying the psychological depth of the idea, in perfecting each little detail and in portraying emotional fervour.

In Rimsky-Korsakov's *The Maid of Pskov* I was one of the crowd in the first act in which Ivan the Terrible (Chaliapin) enters the rebellious town. We were being pushed back by the *ryndas*, on horseback and on foot. Then, the tsar himself appeared, hunched though majestic on a white steed. He looked grimly at the rebels, and it seemed that his old eyes were filling with blood. Chaliapin did not say anything; yet he created a perfect image of his hero, physically and spiritually.

In Massenet's *Don Quixote*, I doubled for Chaliapin in the battle with the windmills. He made an extremely light and graceful Don Quixote, and although I appeared in the rear of the stage and then only for a very brief spell, I did my best to look and act like Chaliapin. Little by little I penetrated the secrets of his style and many years later, when I was playing Ivan the Terrible and Don Quixote, I often resorted to Chaliapin's little mannerisms.

I also had many an opportunity of watching Chaliapin in comedy, or rather in humorous character roles. In those years he often sang the role of Varlaam. Mravinsky and I played the bailiffs, and our job was to grab him by the hands. He would free himself and slowly read the tsar's order to arrest Grishka Otrepiev (Pseudo-Dmitri). I also appeared with Chaliapin in *The Barber of Seville*, as the notary drawing up the marriage contract between Rosina and Almaviva in the last act. Holding a lantern, I would wait for Chaliapin at the entrance to the stage. He always appeared in good time, greeted me, soaked his hat with water (it was supposed to be raining outside) and saying "Some weather in Seville!" preceded me to the stage. This opera, incidentally, was one of the most popular at the time, and Chaliapin was always in a good mood when he sang in it, especially in the last act in which he introduced his own gags, joked with the audience and generally behaved in such a manner that even we found it hard to refrain from laughing.

Towards the middle of the 1919-20 season Chaliapin decided to stage Serov's *Dark Power*. He knew all its roles by heart, bossed everyone at the rehearsals and showed the singers how to sing their arias. He would softly hum the piece, but with all the necessary intonations and inflections. His knowledge of music and the highly expressive timbre of his voice were well-nigh perfect, and it was equally easy for him to direct and interpret all the parts in the opera. He was always willing to share his stage experience with others. He would show the choristers and pantomimers how to behave, how to group mises-en-scène, mould players into characters, without showing them twice how to do it. People who harkened to him gained much from his experience.

At one of the rehearsals, Chaliapin told the conductor that he wanted a pause after a certain remark, and the latter asked how long it should last.

"Never mind that," Chaliapin retorted angrily. "Follow my acting and you'll see for yourself when it should end."

He wanted the players and the conductor to feel the music. That was one of the unwritten laws of his art.

There was one episode in *Dark Power* I shall never forget. I was playing in the Shrovetide scene in the fourth act. The action takes place at a fair and it was necessary to clear the forestage to make way for the hero, Pyotr, and blacksmith Yeryomka (Chaliapin). That had to be done without driving the crowd off the stage. The task was entrusted to me; dressed as a spieler I appeared on a platform at the entrance to a tent, and harangued the crowd into going in. The people trooped around me, leaving Pyotr and Yeryomka on the forestage where they spoke their dramatic lines.

The role was a comedy one and I did my best, extremely flattered that I had been given a real bit part to play and that such a well-known artist as Boris Kustodiev had designed my costume.

Kustodiev had agreed to design the scenery and costumes for the opera only because he had been asked to do so by Chaliapin himself. His legs paralyzed, Kustodiev never left his wheel chair. He soon became a well-known figure at our rehearsals, and one day asked to see how I looked in my costume.

He was quite young-looking, moved about quickly in his wheel chair and delighted everyone by his wit. After a careful look-over he declared that my make-up was good though not well applied, and then remarked on the way the costume was cut. The dress rehearsal passed off well, but at the première I gave full rein to my latent comedy temperament and did things that my role did not call for.

As I appeared on the platform, I began to make the crowd laugh by grimacing and gesticulating, and the laughter spread to the public. There was a pause, and I saw Chaliapin signal backstage without, however, betraying the slightest sign of annoyance. I realized right away that he wanted me off the stage. Almost simultaneously régisseur Mikhail Zimmerman crept up from behind and tugged at my coat. I tumbled off the platform and hastened to the dressing-room. Scared by what I had done and certain I would be dismissed, I returned home early that night.

The next day Zimmerman caught me as I was passing his office, although I had done my best to evade him when I saw the door open.

"You're just in time," he cried. "Feodor Ivanovich wants to know how you managed to make the public laugh so much last night. Come in!"

He pulled me by my hand into his office, which he was sharing with Chaliapin, then art director of the theatre.

Chaliapin was reclining on a sofa, just as majestic-looking and handsome as he was on the stage. He was in knee-high white felt boots, a well-fitting fluffy blue sweater, and had a diamond-studded pin in his tie. Frankly, I was scared stiff, expecting a real scolding. I was afraid even to look in his direction.

"Well, well," he said. "How're you, young man! Show me how you entertained the audience last night. It's interesting, you know!"

Happy at the thought that I would not have to explain my behaviour in words, firstly, because I was afraid and, secondly, because in those days I stuttered quite a bit, I reproduced the scene, with grimaces and gestures.

In my childhood I liked burlesque and buffoonery. I don't remember when that actually began, probably in my school-days, but at any rate I delighted in imitating my friends, burlesquing them, entertaining my class-mates with tricks and stunts. I liked the circus with its clowns, and the vaudeville comedians whom I often saw perform in parks and cinemas.

Thus, I accumulated a large store of antics with which I entertained my friends at the theatre. Playing the spieler I unexpectedly, even for myself, let loose my store of tricks—and here I was waiting for the pay-off.

I showed Chaliapin all I knew and his laughter encouraged me. I was very thin in those days and my arms were so long I could embrace myself. I could really double up and stretch my arms out of the sleeves to an incredible length or swing my arms so fast at the elbows they looked as if they were hinged, and do many other tricks.

Chaliapin, laughing louder and louder, tried to do some of my tricks, but failed. Then, suddenly becoming serious, he said:

"Thanks. Only listen, young man, let's agree not to steal each other's scenes in the future."

That was an object lesson in relations among actors and I have never forgotten it. To this very day I am thankful to Chaliapin for this lesson and for his tact.

Whenever my thoughts turn back to my early days on the stage, to the beginning of my long and tortuous path as an actor, I am always grateful to the Academic Opera and Ballet Theatre.

I entered it as a sixteen-year-old boy and played in it for more than four years, and although my roles were not important, still it was there that I was initiated into the art of acting.

The October Revolution opened the theatre's doors for me, first as a spectator and then as one of its young actors. The new audiences who filled it inspired it to greater achievement.

I shall never forget the concerts we gave for the Red Army and Baltic Fleet units defending Petrograd. Our audiences in those days were made up mostly of soldiers and sailors. They would pack the cold, unheated auditorium, often with rifles in their hands, the bayonet unsheathed. Sometimes up to 20 servicemen would crowd into the six-seat boxes, and we feared that one day they would collapse.

Neither shall I forget our tours—the concerts we gave at various army and navy units and factories. I particularly remember our show at the Putilov Plant in the winter of 1920. It was the theatre's day-off, but to mark the opening of the workers' club we presented *Boris Godunov* with Chaliapin singing the title role. The company travelled to the factory in a horse-drawn tram and was welcomed by a large delegation of workers. The stage of their club was very small, the dressing-rooms were ill-equipped, and we had to dress and make up standing. But we did not mind that: it was the first time our theatre was presenting an opera outside its doors expressly for such an audience. After the performance we met the workers' delegates at the factory canteen where we were invited to a dinner of boiled potatoes and millet gruel. Then there was an exchange of opinions. That meeting marked the establishment of ties between the future Kirov Theatre and the future Kirov Plant, as our theatre and the Putilov Plant were later renamed.

I shall never forget the extremely cold days that year, so cold that the radiators in our theatre burst and the lobby floor was covered with such a beautiful layer of ice one could skate on it. We young actors, volunteered to go to the woods to get fuel. Working in a blustering snow-storm, we felled trees, dragged them several kilometres to the railway line, loaded them on to flat-cars and triumphantly returned to the theatre.

I shall never forget how the theatre looked nor the square with its shops closed down, with snow piled up so high we had to break a path to get into the theatre. Desolation seemed rife, yet the theatre was pulsating with creative life.

I shall never forget my heated arguments with Mravinsky nor our dreams. We were young and so in love with the theatre that one evening, with the permission of the firemen on duty, we spent the whole night there just to enjoy its atmosphere. Mravinsky made believe he was conducting an orchestra, while I recited monologues and sang arias to the deserted auditorium. On the backdrop illuminated by a few lamps hung a décor—a mountain with the ruins of a castle in the distance, and this detail added to the fantastic character of our impromptu performance which so originally reflected our dreams of the future.

And now, whenever I think of those days, I realize how much my modest roles at the Mariinsky Theatre had meant to me. I entered it at the turning point of my life, when I was maturing and my character was forming, and left it a full-grown man and an actor in the making.

I had made the first decisive step in my career in the creative atmosphere of this theatre, a theatre famed for its bold plans and accomplishment. Here with all my youthful fervour I studied the characters of Russian classical operas as portrayed by the theatre's outstanding singers, particularly Chaliapin. I tackled enthusiastically all the little tasks that were leading me to the goal I had set myself and educating me in the finest traditions of stage realism. By doing my best in the theatre, I tried to be a worthy citizen of my country. My consciousness of a Soviet patriot matured under the influence of the revolutionary era which showed me the way to art, and I now realize that this was the greatest achievement of the four years I had spent at the theatre named after Sergei Kirov.

AT SCHOOL

Time passed. The Civil War was over, and the country had set out to rehabilitate itself. Life changed completely, and the younger generation faced the problem of choosing their professions.

Mravinsky and I continued to play bit roles, such as officers in the ballet scene in *The Queen of Spades*. In the intermissions we discussed our prospects.

"It's time we gave up pantomime, at our age it's no longer a profession," we would tell each other.

At that time this was the only worth-while conclusion we had reached. But what next? Where to begin? The question was urgent. For a long time we could find no answer.

Theatre work was tempting all right, but my modest abilities seriously restricted my field of action.

I enjoyed a good reputation as a pantomimer, and the régisseurs gave me important bit parts. When Vladimir Lossky was staging Verdi's *Aida* he cast me as the master of ceremonies. Standing on the forestage I gave the signal for the procession to begin and that marked the turning point in the acting on the stage. There was an orchestra when I was tested for the role, and Lossky praised me for the way I had done it. But I was out for more than just praise.

I wanted to be an opera singer. I had long dreamed of it, but that dream never came true, for my voice was too weak. I could have sung in the chorus, but that held out no attraction.

There was another profession I could choose—that of a ballet dancer.

The small pantomime roles I was doing in ballets and operas had attracted attention, and in 1920 I was asked to join the newly-established Petrograd Young Ballet Studio, which was staging shows in parks and workers' clubs. I joined it without severing my ties with the Academic Opera and Ballet Theatre. At first I played character pantomime roles in classical ballets, among them the part of Father Colin in *Vain Precaution*, the Brahmin in *The Bayadere*, the evil genie in *The Swan Lake* and, finally, the title role in the popular ballet *Don Quixote*. After that I appeared in comedy dances. I liked this genre, and the choreographers encouraged me. In *Coppelia* I did a somewhat grotesque Negro dance and always had to encore it. In my last studio presentation—a pantomime review called *The Misadventures of Mr. Hughes*—I did an eccentric acrobatic solo dance.

In short, the ballet test proved successful. My search for a place in the theatre revealed that my best prospects were in the pantomime and dance, particularly in the eccentric dance which was becoming more and more fashionable. And so I decided to try my luck in that.

It was precisely at that time that the Institute of Art History, a research organization of high repute, established its "Experimental Ensemble." Its organizers set themselves the task of experimenting in the sphere of "purely expressive movement and gesture." There was something new, scientific and at the same time mysterious in their curriculum. All that was known was that the scientific researchers intended to create a "new actor" in their "laboratory."

Tempted by the vague but seemingly far-reaching plans and thrilled by the fact that I had been noticed by ballet "scientists," I eagerly joined the ensemble which was made up mostly of the younger generation.

For its début the ensemble chose extracts from the latest West-European operettas. In one of them, by Franz Lehar, I appeared as a Papuan and, surrounded by "African" girls, danced and sang an absurd "exotic" ditty that started with the following words:

> I want to hide in the tropics,
> That's what I'm dreaming of....

After that we staged two pantomimes: *Colombina's Shawl* and *The Ox on the Roof*. In the first I played the role of a dance director—an eccentric who would become as one "possessed" whenever he staged dances. The régisseur insisted on eccentricity and abrupt movements and gestures, and I obediently did everything I was told. In *The Ox on the Roof*—which was silly beyond words—I was cast as a foolish policeman who got himself into all sorts of incredible situations. The whole thing, and especially my part, was packed with ridiculous stunts. In the finale, one of my "enemies" knocked my head down the collar and, "headless," I contorted to the rhythm of syncopated music.

My youthful enthusiasm for pantomime, movement and gesture, burlesque and buffoonery, grotesque and eccentricity was used for purely formalistic purposes. The numbers in which I appeared were devoid of any idea whatever and, more often than not, of common sense.

The "Experimental Ensemble" shows were staged at the scientific research institute and were attended by actors, régisseurs and producers. They "noticed" me and claimed that I was an "almost full-fledged actor." I soon became a name in the theatrical world and was pleased to read press reviews of my performances. I was thrilled by the praise, written and oral, chiefly because I was persisting in the search for my true place in art and needed advice that would set me on the right path. And so I listened to fashionable régisseurs, who used me in their burlesques, with the result that very soon I came to the very edge of formalism.

But I did not realize the danger that implied.

"Fashion" was the word I heard all around me, the word that the so-called innovators used to justify the formalistic trends in art and quest after refinement.

For us, the younger generation, to follow fashion seemed natural, logical, progressive, and even revolutionary. Most of us did not understand the real meaning of this blind following of fads, and yet it was under its guise that attempts were being made to degrade art.

Fortunately, the "Experimental Ensemble" soon fell apart; my connections with it proved short-lived. And once again I faced the choice of profession.

Mravinsky and I often played piano duets from the operas and symphonies by Glinka, Chaikovsky, Moussorgsky, Borodin and Rimsky-Korsakov, and discussed our careers, dreamed of our place in art and usually came to the conclusion that our future lay in music.

By that time my friend had overcome his hesitations and made up his mind about his profession. He had given up the idea of becoming a geographer and applied to the conservatoire, and was now trying to convince me to do likewise and start with the piano class. I eventually agreed and filed my application.

But as I thought over and over my stage experience and carefully went over my impressions of the last four years, I realized that my true vocation in art was acting. It had been awakened in me by

Chaliapin, by the variety and perfection of the images he had created. It was his skill at impersonation that had impressed me most and stimulated my imagination. And this finally convinced me that my place was in the drama.

But although convinced, I was not yet sure what theatre I should choose. I could not imagine a theatre without music. I thought I would be best in strong character roles in the synthetic theatre, in plays that had music, songs and dances. I also thought of films, of comedy roles in which I could make good use of my large store of stunts and tricks and of my natural humour. And if the worst came to the worst, I thought then, I could try the drama.

I must stress, however, that in those days I did not know and did not understand the drama. The plays I saw in Leningrad left me indifferent (with the exception of the early productions of the Bolshoi Drama Theatre), and I knew nothing of any other dramatic art. If I could have seen the Moscow Art Theatre and its highly realistic productions, I would have probably asked to join it. But then, I had no opportunity of seeing genuinely realistic plays, and so in my plans for the future the dramatic theatre occupied the last place.

The decision to devote myself to acting prevailed over my doubts and in the autumn of 1923 I entered the drama department of the Leningrad Institute of Stage Art.

This institute was still in its infancy. It was established in the first years of the Revolution as an antidote to the old school that existed in the former imperial theatres, as an antidote to its routine and inertia, and played an important role in smashing the old, obsolete traditions in the education of young actors.

It was then that régisseur Leonid Vivien was making a name for himself as an instructor. One of the founders of the institute, he strove for realism from the very first. Some of his pupils had already achieved renown, and his productions were attracting wide attention, particularly A. N. Ostrovsky's *Truth Is Good, But Happiness Is Better* in which twenty-two-year-old Vasily Merkuriev (now one of the leading Soviet film actors) gave a superb portrayal as seventy-year-old ex-Sergeant-Major Silas Groznov.

As Paganel in the film *Captain Grant's Children.* 1936

As Varlaam in *Boris Godunov.* 1934

But although the institute was waging a bitter struggle against the old, obsolete traditions that were hindering progress, it failed to prevent the penetration of certain exponents of formalistic and aestheticist trends who called themselves revolutionary innovators. Their pseudo-revolutionary phraseology confused the younger artists, and I myself fell under their influence, though I did not understand it then. These "innovators" were doing their utmost to deprive art of ideology.

We were told very little of the Russian classics, the rich traditions of our progressive theatrical art or the history of our theatre. The main subjects were rhythmics and plastics, fencing and dancing, gymnastics and acrobatics. We were taught how to walk, run, assume the most intricate poses, dance in groups on sharply sloping platforms, cubes and stairs. In the acrobatic class we were trained to do all sorts of tricky stunts such as twisting our arms, legs and the whole of the body. I must admit that I did all this quite enthusiastically, but the experience I had gained at the opera soon opened my eyes to the utter untenability of the ideas propagated by the formalistic "innovators" who were setting the pace at the institute.

A theatrical school, naturally, does not and cannot produce an accomplished actor. It only discovers and develops his talent, his abilities, his latent potentialities, and then passes him on to the professional stage where he accumulates experience and eventually becomes a master at his art.

But the fashionable "innovators" who were monopolizing my class merely developed our physical abilities or, as they were wont to call them, our "outer texture," our "physical expressiveness."

I had a very flexible body, was good at imitating people, and interested in burlesque, grotesque and circus antics, and these talents of mine were used merely to create an effect, irrespective of whether or not they fitted in a play or an étude. My formalistic instructors were definitely coaching me to become a comedian.

Highly characteristic in this respect was the first play produced by the institute, Shakespeare's *Twelfth Night*, in which I was given a comedy role.

The play was staged as a burlesque, simple and pure, and the régisseur set out to stun the audience with a kaleidoscope of the most extravagant and absurd stunts.

There was a sort of a prologue in which a young man appeared on the stage, dressed à la Tolstoi in a long blouse, with a cigarette dangling from his mouth and a whistle in his hand, and pertly announced that Shakespeare really had nothing to do with their play, for his comedy was too outdated and was only fit to serve as a pretext for a comedy about a touring circus troupe. The young man, a sort of master of ceremonies, made similar remarks before each act, and would then whistle shrilly to signal the beginning of the act. The young actor was Sokolovsky, one of our students and later director of the Leningrad Young Workers' Theatre. Undoubtedly a gifted player, he was early corrupted by this contemptuous, nihilistic attitude to the cultural heritage of the past.

The main object of the performance was to astound the audience by its crazy antics and stunts, and for this reason the locale of *Twelfth Night* was shifted to a modern circus. All the characters became circus performers, irrespective of the people they were impersonating or the lines they had to speak.

The formalistic "innovators" presumed that the incompatibility of the text with the characters, their costumes and the environments, were bound to enhance the comicality of the play, which they considered "too out of fashion."

The duke became a circus manager and concurrently animal-tamer, and appeared in a scarlet tunic with a whip in hand. Poetic Olivia became an accomplished bareback rider, the jester emerged as a clown, and Sir Andrew Aguecheek as a sword-swallower. That was my role, and it was packed with incredible stunts. The performance represented an uninterrupted flow of absurdities which ridiculed the immortal playwright's idea, taught the student-actors bad habits and made ill use of their abilities.

I was still blind to the danger facing me—this time at the institute. The newspapers carried glowing reviews of *Twelfth Night*, singling me out as "a full-fledged actor of great eccentric talent." Many of the instructors also praised me. My reputation as a comedian of the grotesque and eccentric type was growing, particularly in my own class and among the senior students, and I must admit that this pleased me very much.

It was at the institute that I was first warned against it by Vladimir Maximov, the newly-appointed director of our studio.

Twelfth Night was staged after he had become our director and, therefore, he was to a certain degree responsible for it. A few days after the première, Maximov called me in and advised me to work on a role from Chekhov's *Uncle Vanya,* to create a character as realistic and psychological as Chekhov had intended it to be. The suggestion came as a surprise for the role was completely out of keeping with anything I had been taught to do.

Maximov came to his suggestion in a roundabout way. He first praised me for my comic movements and gestures and for my sincere interest in comic and eccentric roles, and added that I was undoubtedly quite gifted. But, he went on, one who has decided to devote himself to dramatic art should not indulge in such trifles. He firmly advised me to think of my future in art, to realize that the theatre was not just a pastime, but a school of emotions and thoughts, and that the actor was the medium who gave them a concrete form through his interpretation of the role. Maximov spoke warmly and enthusiastically and yet very cautiously, careful not to hurt my feelings and to convince me that he was right. He achieved that, and I readily agreed to work on a small scene in *Uncle Vanya*—the dialogue between Astrov and Sonya.

The task demanded no little effort, but I was quite prepared for what Maximov was urging me to do. The experience I had accumulated in the four years at the theatre and the impressions I had gained from Chaliapin's performances stimulated my interest in realistic acting and helped me correctly to understand the fundamentals of stage realism.

I did the Astrov bit successfully, and my fellow-students were surprised when they heard me speak my lines simply and naturally. As for me, the fragment from Chekhov's play convinced me that I could captivate the audience without resorting to silly tricks, but simply by using the ordinary means of realistic art based on life itself.

After Maximov's appointment as instructor of our class I began to study dramatic art more thoroughly and soon came to like it. He took a particular interest in me, helped me with advice, and that is why I consider him my first teacher.

Maximov was one of those persons who devote themselves wholly and fully to art. Tall, elegant and handsome, with easy movements and gestures, he was charming both on the stage and in private life. In his younger days he was connected with the Moscow Art Theatre and successfully played Treplev in Chekhov's *Sea-Gull*. Later he joined the Maly Theatre and on the eve of the Revolution was one of its leading actors. He had appeared in several plays with the famous Russian actress Maria Yermolova, and always spoke of her with enthusiasm, tenderness and at the same time filial respect, never tiring of citing her as an example of high morality.

Maximov became especially well known for his leading roles in the early Russian films. His appearance in those artistically weak pre-revolutionary pictures brought him country-wide fame, but at the same time created a completely wrong impression of his skill as an artist.

After the Revolution, Maximov was invited to the Bolshoi Dramatic Theatre in Petrograd where he played in almost all the romantic plays starting with the title role in *Don Carlos*. Ardently in love with the stage, always seeking for new forms, Maximov tried his skill in every sphere of theatrical art. He played at the Narodny Dom and the Comedy Theatre, gave dramatic readings on the variety stage, worked as a régisseur and producer, and as an instructor; it was at our institute that he first worked in this latter capacity.

Thoughtful and tactful, Maximov soon won the sympathy of the students. Without openly opposing the formalists, sundry "leftists" and pseudo-innovators in our studio, he waged a consistent though covert struggle against them. He familiarized us with drama and dramatic art, with the fundamentals of stage realism, and developed in us a sense of responsibility towards our creative work and an understanding of the magnitude of our tasks. His talks in class and private conversations soon convinced me that the old masters of the pre-revolutionary theatre were much better instructors than many of the young innovators who, while claiming that they were exposing the evils of old art, were in reality making use of pseudo-revolutionary phraseology to kill ideas and lead us to formalism, absurd stuntery and affectation.

There is no doubt that I could have corrected my ways and done away with all the misconceptions I had amassed at the institute if I had had more faith in my instructor. But the prevalent atmosphere, the presence of the "leftists" who enjoyed the reputation of progressives, the influence of the senior students with whom I played in our studio productions and, finally, the climate of the New Economic Policy period and the complicated ideological struggle waged by the reactionaries under various guises—all this kept me at the cross-roads of healthy realism in theatrical art and formalism masked as innovation.

One day I would be cast in the realistic role of landlord Milovidov in Ostrovsky's *At a Lively Spot*, and the following day I would be given the leading role in Emile Zola's *The Heirs of Rabourdin* and told to make my character grotesque and eccentric even if that was completely contrary to the playwright's idea.

At that time there were few Soviet plays, and most of them rather poor. They could not serve as study material and, therefore, we did not work on modern Soviet themes, nor did we work enough on Russian classics. In fact, I was much oftener engaged in such foreign plays as Oscar Wilde's *The Importance of Being Earnest* and Labiche's *Money-Box* and *The Straw Hat*. Our pseudo-innovator instructors, the majority of the senior students and especially the critics praised me most when I played comedy roles. Newspaper reviews continued to single me out, insisting that I was a comedian of the grotesque and burlesque type, a "full-fledged eccentric."

The institute was allowed the use of a little theatre to stage its student plays, and the shows we put on there—a sort of tests—were usually attended by a not-too-numerous, but a highly qualified audience made up mostly of régisseurs, art directors, theatre managers, players and instructors. They studied our performances and criticized us. On our part, we learned to associate with our audiences, appreciate our profession, value the possibility of appearing in public and draw conclusions.

Our performances were not limited to this little theatre: we did not think that we had enough practice at the institute and made up for it by staging ex-curricula shows.

On the initiative of our Komsomol organization we began to appear in May Day and October Revolution celebrations at various Leningrad youth clubs. These shows demanded a repertoire of agitational character on contemporary problems, and we spent our free time rehearsing satirical playlets, one-act plays and items from "live" newspaper.* Once we even staged a "polit-operetta"—*Ivan's Venture*—a gay musical piece about the collapse of the White émigré society. I played the lanky, weak-minded Grand Duke Nikolai Nikolayevich, one of the pretenders to the Russian "throne," and spared no effort to caricature him as grotesquely as possible. The audience liked our shows, and we were very popular at the youth clubs.

This gave us an idea of spending our 1926 summer vacation usefully on a concert tour of Central Asia and the Caucasus. Some time earlier it had been decreed that students could travel free of charge, and we worked out an interesting itinerary that would start in Tashkent, take us to several towns in Uzbekistan and end in Baku. Our idea was readily approved by the institute.

We prepared a special issue of a "live" newspaper on various contemporary political themes, but as that was not enough for an evening's programme, we decided to present some other numbers as well.

In our spare time at the institute we often gathered in the music salon and staged impromptu performances that included comedy scenes, parodies, satirical songs and dances. We joked and laughed and played with the abandon that is so natural in young people.

I used to entertain my friends by doing comic dances. In this I was soon joined by two other students, Boris Chirkov and Pyotr Beryozov, and the three of us always tried our best to "outdance' each other.

* "Live" newspaper—an oral newspaper dealing with contemporary themes.

Little by little we worked out humorous steps, funny poses and acrobatic stunts.

When it became obvious that we had to have some more numbers for our tour, we three offered to work out a comedy dance.

Our proposal was accepted and we set out on integrating all the humorous movements and steps each of us had mastered. At first we wanted to come out as sailors, but gave up this idea because our dance was anything but a sailor dance. Then, a few days before our departure, we decided to impersonate the three most famous film comedians of the day: Charlie Chaplin, Pat and Pataschon. The number, in which we appeared made up as these comedians, was a burlesque, pure and simple, and eventually developed into the well-known acrobatic dance "Pat, Pataschon and Charlie Chaplin."

It is difficult to describe the dance and its composition, particularly since with time it underwent so many changes that nothing remained of the original.

Beryozov was Chaplin and Chirkov Pataschon. As Pat I tried to copy his mannerisms, and movements, and gestures, twisted my body, shook hands with myself behind my back, embraced myself and made believe I was dancing with a lady, and stepped absent-mindedly over my partners. I would pretend to envy their successful steps and stunts and try to outdo them by a fast eccentric dance packed with acrobatics. The number was previewed and accepted.

Never shall I forget my first tour of the country!

For many of us, including myself, this was the first time we were away from Leningrad, and we were thrilled and impressed as only young people can be.

The journey to Tashkent was long. We went out at each stop and often did not sleep at night lest we miss some interesting place. Tashkent's architectural monuments, the old city and the numerous construction sites fascinated us. In Baku we spent the first night walking up and down its water front and singing—true, it was not so beautiful then as it is now. The next morning we went to Surakhany and were deeply impressed by the scale of mechanized oil-extraction work. We matured considerably in the two months we were away from

Leningrad and saw for ourselves how the peoples of our country worked and lived.

Our audiences were people of different republics. In Uzbekistan we gave shows in Tashkent, Andizhan, Ferghana and Samarkand, as well as in many neighbouring villages, big and small. There were difficulties too: at first no one wanted to invite our "live" newspaper. Then we managed to stage a public review at one of the leading clubs in Tashkent and immediately got several engagements. We followed events closely, drawing material from the central and local newspapers for the political satire which we worked into our programme.

Our acrobatic dance proved extremely popular and received favourable notices in the press. We improved it on with each performance, striving for greater precision and dynamism. On our return to Leningrad we received many invitations from clubs and eventually from the professional variety theatre, and there were days when we had to give as many as four performances.

As soon as he had heard of it, Maximov called me in:

"Listen, Cherky," he said, "if it's easy success you're after, you can get it all right in the vaudeville, music-halls and circus by doing your eccentric dance or clown stuff. Yes, you can always find yourself a place there. But you'll never get real satisfaction, never achieve the real creative happiness that one gets from working on important dramatic roles. A real actor, a real artist, strives not so much to make his audience laugh or to astound it as to convince it of the truth, of the power and depth of the ideas proclaimed from the stage. He captures its attention and wins its recognition by bringing out the significance of the ideals he serves. That, of course, is the hard way, but it is precisely the road the best representatives of our theatre have travelled."

Although I listened attentively to Maximov's insistent advice, I was not persuaded. I just could not see what I should do.

Most of the instructors, some of them leading régisseurs, guided me in the opposite direction and lauded my experiments in the burlesque and eccentric genre. So did the senior students. Our clownish dance was in great demand and had become one of the most popular numbers on the variety stage. Why give it up? And if I did, what then?

So we continued to polish it up, and for several years it was our inseparable companion, especially mine.

I did this number for the graduation exercise, and I did it also when given a test by the Leningrad Young Spectators' Theatre. I continued to perform it in vaudeville during my first years at that theatre and re-created it in one of my first films, *My Son*.

Then ten years later, after a long interval, we were asked to do it again for Lenfilm's review *Concert No. 1*. This time we performed it before the cameras and, counting the rehearsals to a phonograph record and the close-ups, we had to do it about thirty times.

In a word, this dance, born as an impromptu number at one of our student soirées and perfected in the course of many years, remained my trade mark for quite some time. That is why I have dwelt so long on it, and that is why whenever I appear publicly and speak to my audiences about my professional life, the first shots of the film illustrating my talk invariably show the "Pat, Pataschon and Charlie Chaplin" number from *Concert No. 1*.

There is a thirteen-year stretch between the day I first did this dance at the institute in 1925 and the day I performed it under the kleig lights in 1938. In those thirteen years my impersonation underwent many changes. At first I indulged in pure burlesquing and eccentricity. Then gradually I began to subordinate my movements and gestures to the character I was impersonating. I ridiculed Pat, thus stressing the utter absurdity of some of his films. My ironic attitude towards Pat was all the more obviously reflected in the little dance we did for an encore, which left no doubt as to the idea the dance pursued. Thus, little by little, I came to look critically upon external grotesque and empty burlesque, to realize that ability was not an aim in itself, but only a means of achieving better results.

To grasp this truth I had to traverse a long and arduous path, and often strayed. It was the path of a professional actor and it took me, as will be seen in the next chapter, through various theatres and genres, and through the cinema, and was influenced by the life around me, by our socialist construction, by the tasks the people and the Party set us.

IN SEARCH OF A HERO

My path as a professional dramatic actor started at the Leningrad Young Spectators' Theatre. Before joining it, I had been one of its regular patrons, since I loved its youthful spirit, its interesting, colourful and lively plays, and especially the warm reaction of the audiences.

There was always something merry going on on its stage, and it was always noisy in its auditorium. The plays had music, lots of songs and dances. It closely resembled the type of synthetic theatre I dreamed of from my very first day at the institute. Here was an atmosphere, I thought, that would best suit my abilities as a comedian, singer and dancer, that would help me to create original eccentric types, though at that time I had only a very vague idea about them.

It was no easy task to get into that theatre. There were some 100 entrants for the competition test and only seven were passed, among them my class-mate Vitaly Politseimako, now a well-known stage and screen actor, and myself. Another friend of mine, Boris Chirkov, who had graduated from the institute a year earlier, was already a member of its company.

The Leningrad Young Spectators' Theatre was organized and managed by Alexander Bryantsev, a former actor and régisseur of the Gaideburov Travelling Troupe which later settled down at Panina's Narodny Dom. After the Revolution, Bryantsev devoted himself wholly to children's art education. The Young Spectators' Theatre, he would say, should unite artists who think like educators and educators who think like artists. For his assistants he chose like-thinkers and moulded them into a well-knit collective. He boldly pushed young actors to the fore and entrusted them with responsible roles. We held him in high esteem as managing director, although most of us, perhaps, did not understand the artistic and educational tasks he set himself, and joined the theatre for purely personal reasons.

I regarded the Young Spectators' Theatre as a sort of extension of the institute. I had joined it shortly before graduation. I went through all the disciplines an actor has to go through to fit his body for the stage, develop his musicalness and enhance his professional knowledge. I lived—yes, virtually lived—three years in the theatre, giving it all my time and being utterly devoted to it.

One of the merits of this theatre, its youthful collective and its experienced managing director, was that they strove not only to develop an actor's abilities, but also his outlook and, above all, his sense of responsibility to the audience and understanding of the importance of his profession. Every Thursday there was a special meeting attended by the members of the company and guests, sometimes adult spectators, to review and criticize performances. We also discussed the urgent problems facing Soviet art, the new plays staged by other theatres and the tours of Moscow artists. Sometimes we met with the leading players from the Art and Vakhtangov theatres.

Soon after joining the theatre, I was cast in the title role in *Don Quixote*. The day I learned about it was a red-letter day, and I shall never forget it.

The scenario was by Alexandra Brustein, a well-known writer of children's plays, and régisseur Boris Zon. Making use of a stage model, he described the production plan. We were told that it was up to us to make the play colourful, to expand the régisseur's ideas with our own. The Cervantes novel was to serve merely as a skeleton of an entertaining and merry play for children in their early teens.

The shows staged by the Young Spectators' Theatre were different in form and character from ordinary plays. One of the reasons was that the stage was not separated from the auditorium by footlights, but was part of it. The régisseur often made use of this peculiarity to stage scenes in the auditorium itself, thus fusing the action of the play with the spectators.

That was how *Don Quixote* was staged too.

There were four proscenium attendants, two girls and two boys in Spanish peasant costumes, but speaking in the language of Soviet school children. They would draw the spectators into the play, into the conventional theatrical game unfolding to Nikolai Strelnikov's loud and merry music.

The action would alternately take place on the stage and in the auditorium. Followed by Sancho Panza, Don Quixote would run down the aisles looking for the little ass a gang of convicts had stolen from him. It was in the auditorium, too, that Sancho Panza hid from his wife Teresa. The four little attendants would volunteer to help her to find him and would start the popular game of "hot and cold" with the entire audience participating. The cries of "hot" and "cold" served to indicate where Sancho Panza was, for he kept popping up in the most unexpected places of the auditorium. In the end Teresa would find her cowardly husband and drive him down the aisle to the stage amid the cheers and applause of the youthful spectators.

In the scene where Don Quixote fought against the magician Malambruno, barber Nicolas would bring out the villain's huge head on to the stage. When Don Quixote imagined he was serenading the princess, the person on the balcony was padre Antonio, disguised as the princess and speaking in a falsetto. The scene which shows Don Quixote preparing the knightly balsam was stretched out into an added attraction in which each performer introduced some humorous element.

In another sequence, Don Quixote's fellow-villagers and friends, disguised as dukes, princesses and beasts, would surround him and try to talk him into returning home, singing the following little ditty:

> Señor, don't mourn your fate,
> Your return we all await.
> There's no good in that you roam,
> It's high time you came back home.

The song was followed by a mass dance, with the hero participating.

Don Quixote was presented as a buffoon, a lovable crank who got himself into all sorts of silly situations because he believed all and sundry, because he let his imagination go wild, and not as a clever man or as a man of ideas and heroism.

His costume was exaggerated: he was dressed in a black singlet, black tights, shorts of silver brocade and jackboots with high heels. His armour consisted of a small trough on his chest, for a spear and

44

shield he had a long poker and big tray. His oval head was crowned by a small basin.

I did my best to make him seem still lankier and caricatured every one of his movements. I tried to amaze the audience by twisting my head, bowing and leaping in a most unnatural manner, and to captivate its attention with dances, songs and clownish antics. I succeeded and won recognition as a professional actor, and before I had graduated from the institute at that. My youthfulness and the sincerity and enthusiasm with which I tackled my first leading role brought me success, while my interpretation of the Cervantes hero brought me the reputation of a burlesque comedian, of an eccentric buffo.

But this success failed to satisfy most of us.

The play was dynamic, the pace too fast and the final curtain always found us exhausted mentally and physically.

By that time I had acquired certain stage habits, but technically I was still raw, and that was why I had to put in so much physical effort into my role.

I always managed to tear my tights with the armour and was blue and black with bruises. The movements distracted me, put a heavy strain on my capacities, and I always felt worn-out particularly since the "convicts," in their desire to achieve realism, often pummelled me too hard. My friend Chirkov (Sancho Panza) did not fare any better.

And that, as I have said above, was because we still lacked professional technique. We tried to make up for it by a purely physical effort, and the result was that our performances were immature.

Frequently, facing the audience, I would start worrying about how to play a scene, take a bow, jump to amaze the spectators, fold myself in two and dance to make the auditorium laugh. I would avail myself of every possibility to see how the audience reacted to my antics—and my role was replete with them. In short, I was anxious to please my young audience.

After we had performed dozens of times, we tired less and less. We worked out new elements in our movements and made them easier and more plastic. Our speech and singing acquired new intonations.

As a result of this improvement in our technique we became more collected and learned to improvise and surmount difficulties.

One day, when I was concocting the knightly balsam, singing lustily and dancing, my moustaches fell off. It was only when the audience burst out laughing that I realized what was amiss. I quickly found a way out of the predicament.

"Oh, these damned magicians! They have ripped my moustaches off, roots and all!" I shouted to the delight of the young spectators.

The role gradually became easier, the performance more polished and colourful, the speech smoother. The image of Don Quixote became more human and lyrical. Without noticing it myself, I progressed from a purely physical impersonation of Don Quixote to one revealing his moral qualities and the loftiness of his ideals. There was also more warmth and lyricism in my serenade:

> Oh, princess my dear,
> Sleep easy, my heart
> You've nothing to fear.
> Don Quixote's on guard.

I put much more feeling and understanding into the scene in which Don Quixote bids farewell to his armour and weapons. Eventually I succeeded in bringing out the underlying idea—the hero's attitude to his weapons, which could be summed up as follows: "Do well unto all and evil unto none."

My sincere portrayal of Don Quixote's emotions deeply moved the spectators, and I was happy at the thought that it was not only by clowning that I could hold their attention.

Little by little we weeded out buffoonery and eccentricity—in which we had indulged with all our youthful enthusiasm—from various scenes and episodes.

In the first three years I played Don Quixote some 150 times. After that there was a break, and then I appeared in the play for another season. And all this while, perfecting and enriching the role, I kept improving my acting, singing and dancing technique so necessary for synthetic plays.

The Young Spectators' Theatre taught actors to regard every bit of acting as important, no matter how small, even a single appearance in a crowd. While playing the lead in *Don Quixote* I did a bit as a guard in *The Prince and the Pauper*. Dressed in armour, with the visor down, I had to stand motionless all through the act without uttering a single word, yet I felt that my part was just as responsible.

Practical work gave me much more knowledge than any theatrical institute.

One day, the actor who was playing the leading role of Sylvestre in Molière's *The Escapades of Scapin* fell ill and Bryantsev chose me for the part. There were only three or four days left to rehearse the role in this comedy packed with humorous situations, clever mises-en-scène and entertaining dances.

A comedian should sincerely and firmly believe in what is going on on the stage, however incredible it may seem, and look serious even when doing utterly ridiculous things. That was how we were supposed to act, and did, in *The Escapades of Scapin*.

By that time I had accumulated quite a bit of experience in dancing and burlesque and had an almost perfect control of my body, but at the very first rehearsal I just could not put my heart into the episodes in which buffoonery prevailed. Somehow I did not feel like doing any stunts, somersaulting or frightening Argante with my huge sword, or donning an extremely wide-brimmed hat and unnaturally large medals. I had to force myself to rehearse.

"What's the matter? Feeling sick?" Bryantsev asked me, noticing my discomfiture.

Not knowing what to say, I kept quiet. The rehearsal was called off. Returning home, I realized that I had failed in the task set by the régisseur because I had not been sufficiently attentive and had not worked up the creative mood necessary on the stage.

The next morning I returned to the theatre much more collected and calm, in a creative mood, and set out with determination to satisfy the régisseur. I knew my role well by the time the play opened, and it became a favourite with me. The lesson was not in vain: I realized that it was necessary for the actor to work up the mood long before

47

the rehearsal or performance, that he should come to the theatre collected and confident, though not overly so, in his abilities.

Apart from *Don Quixote*, which enjoyed an extremely long run and in which I had no understudy, the list of the Young Spectators' Theatre productions in which I played included *The Robbers, Thyl Uylenspiegel, The Escapades of Scapin, The Prince and the Pauper, Uncle Tom's Cabin*, the fairy-tale *The Little Humpbacked Horse*, the first two Soviet plays for children—*Timothy's Mine* and *Underwood*, and the two extremely popular plays that carved themselves a firm niche in the theatre's repertoire—*Yeryomka the Slacker* and *We'll Catch the Sun*.

The performances usually ended shortly after eight, and from the theatre I would hurry to some workers' club where I took part in the "live" newspaper review entitled "Komsoglaz."* Its initiators were a group of young actors of our theatre and Chirkov, Politseimako and I immediately joined them. The task we had set ourselves was to dramatize all the important Komsomol events concerning studies, social activities and vocational training. Most of our material came from the newspaper *Komsomolskaya Pravda.*

I liked taking part in these reviews, for they dealt with the urgent political questions of the day, but at the same time I was somewhat dissatisfied because they were dry and colourless. That, incidentally, was true of all our "live" newspaper reviews. What I wanted to do was to create characters, master the art of "embodying" images, and there was none of that in these reviews. And I felt at home on the stage only when I was impersonating some character.

The "Komsoglaz" gradually developed into an original Soviet operetta company that came to be known as the New Operetta Theatre. Our aim was to produce merry musical plays on Soviet themes at workers' clubs. We proceeded cautiously at first, often vamping up old shows. Our youth, sincerity and enthusiasm saw us through, and our first experiments in this field won the acclaim of the workers and especially of the Komsomol members.

* *Komsoglaz*—the eye of the Komsomol.—*Tr.*

As Tsarevich Alexei in the film *Peter I*. 1936

Scene from *Peter I*. 1936. Author is in the centre

The most successful production was *The Three Pines* about a dreamy young worker, who studies at an institute in the evenings and writes poetry in his leisure time, looking for a heroine for his poem among his fellow-workers and eventually finding her.

The scenario was by Leonid Lyubashevsky, an actor of the Young Spectators' Theatre, who wrote it under the pseudonym of A. Zhulengo, and at my request he added the role of composer Zvonaryov—a role he created to suit my talents.

Zvonaryov was a failure as a composer. An absent-minded, melancholy-looking, unpractical and faint-hearted man, he made himself all the more ridiculous by attempting to conceal his timidity. He was almost the living picture of Pat, and in the operetta people took him for the famous film comedian. Finding himself in all sorts of predicaments, often incredible, Zvonaryov had to pretend he was Pat and to sing and dance as Pat did.

I decided to make use of the character I had created in the vaudeville to build a new comedy image whose conduct in the operetta was determined by the necessity of passing himself off as the popular comedian. I was sure that by developing this image I could improve my acting.

Somewhat unexpectedly the Young Spectators' Theatre offered me the realistic role of Zvezdintsev in Lev Tolstoi's *The Fruits of Enlightenment*. It was necessary to concentrate all my attention on the inner qualities of the character, on the psychology which determined his conduct, on the environments in which he lived and in which his individualistic traits formed. A task of this kind was new to me and as such it represented a step forward in my career.

I should point out that, despite my enthusiasm for burlesque and eccentricity, I had played several straight, realistic roles in the institute's productions.

In *The Fruits of Enlightenment*, for the first time in my life, I was given a psychological role to play, the role of a realistic comedy character. The task was to define clearly Tolstoi's idea, and we set about it in all seriousness, learning much in the process of its fulfilment.

My Zvezdintsev was a foolish rich idler, a man of ludicrous super-stitions, though outwardly cultured. Of aristocratic bearing and perfect manners, with a comely little beard, he dressed elegantly in a frock-coat and a blue velvet waistcoat. Incidentally, it took me quite some time to get accustomed to this attire, to rid myself of the habit of moving briskly and to learn to depend as little as possible on outer expressiveness.

The habits I had formed caused me no end of trouble as I proceeded to mould the Tolstoi character. Everything worried me: how to act in this or that scene, how to round out an episode, how to talk with the muzhiks, how to communicate with Nicholas's spirit, how to run away in confusion when upbraided by my wife.

And while I did commit some errors, particularly because I was paying too much attention to the questions "how to do this?" and "how to do that?" nevertheless I succeeded in making certain episodes realistic and lifelike, and the encouraging applause showed that I was doing the right thing.

One of the scenes I shall always cherish was my dialogue with Tanya, the maid, at the end of the first act—the place where Zvezdintsev smugly tells her about butler Semyon: "I have long known that he is a medium!" Another memorable episode, towards the end of the act, showed Zvezdintsev dance up to his valet, Fyodor, order him to prepare everything for a séance, and happily and naively exclaim:

"We shall have our own medium at the trial séance today!"

The curtain came down as Fyodor threw my fur coat over my shoulders and I rushed off the stage.

These two exclamations were extremely important because they explained the meaning of the episode and anticipated further developments. I hit upon the necessary intonation—and rather unexpectedly too—at the première.

However much I tried, I could not repeat the intonation at the subsequent performances. My dance steps and my exclamations "I have long known that he is a medium!" and "We shall have our own medium at the trial séance today!" left the audience cool:

the curtain came down, but there was none of the applause I had expected.

Disappointed and puzzled, I decided I would not stop trying to achieve the effect I had so successfully hit upon the first night. I rehearsed the lines at home and at the theatre, but all in vain. I worked out the rhythm of the scene and all the movements to the last detail, repeated the two lines hundreds of times, but the intonation was just not there. The second line, in fact, became an anticlimax. Things were going from bad to worse. Utterly dissatisfied with myself, I came to the conclusion that realistic and psychological roles were beyond my abilities. Exhausted by the search for the missing intonation, I reconciled myself to defeat. And then one evening, after I had stopped thinking of the scene and the two lines, they unexpectedly resounded with the same force as at the première and were drowned in applause.

That evening I understood that in a realistic play one should never think of how to play an episode if one wants it to be true to life. Realism, I saw, comes with the proper understanding of the situation and of the psychology of the character portrayed.

This found confirmation in Konstantin Stanislavsky's wonderful book *My Life in Art* which considerably enriched my knowledge and forced a change in my opinion of many things, primarily of realistic dramatic art.

It was in those days that I came to know the Moscow Art Theatre, its leading players and the creative art of Stanislavsky. Deeply impressed by all I had seen and experienced, I read and reread his new book.

Like many others of my generation of actors, I had an entirely distorted idea about the Art Theatre. That idea was instilled in me when I was at the institute under the influence of the "innovators" and formalistic régisseurs then so in vogue in Leningrad. They did not like the Art Theatre; in fact they considered it their mortal enemy and accused it of being backward, conservative and even... politically unreliable. When it staged *The Days of the Turbins*, these "leftists" went so far as to demand that machine-guns be mounted outside the theatre and that spectators be shot for daring to see such a "counter-revolutionary" play. At that time, the political meaning of the struggle waged by these "leftists" against the Art Theatre and Stanislavsky's ingenious creative methods was incomprehensible to me.

I saw my first Art Theatre play in Leningrad, where the company came for the first time after the Revolution in May 1927, and it left an indelible impression.

The production was Anton Chekhov's *Cherry Orchard* with an all-star cast. The packed auditorium sat spellbound, and so did I, by the highly realistic acting all through the play.

I remember the most minute details well because the players lived their parts and also because every one of these details served to characterize the personages of *The Cherry Orchard* and the environments in which they lived.

"Dear and venerable bookcase! Honour and glory to your existence, which for more than a hundred years has served the noble ideals of justice and virtue," exclaimed Stanislavsky (Gayev), revealing the essential features of his hero in the ensuing monologue. In this one little episode the great actor disclosed Gayev's characteristics, his original way of thinking, his habits and inclinations. He gradually developed the image, and although he did not condemn the character outright, he showed the audience that Gayev was a social nonentity, a doomed man.

I remember Gayev's return from the auction, his awkward gait as he entered the hall with a package in hand and the tone of his voice as he said: "Here are some anchovies and Black Sea herrings. . . ." and then wiped a tear from his eye, unable to say the main thing—that the cherry orchard had been sold. I remember how Chekhov's widow, Olga Knipper (Ranevskaya), asked: "Is the orchard sold? . . . Who bought it?" and the sweeping gesture of actor Leonid Leonidov (in the role of Lopakhin) as he declared: "I did!" I also remember how near-sighted Trofimov (played by Vasily Kachalov) calmly and haughtily told Lopakhin:

"I can do without you... I'm strong and proud. I'm in the foremost ranks of mankind which is advancing towards the highest truth, the highest happiness possible on earth."

The play had dozens of similar gems of realistic art and captured my imagination because it was true to life, more so than any play I had ever seen before.

As the final curtain fell I found myself among the young enthusiasts who rushed towards the orchestra pit, applauding and cheering Stanislavsky.

The maestro took about twenty bows, first with the entire company and finally alone, smiling shyly and clasping his hands in gratitude.

Deeply moved by all I had seen, I was one of the last to leave the theatre. After the superb acting of Chaliapin I had seen nothing to equal the performance given by the Moscow Art Theatre and especially by Stanislavsky. I began to compare Chaliapin and Stanislavsky and came to the conclusion that the latter's artistry was just as significant and powerful as Chaliapin's, that it had the same roots and was nurtured by the same ideals. The only difference was that Chaliapin was an opera singer and Stanislavsky a dramatic actor.

I was no less thrilled a few days later when I attended *The Lower Depths,* the first of Gorky's plays I saw on the stage.

"Man is free.... Man—there's your truth!... All things are part of Man; all things are for Man!... Man!... How marvellous is Man! How proud the word rings—MAN!" Stanislavsky, who played Satin, spoke these words convincingly, passionately and yet with unusual simplicity, as if sharing his cherished thoughts with the inmates of the doss-house. And once again he truthfully depicted the character of his hero, his noble and lofty nature, oppressed by capitalist society, and once again the image he created grew tremendously in scope and inner significance.

The revolutionary fervour of Gorky's drama was faithfully preserved in the play, whose cast included the finest actors of the Art Theatre: Olga Knipper-Chekhova (Nastya), Vasily Kachalov (the Baron), Ivan

Moskvin (Luka), Vasily Luzhsky (Bubnov) and Alexander Vishnevsky (the Tatar).

Just like after *The Cherry Orchard*, I left the theatre thrilled and elated. A new sphere of art, vast and unknown, seemed to open up before me. "That's what one can achieve by hard work!" I said to myself, although, frankly speaking, I had no idea how it was done.

That year and the following spring I saw all the plays the Art Theatre staged in Leningrad. Its highly realistic art made me one of its most ardent admirers. "If I could play like that!" I often told myself. But then I still lacked the necessary grounding for that.

It was becoming more and more obvious to me that I was impersonating, but not "incarnating" my characters (in those days I probably did not use such terminology). But though still a comparative novice on the professional stage I had achieved some measure of success precisely through impersonation. I had the reputation of a player of the eccentric type, and it was as such that I played my first film roles—barber Charles in *The Poet and the Tsar*, the clown in *His Excellency* and Pat in *My Son*. These roles won me a following and it was because I was known as an actor of the eccentric type that I received offers from the film studios, variety and music-halls.

I yearned to get away from this reputation, to find a new path in art, to master the secret of realistic art which had thrilled me so in the Moscow Art Theatre plays. Could I do it? Could I achieve realism as a dramatic actor and would it not take too long before I was recognized? Should I throw up the reputation that I had already built for myself, even if in another field of art?

It was while I was weighing the pros and cons of the situation that I received an offer from the Leningrad Music-Hall. It appeared that this theatre was seeking for new synthetic forms, and I was convinced it would find them. I hesitated to join it, but the desire to find new, original and vivid forms in variety was too strong. I finally decided to continue along the path I had taken, along the path which, I thought, best suited my abilities. So I joined the Music-Hall, certain that it was holding out a possibility of perfecting my skill as an actor of the burlesque and eccentric type.

Later I shall dwell at length on my conception of eccentricity, on its tasks and on the assistance it gives me even now in portraying certain roles. Here I will simply say that hollow eccentricity then in vogue in our music-halls left me dissatisfied. More, it ran counter to my intentions, my conception of eccentricity in dramatic art. I was not happy at all about the leading roles I played, in *Odyssey*, for example, or about the parts especially written for me, like that of the waiter in *Out of the Blue*. I just could not feel at home in these gaudy reviews. Disappointed and looking for a way out, I returned to the "Pat, Pataschon and Charlie Chaplin" dance number.

My partners and I performed it in summer at the Gorky Park in Moscow and in the circuses at Kazan, Kuibyshev, Saratov and Stalingrad. We would run out to the edge of the ring, start our dance there and continue it in the ring itself on a special platform. The number was very popular, but it no longer satisfied the three of us: we had grown out of it.

It was at about that time, or perhaps a bit earlier, maybe in 1928—anyway, it does not matter exactly when—that we were performing the number at one of the Leningrad parks. We had been told that Gorky was in the audience and, excited, did our best to outdo ourselves. The applause was deafening. We stole glances at Gorky, who was sitting in the second row, to see how he reacted, but the famous writer did not smile once; it did not look as if he approved of our number. Little could I imagine then that a few years later I would be playing him on the stage and screen, and that this role would represent one of the landmarks in my transformation as an actor.

The necessity for such transformation was becoming more and more evident, dictated by the general development of our art.

The early thirties, which saw the country launch on vast socialist construction, were marked by decisive achievements in art. The pseudo-innovators were suffering defeat after defeat in art, literature and theatre. Realism was becoming the basis of the development of the Soviet theatre and of the genuine creative achievements of Soviet actors, called upon to portray their contemporaries—the builders of socialism.

Feeling more and more dissatisfied and seeing no way of finding my real place in the theatre, I again turned to Stanislavsky's book. I read and reread it, looking for the places I had marked before—paragraphs that might well have been written expressly for my generation.

Speaking of the young actors who came to the fore in the mid twenties, Stanislavsky wrote that he was frankly astonished by the many major achievements in the field of expressive acting. There was no doubt, he said, that there was a new type of actor, so far with a small "a": the actor-acrobat, singer, dancer, reciter, pamphleteer, wit, orator, master of ceremonies and political agitator all rolled in one. The new actor could do anything: sing a couplet or a love-song, recite a poem or a monologue, play a piano or a violin or football, dance foxtrot, turn somersaults, stand and walk on his hands. Speaking of "multiform patterns of movement, flexibility of body and balance, diction and the whole expressive apparatus," Stanislavsky emphasized that so long as the physical culture of the body assisted the main creative tasks of art, i.e., so long as it helped to express human spirit in an artistic form, he welcomed the new expressive achievements of the contemporary actor with all his heart. But when physical culture became an end in itself in art, when it began to slow down the creative process and engendered a split between spiritual aspirations and conventions of external acting, when it suppressed feelings and experiences, then, he said, he became an ardent opponent of these fine new achievements.

It was necessary to stimulate as quickly as possible the spiritual culture and technique of the actor and to raise it to the level of his physical culture. Only then, Stanislavsky said, would the new form receive the necessary inner basis and justification, without which it would remain lifeless outwardly and lose its right to existence. This work, of course, was incomparably more complicated and longer. It was far more difficult sharply to define feelings and experiences than the outer form of embodiment. But the theatre was in greater need of spiritual creativeness, and it was therefore necessary to tackle the job without delay.

Practically speaking, there was nothing new in that for me. It was more or less what Maximov had told me when I was at the institute. And if now I was poring over these words and critically re-examining my own experience, I was doing it as much because I was influenced by the times, the successes of our socialist construction, the social and political upswing it had entailed in every sphere of endeavour, and the growing demands for higher artistic levels made by the people and the Party.

Confined to variety and the circus, I started seeking for a way out of this narrow circle. In the two years I spent at the Leningrad Music-Hall, my ties with the theatre and the cinema—in my latest film *The Moon Is to the Left*, adapted from Vladimir Bill-Belotserkovsky's play of the same name, I had my first important part—became completely severed. My last year in variety, at the Moscow Music-Hall, where I had been transferred, was particularly difficult morally, and although the shows were staged by top-notch producers, they gave me no satisfaction. I realized that I had taken the wrong path and began to look for an opportunity to return to drama where, I knew, I could best use my abilities.

This decision of mine was final, and all I needed was a chance to put it into life.

And that chance came very soon in the form of a contract offer from the newly-established Leningrad Comedy Theatre. At my first interview with régisseur Boris Dmokhovsky, at whose instance the offer had been made, he told me that there definitely was a place in drama for my type of grotesque and eccentric acting. I eagerly availed myself of the opportunity offered and immediately left the Moscow Music-Hall. That was in the spring of 1931.

I was given straight parts at the Comedy Theatre and set myself the task of mastering the psychology of the role. With time I made this my main task.

I performed in several classical and Soviet vehicles. My biggest role was as Bywaters in the anticlerical play *A Million Anthonys* by Grigory Gradov and Vladimir Orlov.

Despite all its shortcomings, this play had its merits, for it exposed, in an exciting and entertaining manner, the hypocrisy and venality of some spiritual fathers. The exposé was done very skilfully. Bywaters, a bold bandit, kills a priest, takes his place and eventually becomes a church dignitary. In this role I did my best to give a realistic portrayal. The task was all the more difficult because the play, clearly an agitational one, was melodramatic, and at the same time could be staged as a satirical burlesque. For that reason, I tried to create a sharply-drawn and clearly-defined character, both spiritually and physically, and this gave me a chance to use the most unexpected methods of expression. The agitational character of the play ensured its success, and in a comparatively short period I played the part more than 250 times.

I recall the days I spent at the Comedy Theatre with gratification. It had no stage of its own and performed mainly in suburban workers' clubs. The majority of the spectators we played for seldom saw the inside of a big theatre. They invariably gave us a cordial reception and we could well judge the agitational value of such plays as *A Million Anthonys* from their lively reaction. I had never played the role of such an active agitator and propagandist before, and I tackled it enthusiastically.

At that time I became keenly interested in social activity. Heading the theatre's trade-union committee, taking part in conferences and discussions with the spectators, I found life much more full-blooded. That enabled me to escape from the narrow circle to which I had until recently been confined and helped me to mature. My faith in my abilities as a dramatic actor grew, and I waited for a chance to test them in a realistic play, in an important and true to life role.

That was the reason why I eagerly accepted Boris Sushkevich's invitation to come in for a chat.

Sushkevich, who had just been appointed managing director of the Pushkin Theatre, greeted me very warmly, spoke to me of his plans and told me that he was looking for an actor to play Varlaam in *Boris Godunov*. He offered me the role, adding that he was convinced I could play it well and that it would be sort of a trial job before I joined his company. I readily accepted his offer.

Sushkevich's faith in me was not shared by the others. The reason: my reputation of a burlesque actor, my connections with the Music-Hall, my well-known clownish portrayal of Pat on the variety stage. The first time I went to the Pushkin Theatre I overheard two persons speaking about me, and none too flatteringly.

"Cherkasov?" one of them exclaimed, feigning surprise. "The one from the Young Spectators' Theatre? You mean Don Quixote and Pat of the vaudeville fame? What do we need him for?"

"Well, why shouldn't our theatre have such actors?" was the reply. "Maybe he'll come useful."

Not too promising a beginning.

I would not have mentioned this attitude had it not affected my very first steps at the Pushkin Theatre.

It was precisely because of my reputation as a burlesque comedian that I was first cast as Senechka Perchatkin in Vasily Shkvarkin's popular vaudeville play *Strange Child*. The character was unnatural, vulgar and did nothing to advance me towards my goal.

In the review of the play I did for a Leningrad newspaper, I pointed out that my performance was not a creditable one and that the role was too trite and shallow. A young actor, I stressed, needs psychological, subtle and creative parts, otherwise he faces the danger of getting accustomed to stereotyped roles and forgetting that our age above all demands lofty ideas, sharpness and freshness of thought, and wealth of expressive means.

I deemed it necessary to say frankly what I thought of the play and my role, which I considered both insignificant and uninteresting. I was trying to forget the past, and here it was pursuing me and pinning me down to parts I did not want to play.

It was no easy task to rid myself of the reputation I had acquired, to get others to believe in my dramatic abilities, to find a way out of the situation.

I resumed my ties with Lenfilm, but the offers that came my way were still for comedy roles bordering on the grotesque and eccentric. And in the films, too, I wanted to play straight character parts, and so I started accumulating the necessary experience.

The early thirties marked a rapid advance in the Soviet talking pictures. They were gaining in popularity. I recall how deeply I was impressed by *The Road to Life*, and not so much by its excellent technique as by its ideological content which technique helped to bring out. The significance of the theme, dealing with the education of people in Soviet society, the highly dramatic situations and true to life characters, especially those portrayed by Nikolai Batalov and Mikhail Zharov— all this convinced me that films held out vast opportunities for an actor. *The Road to Life* stimulated my desire to speak from the screen and persuaded me that talking pictures were a mighty weapon and that actors playing in them were doing an extremely important job.

My first relatively important role in the talkies was Kolya Loshak in *Hectic Days*.

Kolya, an idler and a dunce, last in his class and a not too clever or successful gallant, got into all sorts of situations, at times unnatural and ludicrous. There was much of the comedy element in the role but it was trite. All I had to do was to look funny. And that was not what I was striving for. Nonetheless, it proved useful.

After this role I was offered the part of Jacques Paganel in Jules Verne's *Captain Grant's Children*.

I was very happy playing this tireless traveller and enthusiastic geographer, and not only because I admired his enthusiasm for his profession, but because I had always loved Jules Verne and his heroes.

Lanky Paganel looked like a long nail with a big head. His face bespoke a clever and cheerful man. Though he was silent, it was easy to see that he was a great talker and oh, so absent-minded too. . . .

In my desire to portray Paganel as perfectly as possible, I set out to create a rather exaggerated portrait. During the rehearsals and actual filming, which sometimes were days apart, I was careful not to allow the funny situations to make him look ridiculous, but to make use of them to bring out the peculiarities of his personality.

This role enabled me to apply in the cinema the experience I had accumulated in my younger days in the operetta and at the Young

Spectators' Theatre, and it was with the greatest pleasure that I sang "Captain brave, captain brave, won't you smile, sir?"

I worked on the role for a whole year, and yet I was dissatisfied with the result: for some unknown reason I made Paganel look like a fifty-year-old man when, according to Jules Verne, he was very much younger. I had yet to master the art of impersonation and had constantly to think of Paganel's age to make him act accordingly. I became a prisoner of this thought, and that hampered my effort to bring truth to the screen.

On the stage I played in two Russian classical plays—Varlaam in *Boris Godunov* and Osip in Gogol's *Inspector-General*. Both were produced by Sushkevich, and I must admit that they were not free of vulgar innovations.

The erroneous and frequently false interpretation of the underlying meaning of the play did not affect the tavern scene in *Boris Godunov* and playing Varlaam proved easy and natural. I did it enthusiastically and successfully, and for many years I acted the part without any substantial changes.

I was not content with my acting in *Inspector-General*. I had my own idea about Osip, prompted by Pyotr Boklevsky's illustrations for Gogol's play. I pictured Osip as middle-aged, tall and lean. But at the Pushkin Theatre they still remembered Konstantin Varlamov in this role, and they wanted me to portray him just as this famous actor had done: corpulent and obese. My own make-up was rejected. I was forced to wear heavily padded clothes and felt ill at ease. Later, I worked out my own version of presenting Osip's monologue and often appeared with it on the concert stage. When *Inspector-General* was staged to commemorate the hundredth anniversary of Gogol's death, I was again cast as Osip, but this time I gave my own version of the role.

Despite certain production shortcomings, our classics enriched my experience and helped me to create highly realistic images.

In Ibsen's *A Doll's House* I played Krogstadtes. In this role I tried to give a lifelike portrayal of a humiliated and persecuted man who is compelled to ill-use others. The other play in which I was then engaged, *The Prayer for Life,* also dealt with the decay and collapse of a bourgeois family.

Both of these parts proved successful, considerably enhancing my creative potential and confirming me as an actor of the realistic school, though they by no means fully satisfied me.

It was the films that finally gave me a chance to make use of my experience and that brought me to the wide road of creation.

Speaking of actors' successes, Vladimir Nemirovich-Danchenko, the famous Russian stage producer, said they were determined by three requisites: talent, ability and chance. There's no denying that creation of a character that would agitate an actor's imagination and accord with his desire, depends in no little measure on circumstances and chance. First of all, an actor needs a suitable role. As a rule, the actor is powerless to promote such a role. But when there is a suitable role, it should be given to him, irrespective of his experience or reputation. And when these obstacles—incidentally, it is not the actor who creates them—are overcome, when he is given the role he longs for, then his success in it depends on just two prerequisites: ability and talent.

That chance soon came my way.

One of the most discussed novels in those years was Alexei Tolstoi's *Peter I.* Of great artistic merit, the novel described the historical process of Russia's transformation into a mighty world power, painted an epic picture of the period and its outstanding ruler. Tolstoi showed his hero and his place in Russian history in a new, progressive light.

I became deeply interested in his interpretation of Peter I, particularly when I learned that Tolstoi had agreed to have his novel screened and that he had written a stage version as well. The picture was to be produced by Lenfilm, and the play by the Pushkin Theatre.

I yearned to play Peter I but did not dare apply for the role in the theatre lest they should refuse me. But I did apply to Lenfilm.

When Vladimir Petrov, the producer, heard of my proposal, he laughingly exclaimed:

"What! With that mug?"

But soon afterwards he offered me another role in the film—a completely different role, that of Tsarevich Alexei, Peter's son and chief opponent of his reforms. His offer was a complete surprise to everybody, including myself, but I eagerly accepted it.

There is one unimportant, but thoroughly characteristic episode that is fresh in my memory.

Shortly after the film went into production, a man came to repair my home telephone in my absence. When he had finished his job, he asked what I was doing and was told about my role as Alexei.

"Good. We'll get some laughs!" He smiled.

"Not at all. It's a tragic role."

"That doesn't matter. We know Cherkasov well. He'll make us laugh all right."

When I learned about this, I realized that I would have to convince not only my colleagues in the theatre and studio, but also the spectators who had come to know me as an actor of a completely different type.

I set about enthusiastically preparing for the role. It was not only as a nonentity and weakling that I tried to portray Alexei, not only as a blind tool, but also as a conscious, at times wilful, weapon in the hands of the reactionary elements of Peter's time.

Working on the role, I re-created in my mind the picture of Alexei's childhood, the low, sombre and stuffy chambers, his nurses, his first teachers, the priests, monks, fortune-tellers and quacks, and the half-wits—the God's fools, or *yurodiviye*, as they were called. I re-created the picture of his life—his treacherous flight to Italy, his attempt to find support abroad, his return to Russia and imprisonment, the torture-chamber and his inglorious death. For me, the screened episodes of Alexei's life were not merely isolated events but an integral part of his biography, the logical consequence of his earlier life.

Trying to make the character as realistic as possible, I visualized my hero in all sorts of situations which at times were not even included in the scenario. This search for realism is not difficult when one is portraying an historical character, for one does not have to think up any situations. It is sufficient to make use of historical facts and of the typical characteristics which are not reflected in the scenario. The result is that the portrayal becomes fuller and expressive of the most essential features of the man's personality.

Looking at some of the shots of the future film, Tolstoi noted that Alexei was faithfully portrayed, and this enhanced my confidence in my abilities.

The first part of the film had already been completed and we were working on the second when my long-cherished dream came true: the Pushkin Theatre offered me the title role in its revival of *Peter I*.

I shall dwell on this role later on. Now I shall simply mention that in the evenings I played Peter I at the theatre, and in the mornings I faced the cameras as Alexei, and my colleagues composed a little humorous couplet about it:

> He is busy every day,
> Playing Peter 'n' Alexei.

I should like to point out that impersonating two so diametrically different human beings as Peter and Alexei helped me to bring out in the weak-willed son some of the will-power of his father.

I shall illustrate this with an episode that best reflected the character of Tsarevich Alexei—the scene in which he signs the manifesto urging Peter's overthrow.

On his return to Moscow from abroad, Alexei was pardoned by his father. The scene shows him pacing nervously in a Kremlin chamber, listening to the boyar Buinosov and a drunken priest. Alexei is panic-stricken: the Secret Council has arrested his mistress Yefrosinya, and he is afraid she may reveal the names of his accomplices. Kikin, one of the most reactionary of the boyars rallying around Alexei, suggests that he sign the manifesto. The tsarevich is gripped by fear and hesitates. Kikin shows him the crowd of monks, half-wits and beggars who had gathered at the gates to the Kremlin. To Alexei, they are the decisive force in his struggle against his father. He returns to the chamber with a feeling that he is already tsar. Peter's wilful character awakens in Alexei, and he strides firmly to the table where, with a flourish of the pen, he signs a manifesto calling to mutiny.

As Professor Polezhayev in the film *Baltic Deputy*. 1936

As Professor Polezhayev
in *Baltic Deputy*. 1936

Nikolai Cherkasov with
Maria Domasheva in
Baltic Deputy. 1936

The role opened up new creative perspectives and was another step forward to highly dramatic and even tragic roles—in this particular case along the line of portraying a negative character.

The film was a school in which I studied a number of historical characters, a school in which I worked on epics of my country's past. However much our film industry has advanced, *Peter I,* an early production on a historical theme, remains one of the best, and I am happy that I had the opportunity of playing in it.

As for the role of Peter, which I had thought would help me to create the image of a positive hero, I must admit that I failed: it was beyond my scope.

Many actors, moved by their desire to serve their beloved art, frequently overestimate their abilities. That happened to me too. Sometimes I thought and believed I could play a certain role only to find out later that it was not in my line.

When I speak of overestimating one's abilities I do not mean that actors, especially novices, should tackle only easy roles. On the contrary, I always tell young actors to be bold, to fight for big parts, but only if they see that they have the necessary qualifications, physical and otherwise, to cope with these parts. A Russian proverb says that he is a bad soldier who does not want to be a general. It is fully applicable to the actor, though I would add that for his own good an actor should restrict his desires by his abilities. To understand this is the task of every actor and its successful solution is proof of his creative maturity.

I realized that clearly when I was playing a role that is especially dear and near to me—the role of Professor Polezhayev.

I was still engaged in *Peter I* when I was asked to go through the script of a new film for the title role. I had heard about it and knew that it was about an elderly scientist. Busy with the role of Alexei, I was not overenthusiastic about the new offer, but nevertheless agreed to look through the script, Leonid Rakhmanov and Leonid Dell's *Baltic Deputy.*

The script captured my imagination from the very start.

The period it described I knew well and loved deeply. It was the first years of the Revolution and the heroic defence of its victories. It was in those years that I was in that same Red Petrograd making my first independent steps in life. I was ardently in love with life then and well remember the atmosphere of its revolutionary romance. The script revived in my mind everything I had seen, everything I had experienced and heard, everything my youthful mind had grasped. Only the script painted an integrated picture, moving and lifelike.

I liked every bit of the script—not just the epoch it was describing, but even the surroundings in which the story was laid and the image of the hero himself—Professor Polezhayev. I was carried away by the patriotic ardour of the script, Polezhayev's firmness and enthusiasm, his loyalty to the people and Revolution, his faith in the victory of the proletariat, his dream of an alliance between science and labour, his frankness and charm. I pictured him clearly against the background of the first years of the Revolution, his bitter struggle against saboteurs and counter-revolutionaries in the field of science, his happiness at being able to associate with revolutionary sailors, his militant speech as a Baltic deputy at the plenary session of the Petrograd Soviet, at the Tavrichesky Palace, before the Red Army men leaving for the front. In every detail, big and small, Professor Polezhayev proved just the type of hero I had so long been wanting to play. When I finished reading the script, I was in no two minds about it: I wanted to, could, should and would play Polezhayev!

Sooner or later every actor comes across a role that opens up new vistas before him, that perfectly suits his abilities. I was sure that Polezhayev was just that kind of a role. It was the chance I had been longing for.

The studio tested several well-known actors for the role. I decided to do my best to get the part.

I do not recall any other instance when I tried so hard or worried so much. I spoke of my desire everywhere and to everyone and I am not ashamed to say that I virtually forced myself on the producer, giving him scores of reasons why I was sure I would succeed. I was told, and quite rightly too, that Professor Polezhayev was 75 while I was only 32, but I countered this by saying that he was so young in spirit that only a young actor could play him. In a word, I was practically ready to go to court to fight for the right to play the role ... if it had been within the court's jurisdiction to settle such a case.

My first test was not too successful. But the second proved much better. The producer favoured me and I got the role, despite the fact that the top officials of Lenfilm and certain other film workers had no confidence in me. Thrilled at the thought that the role was mine and that the producer was for me, I set about eagerly to study it.

The highly ideological theme of *Baltic Deputy* carried away the entire company.

The underlying idea was clearly expressed in the script. It dealt with the fate of the progressive, democratic intelligentsia in the early stages of the October Revolution. The task was to elaborate this idea, to complement it with other similar themes—with the theme of the creative cooperation of the best representatives of science with the people, the theme of the role and place of science in the revolutionary transformation of society, the theme of science and socialism. Without these themes the film would have simply been a story of a revolutionary-minded old scientist, and its significance would have been low indeed. The motivating idea could best be expressed through the image of the hero, through his personality and activity.

This is the task I faced, and it was up to me to find a convincing form of expressing the theme through the actions of Polezhayev, through his thoughts and behaviour, in other words, through his character. The idea was to create an image of extraordinary moral integrity and quite ordinary in appearance.

I set out to master the role by reading all I could on the history of the October Revolution, especially the sources throwing light on its first stage. The events which unfolded in Professor Polezhayev's home, in his study, at his lectures and around his manuscript had to be well understood and presented against the background of revolutionary stress. It was only in this way that I could depict the moral aspect of the hero's personality as a scientist, democrat and revolutionary fully and wholly devoted to the cause of the proletariat, and to show him as a true representative of the best section of the Russian intelligentsia.

The film was based on the life story of the great Russian scientist K. A. Timiryazev, and I studied his biography, his articles and letters in order to acquaint myself with his inner world and psychology, and familiarize myself with the features of his character.

Lunacharsky's articles about Timiryazev and particularly Timiryazev's letters to Maxim Gorky did much to help me to understand Polezhayev. Shortly before the Revolution Timiryazev wrote to Gorky: "When will there be an honest newspaper? I am an old man and yet my tongue itches. What then must young people feel?" These words clearly reveal the character of the famous scientist and democrat, who wrote in a preface to one of his books: "In the very first stage of my scientific activity I set myself two parallel tasks—to work for science and write for the people."

The social and political ideals of Professor Polezhayev and his attitude towards the Revolution and the victorious class determined the essence of his whole outlook and the motives behind his actions. After I had grasped this, I started my search for corresponding outer forms of expression, for ways to give my character lifelike and typical features. I sought them in the images, customs and individual characteristics of our scientists, writers and other cultural workers. But my hero was not just a scientist; he was an old scientist who lived in the atmosphere of the first years of the Revolution. It was necessary to depict all these relatively important aspects of my hero's life, aspects which could in no way be ignored.

The closing shots of the film were of momentous significance, proclaiming the alliance of progressive scientists with the revolutionary people in the all-important struggle for socialism. The film thus spoke not so much of the past as of the future. This association of part with the whole represented one of the difficulties in creating the image of Professor Polezhayev.

Gradually there formed in my mind a composite picture of a Russian scientist and patriot which had the features not only of Timiryazev, Mendeleyev and Pavlov, but those of Rimsky-Korsakov and Stanislavsky as well. I borrowed from Kirov the sharpness and firmness of voice for the scene in which Polezhayev, speaking at the plenary session of the Petrograd Soviet, referred ironically to the sabotage tactics of the representatives of the old "academic science" who, to use his words, "have turned their knowledge into a fence to separate themselves from the people." I borrowed Lenin's sweeping gesture for the scene in which Polezhayev sends the soldiers off to the front with the words: "Don't surrender Red Petrograd to the German Whiteguards!"

Portraying Polezhayev as a wise old man, as a man of profound and lucid ideas and of a somewhat "restless" nature, I tried at the same time to show that he was young in spirit and that sometimes he behaved with youthful enthusiasm and eccentricity. This enabled me to paint a vivid picture of his wonderful mischievousness, his original ways and his liveliness and sincerity. In his talk with cinema workers, Maxim Gorky pointed out that Soviet film heroes were not characteristic enough and, what was more, "devoid of humour." The great writer stressed that there is something humorous in every man, no matter how great he may be, and that to create a full character one should not be afraid to show the funny sides.

Gradually I got so accustomed to playing Polezhayev that I could portray him in any situation—for instance, doing physical exercises or dancing mazurka at his birthday, looking for a book that has fallen behind a shelf, or talking with the doorman.

Baltic Deputy was in production for about three months and all this while I virtually lived in Professor Polezhayev's three-room "flat" at the Lenfilm Studios.

I got so used to this "flat" that it became a second home for me, and I felt almost broken-hearted when the carpenters began to take apart the "Polezhayev set" to build a new one.

Baltic Deputy was previewed at the Leningrad Cinema House on January 1, 1937, and released to the general public two and a half months later, scoring a big success.

At our meetings with the audiences, arranged after the première in Leningrad, I had to answer a host of questions which revealed that the spectators were deeply interested in the issues we had raised in the film and in the lofty theme of the alliance of science and revolution. At the end of these meetings I read the speech addressed by Professor Polezhayev to the Baltic seamen, soldiers and workers at the Petrograd Soviet:

"You are the owners, the real masters of a sixth part of the world. . . . I greet you in the name of science, whose task is to think of your happiness, present and future!"

My work on the portrait of this revolutionary scientist was a political school for me. It enabled me to acquaint myself still closer with the struggle waged by our people for their revolutionary development, understand and appreciate still more our Soviet way of life, to see in it the roots of our future.

I left this school with a clear realization that henceforth my favourite hero in the theatre and cinema would be the character through whom we could spread the revolutionary ideas of our historic era.

ON THE STAGE AND SCREEN

I am often asked what I like better, the stage or the screen, and I usually answer: "Both."

The nature of creating roles on the stage and on the screen is the same, but the technology is different.

The theatre gives an actor a longer period of rehearsal. It starts with a round-table discussion of the roles and then shifts to the stage. And the actor spends all this period getting into the inner world of the character he is to portray. It is much later, sometimes only at the dress rehearsal, that the actor expresses the inner world of his hero in outer form.

A theatre première does not mean that the actor has ceased working on his role or that his performance is perfect. It is rather the beginning of a new phase in his creative work which continues under the control and influence of the audience. The spectator is an active participant in the show, and his attitude and reaction to the performance influence the actor's work in perfecting the role.

Very often, unexpectedly for the actor himself, new expressive colours —new ideas and emotions, intonations and movements—emerge during a performance, helping him to improve his characterization. That depends, however, on the attendance, on the reaction and cultural requirements of the spectators and, finally, on the impact of current life. Moments like that give the actor much pleasure, stimulate the initiative in his partners, enrich the play and enhance its artistry. They are, in short, creative discoveries that inject new blood into the play.

I should like to cite two examples from my own practice, connected with the role of Ivan the Terrible in Vladimir Solovyov's historical drama *The Great Tsar*.

When I was rehearsing the play at the Pushkin Theatre, the régisseur and I had to put in quite an effort into Tsar Ivan's monologue at the coffin of the tsarevich whom he had killed in a burst of fury.

The scene was a difficult one. It consisted of that one monologue which was more than 100 lines long, and extremely varied in content.

We thought over carefully the development of the monologue and decided to break it up into six parts, each containing one whole, clear idea. It seemed that the almost ten-minute-long monologue was developing logically, that it was clearly expressing the thoughts of the hero and revealing his emotions.

I was quite nervous at the première, but the scene went off well. In the subsequent performances I made a few insignificant alterations. But it was only when appearing in the role for the fiftieth time that I realized how I should play the scene and how and where I should lay emphasis in the monologue. We now divided it into ten parts; it improved, and became even better when we split it into twelve. The scene flowed more smoothly and monolithically and became richer for that. That climaxed the process of accumulating experience which had gone on uninterruptedly since the première. Without the reaction of the audience I do not think we would have solved this task.

One day, after I had played the role for more than 100 times, I had to perform with a sore throat. It was too late to change the bill. I had to conceal my hoarseness and to do that I decided to change the timbre of my voice and the rhythm of my lines. My hoarse voice had to serve as an organic intonation in the characterization of Ivan the Terrible. That evening there emerged new features in the tsar's character, and this led to new experiences, new inflections and gestures.

How is this to be explained?

Forced to concentrate all my attention on the voice, I naturally relaxed control over the inner development of the image, over its emotions. I thus gave it greater freedom and greater scope to develop, for excessive control, as a rule, adversely influences one's performance. In brief, it hampers true to life impersonation.

Thus, the incident that compelled me to relax control over the inner development of the image really helped me to add new natural characteristics to my portrayal. I retained that in the subsequent performances because the reaction of the audience confirmed that the changes I had been forced to bring into my role were correct and logical.

Consequently, characters on the stage perforce continue to develop with each performance. It is the duty of the actor to enhance his role, unless he wants his performance to doom his artistry to gradual deterioration. An actor is always convinced that with each performance he can bring changes and improvements to his portrayal, and that conviction leads him to progress.

A screen actor enjoys none of these opportunities, for there are no lengthy periods of rehearsal, except—and that is quite rare—in the case of "chamber" films.

Before a film goes into production, the leading players and the producer discuss the roles in great detail, the features of the characters they are to portray, their development, and the main points of the story. Long before the actual shooting begins, the actor must familiarize himself thoroughly with the script and his role, and have a complete idea of the film as a whole so as to be ready to appear before the cameras after three or four rehearsals. He must keep track of the natural, organic process of the development of his character, of the sequence of scenes and of the interrelation and rhythm of various fragments shot, as a rule, at long intervals.

I shall cite just two examples from my film work.

In *Captain Grant's Children* there's a scene showing four courageous travellers crossing the Cordilleras.

The approach to the Cordilleras was filmed against a background of snow-capped peaks at the Chegem Gorge in the North Caucasus in, August. The scaling of the snowy peaks was shot at the Pargolovo Hills near Leningrad the following February, and it was at this juncture that, according to the scenario, I was supposed to fall through the roof of a snow-bound cabin. And it was only in May, at the Mosfilm Studios, that I finally found myself in the cabin. If I had not retained the emotional interrelation between the three sequences, it would have been impossible to whip them into one single scene.

Another, and an even more vivid, example is from *Peter I.*

In the highly emotional and tense scene in which Alexei quarrels and fights with Yefrosinya we had to overcome a lot of difficulties because the scene was fractioned into numerous shots made at lengthy intervals.

The bedroom sequence, divided into many long shots and close-ups, was filmed in five days in January, ending with Yefrosinya breaking away from Alexei and running through several rooms. It is only then that the tsarevich realizes that he was mean to slap her.

Alexei's pursuit of Yefrosinya was filmed two months later, after special scenery had been completed. The next stage of the escape and pursuit on the marble stairs was shot at the Cameron Gallery in the town of Pushkin in August and we had to work ourselves into the emotional mood of five months ago "without any start," so to speak.

The last shots of the scene, in which Alexei goes down on his knees to beg her forgiveness, were filmed at the studio much later. These last scenes were all the more difficult because they ended with Tsarevich Alexei going into hysterics. To ensure a better composition of the scene, the cameraman often placed me in inconvenient poses which I had to justify and in which, at the demand of the director, I had to force myself to shed tears.

Thus, filming this one scene at lengthy intervals, we had to retain the emotional mood of the preceding shot so that all the takes could be cut and edited into one single episode.

These examples reveal one of the technical peculiarities of the work of the film actor which are completely unknown to his stage confrère.

At the theatre, the acting process goes on according to a well-defined and established routine, usually in the evening. Playing on the stage before his public, the actor is calm and collected, and his creative mood is sustained through the play, with only short intervals interrupting it.

In the cinema, filming is done at all hours of the day, very often at night, and sometimes, for purely technical reasons, the actor is forced to sit and wait, all dressed and made up, for two or three hours and then go through five or six retakes. In other words, he has to play the same episode as many as six times, not counting the rehearsals that usually precede the filming of a scene.

At the theatre, the actor plays before an audience. He holds the audience's attention by the thoughts he conveys to it, by varying intonations, and by an unlimited number of other means that present themselves during the pauses and movements. In any case, he has every opportunity of acting according to the dictates of his artistic discretion and creative mood.

In the cinema the actor depends a lot—I would even say up to 90 per cent—on film technique which ties him hand and foot. Appearing before the camera, the actor has to play his part and at the same time be careful to follow the directions given him by the producer, the cameraman and the sound-man. In each separate shot he has to develop his role in the briefest space of time and observe mathematical precision.

Working in difficult conditions, without an audience to bolster him up, his performance subjected to constant, diversified and complex technical control, the actor must develop professional collectedness, improve his skill and accumulate experience, be calm and self-possessed, and always in a congenial mood, for the latter is the main prerequisite for a successful performance.

While on the stage a role is improved with each performance over months and years, in the cinema, unfortunately, the actor plays the role just once, with no further perfecting of the role possible.

While at the theatre the actor starts working on his character at the round-table discussion and then continues at the rehearsals where he fully determines and reveals his hero's inner emotions, in the cinema the actor's work on a character begins with the encounter with the make-up man and costumier, and it is at this meeting that the actor, the producer, the cameraman and the make-up artist decide what the hero should look like. Then comes the test which determines whether the actor suits the part.

While at the theatre the actor gets his role sheets on the very first day and studies them all through the period of rehearsal, in the cinema the actor sometimes gets the sheets almost immediately before the actual filming.

At the theatre the actor's role develops smoothly and consistently and he works towards a climax or a key monologue; in a ballet the dancer step by step prepares himself to perform technically difficult movements—so many bars and so many leaps; in the opera the singer gradually comes to the culminating high note. The cinema actor has no such possibilities.

There is no doubt that creative work in the cinema demands more than just talent, skill and originality. It calls for a special devotion to this art and particularly readiness to surmount numerous difficulties, for film work is hard and requires much patience.

But while the theatre has its advantages over the cinema, the cinema, too, has its advantages over the theatre.

One of these advantages is the much greater freedom in choosing the cast—the producer can engage any actor he wishes from any theatre.

The association of the best actors from different theatres and of completely different types in one film helps them to improve their skill by drawing on each other's experiences.

Another advantage of acting in films is that it gives the actor a fuller opportunity to display his talents and reveal latent abilities which may influence his further development as an artist.

In this sense the Soviet cinema has accomplished much, for it has helped to discover talent in some instances earlier and more fully than the theatre has done.

I would like to mention two of my colleagues at the Pushkin Theatre —Nikolai Simonov and Alexander Borisov. We three owe much to the cinema which had discovered that we had more ability than the theatre had disclosed and which, having tested us, used us boldly in important roles. Simonov, who was very young, was playing all sorts of roles on the stage, very often quite unsuitable, when the cinema singled him out as an actor of greater ability and gave him the title role in *Peter I.* Borisov had long played minor roles in our theatre and was seldom given an important part. The cinema revealed his unique talents first in *Academician Ivan Pavlov* and then in *Moussorgsky.* In the latter picture good use was made of his musical talents, which had found no outlet on the stage, and this enabled Borisov to present Moussorgsky not only as a musician, but also as a singer of his own compositions.

Yet another advantage of the cinema is that it has mass audiences and that makes it possible to popularize an actor's achievements on a scale which is absolutely inaccessible to the theatre.

And then there are other advantages: the cinema can show an actor at his best, especially in close-ups in which he can display his talent through facial expression. All this helps to make his performance rich and full-blooded.

Yet, in my opinion, an actor who devotes himself solely to the cinema is making a mistake, especially as Soviet art offers so many opportunities to develop in all directions. It will be only to his advantage to use his talents in various spheres and genres—primarily at the theatre.

The theatre is a wonderful laboratory which helps the actor to develop his creative talent, learn the mechanics of emotion, reveal his temperament and acting abilities.

The cinema polishes the actor's technique and teaches him to grasp the part he is playing and step into the necessary creative mood at a moment's notice. It helps him to make the best use of different means of expression, and does much to develop his powers of imagination.

The actor should work both in the theatre and in the cinema if he wishes to use his abilities to the full. For me, the theatre and the cinema are more than blood brothers, they are twins.

THE ACTOR AND THE PLAYWRIGHT

No one perhaps reads a play with more attention and interest than an actor. No one is a more exacting reader. And how happy the actor is to come across a powerful and colourful play, how eager he is to act in it when he finds a role that suits him!

The Soviet theatre cannot develop and progress without modern plays and modern themes. A modern play enriches and renovates our art and strengthens its ties with life.

I get excited every time I have to meet a playwright and acquaint myself with a new role. Excited because in most cases acquaintance with a new role in a modern play means learning more about the new man who embodies all the typical characteristics of our time and understanding still better the laws that govern our Soviet way of life.

If the role I am offered gives me nothing in this respect, there is no use tackling it because then I can say for certain that it will mean nothing to my audiences, that it will not move them, that it will leave them cold.

But if the play has an important underlying theme and idea, if the role I am offered will give me an opportunity to portray an interesting and complex character, then I am both excited and worried, and sometimes even alarmed. Alarmed because until the actor has mastered the role, he is always worried, uncertain of himself and afraid that he will be unable to grasp the basic idea of the play and the role.

To master the role and fully understand the character one is to play is no easy task. One must know people, have a good store of life's experiences and a mature world outlook—in other words, one must know life.

How many times, after receiving a play or a script, had I gone through the slow and difficult process of getting into the "feel" of the role, putting to a severe test my perseverance, will and ability to reach people's characters. And I found that the more I broadened my interests, the more I learned of life and the more actively I took part in it, the easier it became to grasp the individual features and the living traits which make a portrayal real and convincing.

Knowledge of life—not abstract knowledge, of course—is the basic qualification of an artist. And it is impossible to know and understand life if one does not possess a mature world outlook. It is the only basis on which an artist can develop his powers of observation, his interest in people, his ability to penetrate the depth of human character. It is the world outlook that guides him in his receptivity, his thoughts and his creative imagination. An actor who has set himself the task of serving his people, the builders of communism, must be a man of firm convictions, a man of ideals and clear purpose. In the Soviet actor's work, the world outlook plays the leading, decisive role, and it is impossible indeed to overestimate its significance.

Unfortunately, there are actors who entertain dangerous delusions: they think that in whatever difficulty they may find themselves, they will be saved by their "sense of truth," and that their actor's instinct will save them from committing ideological errors.

But life teaches us otherwise. It reminds us again and again that only a politically mature artist, an ardent and irreconcilable champion of the people's cause, can fully understand the phenomena of life, see into man's character and create a convincing portrait on the stage or screen. It should be stressed once again that it is impossible to know life without taking an active part in it, by just looking at it from the side-lines. It is impossible to see what is most outstanding in a character or to portray him truthfully without properly understanding his place among men and in society. This is law to the playwright who creates the character in writing, and to the actor who re-creates the same character on the stage.

The actor has the right to demand of the playwright that he follow this law and that the play and its characters be written well and realistically.

It is utterly wrong to suppose that an all-star cast can "save" a poor play. It more often happens that a poor play may spell ruin to gifted actors and keep the audiences away.

The actor knows perfectly well when his creative thought and will are stimulated by the playwright or when, on the contrary, it is he who must help and "prop up" the playwright. He clearly sees the opportunities offered by a play, what it means to him when there is a sharply drawn conflict and a clearly defined character, when the play is a memorable one. And he knows what it is when the play lacks all these qualities.

My roles in *Peter I* and *Baltic Deputy* helped me to bring out the characteristic features of Tsarevich Alexei and Professor Polezhayev in all their versatility because they were disclosed in the acute tense historical conflicts of their times.

Impersonating Professor Polezhayev, I realized for the first time how much a real sharp conflict helps the actor. If the play or the script reflects the period truthfully, if the fate of the hero and his character are depicted in true to life conflicts, then acting is easy and pleasant.

A well-written play or film scenario fires the actor's imagination at its very first reading, offers great possibilities, stimulates his desire to bring out in detail all its motivating ideas, and inspires him to creation.

The more full-blooded the image is, the richer it is in individual features, the easier and the more fruitful will be the actor's work, and the longer his creation will live.

Nikolai Cherkasov (Don Quixote) and Boris Gorin-Goryainov (Sancho Panza). 1941

Nikolai Cherkasov with producer Vladimir
Petrov on the set of *Peter I*. 1937

Producer Sergei Eisenstein and Nikolai Cherkasov
during the filming of *Alexander Nevsky*. 1938

And vice versa: an actor's consummate portrayal of a character in his play means much to the dramatist in his further work.

Indeed, if one recalls how the portrayal of Soviet types developed on the stage and in films, if one scans the long path traversed in the past three decades and more by the Soviet hero and heroine—from Lyubov Yarovaya, teacher and Communist, in Konstantin Trenyov's play of the same name or from the Siberian partisan Nikita Vershinin in Vsevolod Ivanov's *Armoured Train 14-69* to the heroes of today's plays and films, one will realize that the growth of these literary characters was in no little measure influenced by the players' impersonations.

Whenever I think of Lyubov Yarovaya, I think of Vera Pashennaya who created this role at the Maly Theatre. And when I think of Vershinin, I at once recall Vasily Kachalov who first played him at the Art Theatre. When one thinks of the stage portrayal of so great a genius as Lenin, it is difficult indeed to forget Boris Shchukin, the first actor to play the Soviet leader on the stage, in Nikolai Pogodin's *Man with the Gun* at the Vakhtangov Theatre.

The same comparison holds good for the cinema. When one calls to mind the trilogy about the young worker Maxim, one remembers Boris Chirkov, and when one speaks of Chapayev, one thinks of Boris Babochkin, who gave an inspired performance as the Civil War hero. And I hope that, when the cinema-goer thinks of Professor Polezhayev in *Baltic Deputy*, he remembers me.

Very often spectators identify characters in a play or a film with the actors who impersonate them. That is because actors' performances help to bring out the author's idea truthfully and powerfully.

Belinsky once said that the actor's performance complements the idea of the author and it is this that constitutes his creation. Belinsky correctly defined the peculiarities of acting art, the nature of the relations between the actor and the dramatist, and the character of their cooperation.

In the cinema the actor and the producer very often help the script writer with ideas that bring out the characters in bolder relief.

Sometimes, when the makers of a film see the ready product, they themselves do not know who—the script writer, producer or actor—has developed the motivating idea or spun out the action to improve on the role.

Just like other film players, I have time and again elaborated situations which were included in the picture, enhancing its value.

In *Baltic Deputy* there is a dialogue between Professor Polezhayev and his assistant, Vorobyov, who has sided with the counter-revolutionaries. Polezhayev quotes Darwin, and Vorobyov, obviously bent on hurting his teacher, retorts:

"Darwin has never said that!"

Polezhayev looks calmly at his adversary and answers:

"No, he has not said that to you, but he has to me!"

This episode was an improvisation. We were trying to show the ideological gulf separating Polezhayev and Vorobyov and to stress the difference of their approach to science. Looking for a realistic way of solving this task, I recalled an incident which had occurred at one of Lunacharsky's lectures in the first years after the Revolution. Lunacharsky had then quoted Lenin, and a cheeky young fellow in the front row shouted:

"Lenin has never said that!"

There was an uneasy pause as Lunacharsky sized the fellow up and then replied with his characteristic humour:

"That's right, he has not said that to you, but he has to me!"

My proposal to include this repartee in the film was accepted, and it helped to lay emphasis on relations between Polezhayev and Vorobyov and simultaneously introduced a humorous touch.

The dialogue between Polezhayev and Lenin, which climaxed the picture, was polished up at one of the last rehearsals.

Rehearsing this scene, I could not rid myself of the feeling that sabotage by the counter-revolutionary intelligentsia and the betrayal of his erstwhile friends had left Polezhayev fully isolated. His telephone talk with Lenin—brief, dry, and not sufficiently clear to the spectator—did not define sharply enough the turning point of the story and was inadequate in itself to show that Polezhayev was not isolated, that in a difficult moment he had the support of the great leader of the Revolution.

The dialogue was rewritten. In the new variant, Lenin's words encouraged Polezhayev, showed him that he was not alone, that the leader of the Communist Party was really on his side. We thus laid the necessary emphasis on the development of the action and on the change taking place in the hero's position and thoughts.

In *Peter I*, at a very important juncture, I felt the need for a more precise characterization of Tsarevich Alexei in order to explain why Peter had condemned his son to death. The idea was to convince the spectator that Alexei was incorrigible and thus justify his father's severe verdict.

In this scene, Peter is shown questioning Alexei who stands before him in a plain shirt, his head low, seemingly penitent.

"Who are the senators you wrote to? I want their names!" Peter tells him.

No answer.

"So you won't say?" Peter asks threateningly.

According to the script, Alexei was to leave this question unanswered too. But then his silence could be interpreted in two ways: either that he was persisting in being stubbornly hostile or that, crushed by his father's will, he had nothing to say or could not speak after the torture-chamber. In my opinion, there should be no doubt as to the meaning of his silence.

So I proposed to add one sentence, and after a lengthy pause, replied with fury and hatred:

"No, I will not!"

This answer fully revealed the character of the treacherous tsarevich who remained to the last bitterly hostile towards his father's idea of Russian statehood. At the same time it justified, as natural and inevitable, the tsar's verdict:

"Take him away!"

In the film *Bon Voyage!*—in which I played an instructor at a naval school—I tried to paint a picture of Soviet educational methods and suggested the scene in which Captain Levashov comes across a sleeping sentry.

Seeing the youngster dozing, I pulled at his sleeve, coughed and, when he opened his eyes, asked him:

"You're not feeling sleepy, are you?"

"No, Comrade Captain!"

"Good! A sentry should never fall asleep. If he does, he is punished severely!"

And then, looking at the stars in the sky, I added: "The night is beautiful, isn't it?" and sauntered off. It was a brief episode, but it helped to stress Levashov's tactfulness and kindness.

Each film player could cite similar examples from his practice, even when the script is very good. The power of the actor's imagination and his suggestions are the result of his search for a better way of describing a situation or presenting his hero. Production of a film, in which the actor is the most active participant, is absolutely impossible if there is no team-work.

Speaking of team-work between the actor and the producer, on the one hand, and the playwright and the script writer, on the other, I should like to relate how *Life in Bloom* was staged at the Pushkin Theatre.

It all started with the brief note I received from Alexander Dovzhenko, the author of the script about the famous Soviet botanist, Michurin. "Dear Nikolai," he wrote from Moscow, "I'm sending you *Michurin*. I shall appreciate it if you read the script in the morning. I shall appreciate it even more if you like it. And I shall appreciate it most and will be happy beyond words if you find it charming and say: 'Let life bloom!'"

The letter made me very happy and at the same time intrigued me. It showed that Dovzhenko, producer and script writer, was seeking my cooperation and was confident that I could star in his picture. It is only natural that I read the script with keen interest.

Michurin was lovingly depicted as a patriot and a scientist, as a persevering innovator and a man of wilful character and intensive creative work. The script brought out the sharp conflict between Michurin and pre-revolutionary society, and showed how his struggle and achievements helped to form his character. In a word, I liked the script, for it was extremely interesting and even enthralling. But then *Michurin* was to be filmed in Moscow and I was tied by work at the Pushkin Theatre and at Lenfilm, as well as by my many social obligations, and so I had to turn the offer down.

But my desire to play Michurin persisted. The script had deeply impressed me, and I spoke about it to my colleagues, and to Leonid Vivien, our chief régisseur. We knew that Dovzhenko was writing a stage version of his scenario, and we asked him for a copy. It soon arrived. The title was taken from the closing words of his letter to me: *Life in Bloom*.

Strictly speaking, the play we received was a variant of the scenario and more suitable for the screen than the stage. There were a number of serious difficulties to overcome, ranging from the far too many little scenes to a certain lack of continuity. We saw these difficulties from the very first reading, and they considerably retarded our work.

But there was something in the play that made the fight against the difficulties well worth while: the magnificent motivating idea, the exciting story of a scientist's wonderful endeavours for the welfare of man, the theme of materialism in biology, and the role of progressive science in the construction of socialist society.

These merits roused the enthusiasm of the whole company, Vivien included. We overcame the difficulties at the rehearsals, sometimes appealing for advice to Dovzhenko who was then busy with the filming of *Michurin*. The cast helped him quite a bit to improve the play, and the result was a successful show, despite certain shortcomings.

Heartened by the success, the theatre set about eliminating the defects shown up by the critics, and later it was decided to ask Dovzhenko to rewrite certain sequences. Thus was born a new variant of *Life in Bloom*.

This case may well serve as one of the many examples of fruitful cooperation between the theatre and the playwright.

It was fully justified, too, because the play had everything: an idea and a wealth of material which enabled us to paint a true to life picture of Michurin. On this basis it was possible to work successfully.

In such cases—as the one I have dwelt upon, describing the work we had done on *Life in Bloom*—the actor must devote all his talent, artistry and skill, all his creative power, to help the author to perfect his play.

But the theatre cannot do the playwright's work and cover up the shortcomings of an ill-written play. The task of the theatre and of the actor is to bring out the ideological and artistic merits of a play and to give as vivid as possible an impersonation of its characters.

There is no denying that the theatre must cooperate patiently with the author, but only if his play is not sketchy and slipshod, not just an attempt at something like drama or comedy, but a work of artistic merit—perhaps with certain shortcomings, perhaps not yet polished up, but already a play that reveals the author as a man who knows life, as a man who has both talent and taste. If this is lacking, there can be no fruitful cooperation.

Good dialogue is the criterion by which a play is chiefly judged.

The great playwrights have given us excellent examples of how to make use of language. When we perform in classic plays we thoroughly enjoy the precise, pointed and colourful dialogues. The actor feels at ease with words that fit the action; for the text is that very plastic material from which images are moulded so naturally.

Soviet plays develop the best traditions of Russian stage dialogue. That applies most of all, of course, to Maxim Gorky's last plays—but then in wealth of vocabulary Gorky stands in a class by himself—and to no little degree to Alexei Tolstoi, Konstantin Trenyov, Leonid Leonov, Nikolai Pogodin, Vsevolod Vishnevsky and Boris Lavrenyov in whose plays the dialogue flows naturally and realistically, helping the actor to bring out the individuality of his character.

I recall how full-blooded, true to life and powerful the character of young Ivan the Terrible appeared to me as I listened to Alexei Tolstoi reading his historical drama *The Eagle and the Eagless*. That was during the war, after we had been evacuated from Leningrad, at the time when I was working on the role of Tsar Ivan, studying his life and activity from all the sources I could lay my hands on. Tolstoi asked us to hear the play he had just completed, and it helped me more than any historical research. He read excellently, changing his voice to suit the character, and that made it easy to form a picture of the personages which he had so vividly portrayed in his play.

The actor is highly sensitive to the speech of his character, and is always dissatisfied and confused when his lines are colourless and impersonal.

It is the sacred duty of a playwright to write good dialogue. Just like a composer must be a musician above all, just like a régisseur must know and understand the actor's mind, just like a scene painter must be an artist, so must a playwright be above all a master of dialogue and language.

Stage characters and conflicts are inseparable. A playwright's inability to depict acute conflicts deprives the actor of the possibility of bringing out and developing inner emotions. Without a conflict and struggle there can be no action, and the actor, given a smooth, schematic role, cannot create a full-blooded and lifelike character.

The conflict in a play arises from a clash of characters, and to weaken it is to weaken the characteristics of the heroes. There are plays in which conflicts are not developed nor based on clashes between well-defined characters. In such cases, there seems to be action aplenty, but it is action that is neither justified nor realistic.

Plays of this sort show the outer aspects of things without bringing out their essence, and lack motivation.

Another shortcoming that one often encounters in a play is inconsistency of action caused by the artificial transplantation of the hero from one situation into another. Playwrights often put actors in a difficult position by failing to justify psychologically the way in which their characters develop or, what is even worse, by making their characters act quite irrationally. That can be compared to something like this: say, a man has to change a ceiling lamp, and to get to it he first steps on a chair, then climbs on to a table, lifts his arm and does the job. Well, on the stage the actor also needs such logical and consistent steps to explain his conduct. But there are certain playwrights who completely ignore logic and consistency, proposing that the actor jump from the "floor" right up to the "ceiling."

Some of our dramatists fail to reveal the rich spiritual life of Soviet people.

Now and then we hear the groundless argument, unfortunately still put forward by some of our playwrights, that the "villain" is more colourful than the hero. This "argument" has prevailed in a whole number of plays. In real life, however, the hero is always a more striking personality than the villain, whose outlook generally is limited and shallow while that of the hero is broad and noble. It is necessary, however, to depict all the aspects of the hero's life, describe his interests, aspirations and conduct and not just show him discussing production processes and quotas.

In presenting his characters, the dramatist must show their development consistently and logically through their deeds and actions, without disclosing the denouement in the very first act.

The Soviet actor expects new plays and scripts covering a wide variety of subjects. What the Soviet actor wants to do is to depict the new worker, born of the Soviet age, to portray the Soviet scientist as a man who brings science and production together, to play collective farmers, those wonderful Soviet men and women who are struggling against all that is old and outdated, and for all that is new, progressive and communist, to present a Party functionary as a man who is closely connected with the masses and whose political and organizational work is bringing communism nearer.

THE ACTOR AND THE DIRECTOR

Whenever I am offered a new role in a play or picture, I immediately want to know who is directing it. After I have read the play or the script, the first thing I want to do is meet the director and learn of his plans so that I may cooperate closely and fruitfully.

The actor's success is just as much the director's success. But the director's success is an empty phrase if the actor fails.

I have always placed faith in the director. This, in my opinion, is the professional duty of the actor, while the professional duty of the director is to justify this faith. This must be done through close co-operation with the actor at the rehearsals.

Unfortunately, there are still quite a few directors who do not have a clear understanding of what their task is.

These producers may be divided into three groups.

To the first group belong "gas-bag" directors, the great talkers who will speak long and eloquently on the play, but will do next to nothing to help the actor to step into his role. Long talks on historical, philological and philosophical themes, thickly interspersed with quotations from literary works, only tend to tire the actor when he rehearses. They only hamper him in his search for characterization. At the beginning, when I was inexperienced, my association with such directors led me to lose confidence in myself, and I even thought at one time that the acting profession was beyond my scope and abilities.

The second group is that of dictatorial directors: they do not give the actor a chance to really concentrate on the role, to accumulate experience and satisfy his artistic longings.

To have the right to play, the actor must accumulate much experience, develop his skill and gradually learn to create a character. This process cannot forcibly be curtailed.

But the dictatorial directors refuse to take that into account. They often demand that the actor master the role in the shortest possible span of time, at times not even realizing that their plan does not accord with the actor's abilities and personality. At the initial rehearsals they want the actor to improvise and offer to show him how some episode should be acted. At subsequent rehearsals they very often insist that the actor play the role exactly the way they want it played. Not being mature enough and still lacking confidence, the actor very often loses heart when he comes across great difficulties in building up his role.

Lastly, the third group. It comprises "passive" directors. Very calm and collected, they never bother themselves or worry the actor, never take too great an interest in his work at the rehearsals. There are actors who are pleased to work with such directors because they make no demands on them. But with such directors the actor rarely feels the joy of real creation.

The task of the director is to grasp the idea, the thought of the play, to see it with the eyes of a Soviet artist, to work enthusiastically and to help actors to create vivid artistic images that will captivate the imagination of the audience.

The task is not just to show an actor how to play a scene, but to direct him along the right path so that his performance will bring out the basic idea of the play. The producer must clearly define the actor's task in interpreting the character generally and in each of the sequences separately without ignoring any detail. He must help the actor to build up the role and, armed with a well-drawn and clear plan, demand that the actor fulfil all the tasks arising from their joint effort. Setting himself the job of bringing out the idea of the play through the actor, the director must consider the latter's potentialities and help him to lose himself in the personality of the character. It was on the basis of these principles that the art of direction developed at the Moscow Art Theatre—under the wise guidance of Konstantin Stanislavsky and Vladimir Nemirovich-Danchenko.

However, it is not only through cooperation that a director helps an actor. He also does so by proposing him for a role.

Watching the actor the director often discovers his latent potentialities and insists on his being chosen for a role no one would ever think he could play. The director thus influences his further development as an actor.

It is difficult, indeed, to overestimate the significance of such assistance.

Speaking of my association with directors I must mention those with whom I have not worked, but whose advice has helped me tremendously.

The suggestion that I should play Professor Polezhayev was made by two Lenfilm producers—Sergei Gerasimov and Mikhail Shapiro. My previous roles on the stage and on the screen, it seemed, hardly justified their choice. But nevertheless Gerasimov and Shapiro strongly supported my candidature. They thus helped me along, opening up new prospects for me as an actor.

The idea that I could play Alexander Nevsky after I had portrayed Professor Polezhayev and Tsarevich Alexei, was suggested by Yeliza-veta Telesheva, director and instructor at the Moscow Art Theatre, who spoke about me to Sergei Eisenstein. I did not accept his offer right away. But my work revealed that I was wrong to hesitate: the film proved another milestone in my career.

As I recall my younger days and the tortuous path I had to traverse, I am deeply grateful to my instructors and directors who saw in my burlesquing and clowning my real abilities and risked trying me in difficult, highly dramatic roles.

Just as with all other actors, my relations with directors developed in their own particular way, and I should like to illustrate them with a few cases out of my practice.

The man who brought me to the Pushkin Theatre in 1933 was its managing director, Boris Sushkevich, who believed in me from the very start. At our first interview he was cordial and charming. His faith in my abilities encouraged me, a physically mature thirty-year-old actor, though in reality a beginner, joining one of the best and oldest theatres in the country.

Sushkevich was undoubtedly deeply interested in young actors and worried when they were not given roles to play and saw to it that everyone had enough to do. He was an excellent actor and possessed all the qualities necessary for a managing director, producer and instructor. I was then striving to master Stanislavsky's principles of acting, and it was Sushkevich who, having been connected with the Moscow Art Theatre and especially with its First Studio, rendered me invaluable assistance along these lines.

But although Sushkevich was kindly disposed towards me, our cooperation was not fruitful. The reason was the difference in our characters and temperament, interests and aspirations.

I cannot say that I was not given enough roles. On the contrary, in the first three or four years, while Sushkevich was managing director, I was engaged in many plays. I played in classics—Varlaam in *Boris Godunov* and Osip in *Inspector-General*. I played modern Soviet roles —Senechka Perchatkin in *Strange Child* and the small role of Besshtanko, a patriotic collective farmer, in Alexander Korneichuk's *The Banker*. And I played in foreign plays, as for instance the role of Krogstadtes in Ibsen's *A Doll's House*. But, strictly speaking, not one of these roles, with the exception of Varlaam and perhaps Krogstadtes, brought me any nearer to the tasks I wished to tackle in the field of dramatic art. In those days I wanted to play as much as possible, and while acting in *Baltic Deputy* and *Peter I*, I rehearsed at least two roles at the theatre. But despite all his concern and friendship, Sushkevich failed properly to understand my aspirations and assess my abilities. These had been brought out by my screen performances of Tsarevich Alexei, Professor Polezhayev and shortly after that Alexander Nevsky.

Thus, what makes for fruitful cooperation between the producer and the actor is the coincidence or, at any rate, the proximity of their creative interests, or briefly, the director's ability to discover and bring out the actor's peculiar gifts.

At the Pushkin Theatre I worked most with régisseurs Leonid Vivien and Vladimir Kozhich. The latter captivates the actor by experiments and his bold search for new forms. There may be much in his production methods that can be challenged, but his work bears the stamp of originality, and there can be no doubt about his ability to create atmosphere on the stage. He is keenly aware of the underlying idea of the play and subordinates everything to this idea, including the innovations in which his productions abound.

When Kozhich starts rehearsing a new play, there are usually many arguments and at the same time many hopes and expectations and bright prospects. At the rehearsals his ardour, his search for new forms and his ingenuity carry the actors away and help them to penetrate the inner world of their characters.

Kozhich and I worked together on several plays, the most memorable being Mikhail Bulgakov's dramatization of *Don Quixote*.

There was an interval of several years between this Don Quixote and the one I had played at the Young Spectators' Theatre. The experience I had accumulated in the meantime, my greater maturity as an artist and the absolutely new tasks Bulgakov's play set us—all this aroused in me a feeling of particular responsibility and made demands which, in my opinion, I could solve only with the assistance of the director. I can say without exaggeration that working with Kozhich on *Don Quixote* was an invaluable experience.

Bulgakov's play, truthfully and faithfully reproducing the best episodes of the Cervantes novel, presented to the actors wonderful creative opportunities.

In bringing out the main idea of the play we proceeded in no little measure from Belinsky's interpretation of Don Quixote. "Don Quixote," he wrote, "is above all a fine and noble man, a true knight without fear and without reproach. Although he is funny through and through, morally and physically, he is not silly. On the contrary, he is very clever. More, he is wise." Those words of the great Russian critic defined the character of Don Quixote and served as a leit-motif for the most important scenes—Don Quixote's monologue about the golden age on earth, his talk with Sancho Panza about a just and impartial court for his fellow-countrymen, the scene in which he speaks pathetically to his squire of his presentiment of death. Our Don Quixote was a tragicomic and, at the same time, human character.

One of the tasks I was given by the director was to stress as clearly as possible the difference between the realistic image of the impoverished Spanish nobleman Alonso Quijano and, the product of his imagination, the fantastic image of Don Quixote, the "knight without fear and without reproach." What I had to show was that Quijano, deeply dissatisfied with the squalor of his life and influenced by the novels about knights, strove to find his ideal in an image of his own creation.

With Kozhich's assistance we succeeded in elaborating all the major episodes of the play—the assault by the muleteers, preparation of the curative balsam at the inn, Don Quixote's battle with Sansón Carrasco and his death.

The scene in which the muleteers attack Don Quixote and Sancho Panza was very well done. Don Quixote and his faithful squire, played by Boris Gorin-Goryainov, stood close together and successfully repulsed the surrounding assailants. The tempo of the scene was fast, one might say even stormy, and when the muleteers finally took to their heels, we fell exhausted, just as the play called for.

Preparation of the curative balsam was one of the funniest episodes, of which, in my opinion, there were not enough. The scene showed Don Quixote enthusiastically concocting the brew and chasing the evil spirits away. In the end he drove away the spirit of his worst enemy, the magician Frestón, thinking that the latter alone could deprive his balsam of its magic properties. Then, in his belief in the curative power of this knightly medicine, Don Quixote drank it, bravely bearing the pain caused by the horrible drug.

In the tournament with Carrasco, Don Quixote was presented as a mighty knight, and in the first encounter he emerged victorious, striking Carrasco fiercely on the shoulder. Don Quixote won because of his profound faith in the justice of his cause. It was only later that Carrasco beat him. The scene was rehearsed so well that we could do it blindfolded.

I should like to mention one very expressive detail that was part and parcel of the play—the call signals invented by Don Quixote and Sancho Panza. We decided on the nature of these "knightly" calls during the rehearsals. At first these signals helped Don Quixote and Sancho Panza to meet without hindrance from anyone—the housekeeper, priest, barber or any other of their fellow-citizens. Don Quixote's call was a gentle, friendly coo, while Sancho Panza's was a shrill whistle. It was thus that they signalled each other in the village, in their back yards, when they wanted to meet without anyone knowing it. This detail successfully stressed the fact that Don Quixote was under surveillance, that the whole village was watching him because they thought him a crank, and that it was for this reason that he was using these conspiratorial signals in his relations with Sancho Panza.

Later these signals were used in every situation possible. For instance, when they repulsed the attack of the fourteen muleteers and fell exhausted, Don Quixote, unable even to raise his head, cooed gently as if to ask: "Are you alive, Sancho?" and the latter answered with a soft, though slightly coarse whistle. And when Don Quixote was lying dead, the disconsolate Sancho whistled softly as if expecting an answer from his friend.

Don Quixote and Sancho Panza are perhaps the most complex images in world literature, and rehearsals are not enough to create them. It is necessary to play them before the audience, and to perfect them during the actual performance. Unfortunately, we did not have the chance of accumulating the necessary experience, of making use of the reaction of our audiences, of doing what we had failed to achieve at the rehearsals. *Don Quixote* opened some three months before the outbreak of the war, and we gave only about twenty performances, the last going on during fascist air raids on Leningrad when one could expect alerts at any moment. In those days our shows ended at ten p. m., without the last act. During the war the play was dropped from the theatre's repertoire.

I must admit that the play was somewhat dull, there was not enough hearty laughter that would have gone well with its deep philosophy. I also failed to make Don Quixote dreamy enough, to show him soaring in the clouds of fantasy.

The man I worked most with at the theatre was chief régisseur Leonid Vivien—an all-round actor and outstanding teacher who had reared many prominent stage and screen personalities at the Leningrad Institute of Stage Art. Vivien has been directing the Pushkin Theatre for many years, passing on to its players the best traditions of Russian realistic stage art which he acquired from his teacher Vladimir Davydov.

Although Vivien had known me from my institute days, it was only five or six years after I had joined the Pushkin Theatre that I first met him as a producer.

I remember particularly well one of our earlier meetings at the rehearsal of Carlo Goldoni's classical comedy *The Liar* in which I played the title role—a charming lover and inveterate fibber.

Frankly speaking, I was not the type to play Lelio, a heroic lover, dashing cavalier, very elegant and graceful of movement, temperamental and eloquent. I had to change my manner of carriage and master all the plastic peculiarities of a costume role. Striving to look as elegant and graceful as possible, to appear natural in a fluffy shirt or cape, I concentrated too much on the outer characteristics and therefore gave too little thought to my hero's emotions and to the development of his character. The result was that I failed to bring out Lelio's main characteristics as the satirized liar.

Vivien did not direct this play, but often attended the rehearsals in his capacity of chief régisseur, helped me with advice and explained my errors. He showed me where to lay stress in my monologues, where to pause before lying, as if thinking of a way out of the situation in which I had found myself.

I made good use of his counsel, convinced that it was helping me to master the role, and began to play Lelio in a different way.

Caught unawares, Lelio would pause to think of a way out and then blurt out some ingenious answer. I resorted to these little pauses every time Lelio was about to lie, and they helped me bring out more fully the satire and humour of my lines. In the most difficult episodes Vivien would try to explain the main task as clearly as possible.

Later, after the war, I worked with Vivien when I was doing two important roles, that of Ivan the Terrible in *The Great Tsar* and Michurin in *Life in Bloom*. I shall deal with these roles in the next chapter. Here I wish to say that my association with Vivien has taught me, to use his favourite expression, to "think emotionally on the stage," that is, to control emotion by a clearly and precisely expressed thought and to animate the thought by lifelike acting.

Vivien was already an experienced actor and instructor when he became a director. His interest in teaching went back to the days when he himself was a student at the St. Petersburg Theatrical School. There he was in Davydov's class and wrote down all his lectures and lessons, intending to master his pedagogical system and methods in teaching young actors.

After graduating the school, Vivien joined the Alexandrinsky Theatre where he proved a success, playing with such masters of the Russian stage as Maria Savina, Vladimir Davydov and Konstantin Varlamov. His interest in teaching, however, remained strong as ever. He became an assistant master at the Theatrical School and shortly before the Revolution came forth with a plan for the reorganization of the dramatic course. The plan was rejected because it was considered too bold.

As Alexander Nevsky. 1938

As Alexander Nevsky. 1938

In the first years after the Revolution, holding one of the leading jobs at our theatre, Vivien found more and more opportunity to make use of his pedagogical experience and soon became one of the leading instructors of the College of Stage Art. There he made his début as a régisseur, directing plays that were staged by the students as part of the curriculum. His young pupils formed a company that came to be known as the Theatre of Acting Art. It was headed by Vivien as chief producer, and he staged several important plays there. Later, it became a branch theatre of the Pushkin Theatre, and Vivien began to produce more and more plays for the latter.

At the rehearsal Vivien is invariably cool and collected, confident that his production is well planned, and noticing at once when anyone begins to deviate in any appreciable manner from his plan. He knows where to lay stress, how to bring out the underlying idea of the role, how to guide and help the actor. The clarity of the tasks he sets, his artistic sense, the ease with which he works and his individual approach to each actor, his knowledge of the nature and technology of the actor's art and, finally, his all-round understanding of the complexity of a stage production as well as his pedagogical experience—all this deserves the highest praise.

In the cinema I have worked most with my two old friends, Alexander Zarkhi and Joseph Heifetz, with producers Vladimir Petrov and Sergei Eisenstein.

I met Zarkhi and Heifetz when I was working on *Hectic Days* in which I played the idler Kolya Loshak. The role, a highly comic one, was meant to get as many laughs as possible from the audience. Kolya's grotesque figure, his conduct and the situations into which he continually got himself were calculated to force the spectator to shout with glee: "Look at his lanky figure! What a gait! Have you ever seen anyone mount and dismount a horse as he does! Boy, what a slap he gets from Tonya!" Thanks to my experience in burlesque, in the dance number "Pat, Pataschon and Charlie Chaplin," in the light opera and in vaudeville, the role was easy.

I soon met Zarkhi and Heifetz again, this time when working on *Baltic Deputy*.

In making this film we used stage methods in studying the script and rehearsing, and the result was gratifying. The very first dramatic reading of the script at the Cinema House convinced us that our co-operation would be fruitful. The three of us thought up new situations and bits of dialogue which allowed us to bring out the psychology of the characters. The entire cast took part in the discussion of the script and roles, and in the tests. The preparatory period lasted a whole month in the course of which I rehearsed my role about thirty times in costume and make-up. Our work was an excellent specimen of co-operative effort of the script writer, producers and actors.

The main task was to produce a realistic and at the same time monumental and exciting film in which every shot should glorify the triumphal onmarch of the Revolution, and to show Professor Polezhayev, the Baltic Deputy, as symbolizing the ties between science and the people, between a scientist and the Revolution and the Communist Party.

My job was to convince the audience that Professor Polezhayev was a very old man with a very young heart.

Professor Polezhayev was over 75, while the three of us taken together—Zarkhi, Heifetz and myself—were only slightly older. And so with all our youthful enthusiasm we set about studying the psychology of old age. We read much about famous scientists and artists in their old age. We read about the last years of Lev Tolstoi, Timiryazev, Darwin and Voltaire, studied their portraits, learned of their conduct and habits in that period of their lives. Little by little we succeeded in building up a picture of Professor Polezhayev without forgetting for a moment his true feelings which could be summed up in the following line by Mayakovsky:

In the soul there is not a single grey hair!

The Revolution helped Polezhayev to grasp the purpose and meaning behind his scientific work, and that was why he emerged victorious from his struggle. The producers emphasized this and helped us to convey it to the audiences.

Baltic Deputy was filmed with every regard to sequence from the first shot to the final scene, and that facilitated my task. And although, in my opinion, I was not at my best at the beginning, I soon got used to the role. I realized more and more that the film was not merely a story of the past, but one that spoke of the future. And that was the theme I developed in the closing shots, particularly in Polezhayev's speech at the session of the Petrograd Soviet in the Tavrichesky Palace.

It was not only at the rehearsals, but at the actual filming sessions, too, that the producers explained the relations between the various characters in the story, set us new and bigger tasks, and worked out new variants. All these variants were thoroughly discussed and gradually narrowed down to some vivid, characteristic and memorable detail. Thus, for instance, in the first variant Professor Polezhayev reacted to his talk with Lenin by running up and down his flat and even through the kitchen, excitedly tapping things he came across. In the end, the whole episode was reduced to one detail: the happily excited Polezhayev went through the rooms switching electric lights on.

The producers also helped me by discovering features characteristic of Polezhayev the scientist and by advising me how to show his high intellect. It is said that the producer must work as one with the actor. The work done by Zarkhi, Heifetz and the cast may well serve as a graphic example of such creative cooperation.

The three of us—Zarkhi, Heifetz and myself—became such friends that we jumped at every chance to work together, and when there were no roles for me in their new films, I gladly accepted bit parts, as I did in *Sukhe-Bator*, the film they made for the Mongolian People's Republic in which I played Baron Ungern, or in their *For Life* in which I played a hospital doorman.

The turning point on my path to drama and tragedy was my role of Tsarevich Alexei in *Peter I*.

Vladimir Petrov, a true artist and talented film producer, seemed to have guessed my cherished dream, for he trusted me with a tragic role and helped me to come into my own as an artist.

Having proposed me boldly for the role, he watched my test sympathetically but was at the same time exacting and even captious.

Thrilled and excited I "worked myself into the mood," and when the highly emotional situation called for it, I shed real tears. The film test turned out excellent. I did such a bit of true to life and expressive acting that I got the role.

Vladimir Petrov's production methods are very similar to those of the Moscow Art Theatre, and for his films he usually recruits its players.

A clever producer and a glutton for serious tasks, he successfully tackled such an important undertaking as the two-part epic about *Peter I*. He confidently guided the whole company in its work, learned a lot from the actors and taught them a lot too.

When portraying an historical figure it is not enough to impersonate it correctly. It is necessary to paint a true picture of the period and show class antagonisms. It was not enough to present Tsarevich Alexei as a traitor; the portrayal had to show the audience the reactionary forces behind him. Peter's progressiveness and Alexei's reactionism were exemplified not so much by themselves as by the various social groups they represented. The producer must help the actor not only to portray a man and his place and role in history, but also to describe history and bring out the deep social reasons underlying the event in question.

Petrov knew how to solve such broad problems. He always came to the studio well prepared, with concise proposals and clear-cut tasks for the players. He taught me how to act in close-ups, how to perfect my acting technique before the cameras, how to express big ideas in terse phrases and actions. It was thanks to his assistance that I succeeded in mastering Alexei's complex character and in bringing out his inherent qualities: unbridled fury and cowardice, hesitancy and quick temper, weakness and strength, and at times even majesty. Not content with rehearsals, Petrov often spoke to me just before the filming, and I am deeply grateful for his advice.

I worked with Petrov for almost three years, and our work together added to my experience, enhanced my self-confidence, my ability to play big and difficult parts, and thus enlarged the range of my roles and paved the way to further portrayals of historical figures.

Two of such roles, especially dear to me, were created in close co-operation with Sergei Eisenstein.

In my eyes, Eisenstein, whose early films and especially *Battleship Potyomkin* had brought him world fame, was a giant among producers. He specialized in making historical and revolutionary epics, but his earlier productions showed that he was inclined to impose on the actor, and when I received his offer to play in his new film, *Alexander Nevsky*, that was the thing that worried me most.

When we met, Eisenstein told me briefly the idea behind the film.

"We must show him as a noble, strong and vigorous man!" Eisenstein stressed, pointing out that the epithet "saint" he had been given in history was meant as a superlative of such epithets as "brave," "dashing" and "wise."

"What a task for an actor!" he repeatedly said, and it seemed that he had guessed my fears of which I, of course, dared not bring myself to talk.

I repeat that I hesitated about accepting the role. The epic magnitude of the film, the legendary figure of its hero, the ancient historical events to be screened—all this, in my opinion, presented insurmountable difficulties.

But after reading the script, so forcefully written by Pyotr Pavlenko, and getting acquainted with documents, with legends and historical research, I grew to like the image of my future hero—a tall, stalwart youth, agile, merry, quick-tempered, naive and somewhat uncouth.

The first tests were not too successful. I just could not hit upon the right make-up. I finally found it, thanks to Eisenstein. It was surprising how much attention he paid to apparently minor details which, later on, proved highly significant in filming close-ups. He got some thirteenth-century armour from the Hermitage Museum and ordered exact copies to be made. He often visited me in my dressing-room before the filming of some important sequence and one day spent a whole hour fixing a detail of my costume, while I stood there, surrounded by tailors and costumiers, my knees weak from standing motionless so long. As for Eisenstein, he pretended not to notice that, and joked and laughed, putting my costume in perfect order.

I must admit that I was rather worried and often dissatisfied at the beginning. I wanted to bring out the human element in Alexander Nevsky and his high moral qualities. But at times it even seemed to me that Alexander Nevsky was being drawn somewhat abstractly, that he was not human enough, and that his true image evaded me.

I spoke of my doubts to Eisenstein, but he tried to convince me that I should subordinate my acting to the general epic style of the production, without detailing the various psychological traits of the hero's character. What I should do, he said, was to give a general picture of Alexander Nevsky. In acting, just as in any other art, he told me, one should pay attention to the whole, the general, the main. And it was in this direction that Eisenstein insistently led me, teaching me to seek for the general and widely understandable in my role, to keep within a strictly defined style, and in this case particularly within the epic plan of the production.

We were filming the main episode—the Battle on the Ice in 1242.

This battle was fought on an extremely cold winter day on Chudskoye Lake which was turned into the burial ground of the vanquished Teutonic Knights.

It was impossible to film this episode in winter, and not so much because it was cold as because the winter sun is not bright enough. Hence this episode of almost 200 shots was filmed in summer on a specially prepared ground at Potylikha near the Mosfilm Studios. The ground was asphalted and then covered with sawdust, naphthalene and salt, which created an illusion of snow.

Alexander Nevsky was previewed at the Moscow Cinema House in November 1938 and released the following month.

The final shots of the film showed Alexander Nevsky addressing the people.

"Oh, how I would have beaten you, how mercilessly I would have whipped you had you lost the Battle on the Ice! Russia would have never forgiven you or me, had we displayed cowardice.... Remember that and tell your children and grandchildren, and if you forget, you will be traitors to the Russian land.... My word is firm: should misfortune befall us, I shall rouse the whole of Russia. And if you split up, you will be beaten mercilessly. If I am alive, I shall do it myself; if I die, I shall bequeath my sons to do so," Alexander Nevsky told his warriors.

Then, turning to the prisoners, he said:

"And you, you go and tell in foreign lands that Russia is alive. Let people come to us without fear as guests! But he who comes with the sword, shall perish by the sword! This Russia upholds and will uphold!"

I had a chance to check on the power of the film during the Great Patriotic War. Meeting people on my personal appearances at the front, seeing the film together with them and answering their questions, I saw for myself that Alexander Nevsky was one of their most popular heroes. It was during the war that the Soviet government instituted the Order of Alexander Nevsky, and his portrait, engraved on steel, was soon adorning the chests of Soviet Army men who had distinguished themselves in bitter struggle against the nazi invader.

Working together, Eisenstein and I became close friends.

Eisenstein was an outstanding artist, a man of inflexible will-power and very exacting, but at the same time somewhat reserved with people. I seemed to be an exception. He believed in my acting abilities from the very start, spoke to me of his plans, and there soon grew a sincere friendship between us.

I had complete faith in his abilities as a producer. He not only helped me to portray epic characters, but also taught me a good deal about spacing, the use of gestures and movements. Under his guidance I was able to perfect my acting technique before the cameras. It was he, too, who taught me to be exacting to all aspects of artistic creation. There is no doubt that my association with Eisenstein has helped me to develop greatly as an artist.

That is why I welcomed another opportunity to work with him. This time Eisenstein's offer reached me in Novosibirsk where the Pushkin Theatre had been evacuated in the first days of the war. It was only natural that I agreed right away. The film was *Ivan the Terrible*.

Filming began in Alma-Ata on February 1, 1943. The Kazakh government placed at our disposal the newest and best Palace of Culture in the capital, and its stage and auditorium served as a studio.

Despite war-time difficulties, the company got everything it needed for the production of the two-part epic, from scenery to costumes of all kinds, including the rich attire of the tsar and the armour of his soldiers. There was only one organizational difficulty we could not overcome: we had to do all the filming at night. That was because in the day electric power went to munitions factories.

The picture started with the coronation of seventeen-year-old Tsarevich Ivan. The character of Ivan the Terrible, his keen mind and the dramatic and at times tragic situations, focussed all my attention and effort.

This time Eisenstein was more than just a director: he was also author of the script and to some extent designer.

Formally, it was Joseph Shpinel who was the designer, but Eisenstein helped him a lot with the sketches. Eisenstein the producer and Eisenstein the designer were one. He drew the sketches of costumes, designing them in such a manner as to stress the personality of the characters, and in this he was extremely successful. He went about tirelessly perfecting every detail, no matter how unimportant it seemed, and took great care to get the proper church-plate and sacred images, to achieve unity of style in the picture. The finale of the first part was a complete, perfect picture composed of a sequence of well-planned shots. Eisenstein always tried to reproduce on the film what he had previously drawn on paper. Before proceeding with the filming he would look long and searchingly into the camera's eye to see whether the scene was properly arranged and was never satisfied unless each shot was a complete picture in itself. And many were brilliant in idea and style, particularly those which went into the coronation scene of Tsar Ivan and the religious procession to the Alexandrova Sloboda.

As director, Eisenstein set me a whole series of complex tasks. He demanded that I develop and bring out Tsar Ivan's character, synchronizing the process with the development of the film's action, although this action was spread over more than 20 years of the tsar's

Nikolai Cherkasov in the title role
in *Ivan the Terrible*. 1943

As Ivan the Terrible. 1943

life. I had to show the complex processes that went on in his mind as he developed into a sagacious statesman. The many physical changes alone through which Ivan the Terrible went in the picture—from a vigorous youth to the fatigued, but mighty and powerful ruler—created numerous serious difficulties.

At rehearsals and during the filming Eisenstein never seemed to tire of setting me intricate tasks in movement and action. In the scene in which Ivan the Terrible stands before the coffin of Tsarina Anastasya —a deeply psychological scene—he not only demanded highly emotional acting, but sharply defined outer plastic form, often shackling me by the rigid line of his graphic and artistic thought.

Carried away by his enthusiasm for pictorial composition, Eisenstein moulded expressive, monumental mises-en-scène, but it was often difficult to justify the content of the form he was striving to achieve. In some of his mises-en-scène, extremely graphic in idea and composition, an actor's strained muscles often belied his inner feelings. In such cases, the actor found it difficult indeed to mould the image demanded of him. Eisenstein insisted that his ideas be carried out. This insistence infected us. We had great confidence in him and often followed him blindly, fired by his enthusiasm.

Absorbed in his tasks as director and designer, Eisenstein began to sacrifice the story to their fulfilment, with the result that he failed as script writer.

We noticed and discussed the film's shortcomings after the preview. Almost every shot was a masterpiece in itself, with perfect harmony of composition. But succeeding as designer, Eisenstein failed as director: he did not effectively control the length of each sequence or ensure cohesion. The result was a film that was at times slow and tedious. Some of the scenes—for instance, the poisoning of Anastasya by Boyarina Staritskaya—were monotonously long. Minor episodes and sometimes mere details were given too much prominence.

My confidence in the film waned and my worries grew with each passing day. After watching scenes of the second part run through I criticized some episodes, but Eisenstein brushed my criticism aside, and in the end stopped showing me ready bits altogether. In films, it is the director who has the last word.

Soon Eisenstein revived my interest in the role by setting me complex tasks of predominantly plastic character. Thus, in the scene with Metropolitan Philip, I had to run up to the camera for a close-up to within twenty inches of the lens, taking good care to have my chin, nose and forehead well within the camera's eye, then look wrathfully and speak lines that were supposed to terrify not only the metropolitan, but the spectators too.

* * *

As I come to the close of the chapter I should like to point out that the actor usually trusts the director implicitly, regarding him as a loyal helpmate. Therefore, the responsibility of the director for a stage or film production is all the greater because he is, after all, responsible for the actors who appear in it. For this reason the director must be patient with the actor even when the latter does not always understand what is expected of him.

Yet it does happen that the director loses his temper and raises his voice at the actor during the rehearsal or filming.

In the theatre, where rehearsals sometimes last more than six months, the director-actor contradictions are easily smoothed out. In films, where everything is tied to a schedule and where even a day's delay may upset a monthly plan, there is more ground for disagreement and more chance of it becoming acute.

My own experience and that of my friends have convinced me that shouting and, what is even worse, mimicking an ill-spoken line never bring the desired effect. It is much better for the director to conceal his annoyance behind a smile, for a smile is the best remedy in all difficulties.

And that goes for the actor too.

One day, during the filming of *Peter I,* Petrov lost his temper when things started going wrong and raised his voice. That, naturally, did not help to improve the actors' creative mood.

We did not feel like adding fuel to the fire and pretended not to notice it. Very soon Petrov lost his temper again, and this time we decided that if this recurred, we would leave the studio—not with ill feeling but as a joke. Just before the break for lunch, Petrov again raised his voice, and this time we acted.

The three of us—Peter (Nikolai Simonov), Menshikov (Mikhail Zharov) and Alexei (myself)—unsheathed our swords, threw them down with over-exaggerated indignation, walked out of the studio and went to Zharov's rooms at the hotel where, still in our doublets and make-up, we laughed all through the lunch over our prank.

When we returned to the studio, Petrov met us cordially, and the four of us had a merry time discussing our "misunderstanding." Everyone was in a good mood, and filming that day went on without a hitch.

One of Eisenstein's greatest assets as a director was his ability of working harmoniously with actors and his knack of setting them into a congenial mood. Eisenstein liked to joke. His ready wit delighted everybody and kept people in high spirits.

One day we were filming the Battle on the Ice for *Alexander Nevsky.* The job was physically hard. As I have mentioned, we shot this sequence in July, and the heat was stifling. What made it all the more difficult for me was that I had practised some exhausting physical exercises which were then filmed, and felt I was all in.

The battle scene was being shot near the studio and my friends suggested that we drive there and rest in its cool premises.

The car pulled up at the studio gates, and I alighted, dressed and made up as Alexander Nevsky. The guard asked for my pass, which I had unfortunately forgotten in my jacket pocket at the studio. I tried to reason with him, but to no avail. As I saw that the 15 or 20 minutes I had intended to rest were being taken up by my argument with the man, I unsheathed my huge sword and made as if to assail him.

"What pass, knave!" I shouted. "Do you know who's before you? Prince Alexander Nevsky! I'll behead you!"

That did the trick. The guard ran away in confusion. This funny little incident cheered us and gave Eisenstein food for many jokes, with the result that we successfully shot the rest of the battle episode.

The most collected and cool director I have ever come across is Grigory Alexandrov. I have never heard him raise his voice or seen him sulk—not even when things really went bad.

One day on the set of *Spring*, Lyubov Orlova and I had chatted and joked so much we could not get ourselves into a mood for work, and were holding up everything.

Alexandrov was sitting near by with a thick volume in hand. He glanced at us and dropped the book. It fell with a thud, and he softly said:

"Silence!"

And that was the loudest I had ever heard him raise his voice.

Very often directors want well-known actors to play small but important roles in their films. This tradition has been borrowed from the Art Theatre and does much to enhance the quality of a picture.

One day one of our leading directors asked me to play in a very brief but interesting episode.

"You'll be occupied only two days!" he said, trying to talk me into taking the role.

"My dear friend," I retorted. "How can you, an exacting artist, forget that while actual filming may take only two days, it is necessary to work for a whole month to create a living character, especially for an episode? Without that it will be a stereotyped portrayal, a repetition of some character I had done in the past. Don't forget that the actor who portrays Hamlet and the actor who plays the grave-digger both think of their roles and work on them from the first dramatic reading down to the première."

I have played many small parts in films. Yet I really succeeded only when I worked thoroughly on the part. When I tackled these parts without long preparation, the result was never satisfactory and the performance well below my capabilities.

The actor's is a craft which requires endless perfecting: artistic horizons are boundless. If he works in a group, the actor's skill grows from association with his co-workers, and the man who can do most for him in this respect is the director.

THE ACTOR AND THE ROLE

Russia's leading theatre personalities have always held that actors must keep in step with life and study its developments. However, it is only we Soviet actors who have the possibility to do this, for we are not mere onlookers, but active builders of communist society.

One of the greatest achievements of the Soviet theatre is that it has completely abolished all caste prejudices in regard to actors and smashed the walls which separated them from life and the working masses. For the Soviet actor work in the theatre means active participation in public life and in the nation's effort to build the communist future. Soviet actors do not have "to go out among people." They *live* the throbbing life of the people, their interests are the interests of the people, and they cannot conceive of art without it being an art of the people and for the people.

In tackling our tasks we often encounter difficulties engendered by the novelty of the tasks themselves, by their significance and scale, by the responsibility they place on the actor.

Boris Shchukin, an outstanding Soviet actor, told me that when he was offered the role of Lenin in the film *Lenin in October*, he hesitated to accept it, although inwardly he was well prepared for the part and eager to play it.

"I was afraid I hadn't enough brain, heart, talent or ability to achieve such heights," he said.

Nevertheless, he was the first actor to tackle and tackle successfully the extremely responsible task of portraying the founder of the Soviet state on the stage and screen. Impersonating Lenin in the films *Lenin in October* and *Lenin in 1918* and on the stage in Nikolai Pogodin's play *The Man with the Gun*, Shchukin put all his brain, heart, talent and experience into his work, and his inspired performance thrilled millions of spectators.

I was fortunate enough to play in *Lenin in 1918*, one of our earliest films about the Revolution, and to be the first to portray Maxim Gorky on the screen.

My association with Shchukin proved more than just a pleasant experience; it enriched me infinitely as an actor. This versatile actor's portrayal of Lenin was his crowning achievement. Those who saw him in *The Man with the Gun* at the Vakhtangov Theatre no doubt remember how he gradually overcame the constraint and unnaturalness which were so obvious at first. Evidently afraid of destroying the illusion of resemblance, Shchukin at first passed from one statuesque pose to another in an attempt to create an uninterrupted chain of outer forms. But in doing that he often lost track of the inner feelings. What is significant is that when Shchukin laid less stress on the sculptural pattern of the image, he revealed inner feelings more naturally, more convincingly, and this made the resemblance all the closer.

Shchukin finally achieved complete naturalness in the film *Lenin in 1918*. He succeeded in subordinating outer form to inner feelings and surmounted the barrier which had been hampering him from "incarnating" the role not only physically, but spiritually. And it is only natural that in doing this he introduced certain elements of his own individuality as an artist.

The sight of Shchukin made up as Lenin never failed to thrill me. This feeling was shared by all the others and helped us in our creative work, reminding us of our vast responsibilities.

My role of Gorky in the same film set new problems before me. I appeared just twice—in Lenin's office and at his bedside after he was shot at and wounded. But the briefness of the role did not make it any less important in the eyes of the spectators or in my own. More, it was this briefness that made it difficult, for it gave me no opportunity of gradually bringing out Gorky's inner features which alone could have made up for imperfect physical resemblance. In these circumstances, it seemed, the most important thing was to achieve 100 per cent likeness in looks, movements, mannerisms and gestures. The film was shot in 1938, only two years after Gorky's death, and that made the task more difficult.

To give a lifelike performance, one must find the core of the role. That is why, working on the role, I reread Gorky's novels, stories and articles, and my picture of him as great proletarian humanist grew more vivid than ever. Knowing how much Gorky loved books, I would stop at the bookshelf in Lenin's study and stroke the books, thus reminding the audience of his love of books which he said were a "miracle."

To make the portrayal as perfect as possible I set out on mastering various minor details—the way he talked, walked and gesticulated. From people who knew him I learned that he stooped a little, coughed as he spoke, covering his mouth with his hand, liked to pull at his moustaches, burn paper in an ash-tray, etc. All these seeming trifles helped me to re-create Gorky on the screen.

I taught myself to gesticulate and stoop just like he did and to speak with his particular accent. But when I saw the scenes run off on the screen, I realized that my performance was flat, that while I did look and speak like Gorky, I had failed to bring out the humaneness for which the Soviet people loved him.

Watching myself on the screen I saw that details, however correct, do not always make a correct whole. I did not digress in any measure from the material I had at my disposal, and yet the result was not what it should have been. That happened, I think, because Gorky's part in the scenario had certain flaws and because I had paid more attention than necessary to physical resemblance. Obviously, my impersonation needed considerable reworking, and that could have been achieved if I had defined more precisely the inner line of development and toned down the outer form. It was necessary to find the "golden mean," and I succeeded in doing that with the help of the theatre where I played Gorky in the stage version on more than 100 occasions.

Preparing myself for the rehearsals, I set myself the task of elaborating the dialogue between Lenin and Gorky at their first meeting—the very first scene of the play.

In the early years after the Revolution, Gorky held an erroneous stand in the question of proletarian dictatorship—and this is revealed in the play and film in his dialogue with Lenin. Their talk is important not only because it gives insight into their characters, but also because it brings out the underlying idea of the play which speaks of proletarian dictatorship and proletarian humanism, of dictatorship as an expression of proletarian humanism and of the political harm of abstract "humanism" in the conditions of an acute class struggle. This leit-motif of the play had to be clearly reflected in the Lenin-Gorky dialogue, and the task was to present the latter, despite his vacillation, as an ally and ardent champion of Soviet rule.

Attention was focussed on this scene from the very first rehearsal. New lines were supplied, and it was on the stage that I polished up the role. Some lines we incorporated, bringing the scene to its logical conclusion.

Gorky begins by mentioning Academician Pavlov, then speaks of his needs and relates an anecdote. This little story helped not only to liven up the scene, but revealed Gorky's close ties with scientists, with the best representatives of the old intelligentsia.

And then comes the clash of opinions about proletarian dictatorship.

"I realize that cruelty is indispensable and that without cruelty it is impossible to smash and remake the old world," Gorky replies to Lenin's convincing argument. "But, perhaps, sometimes our cruelty is uncalled for—and that's what is unnecessary and terrible."

"But just imagine two men fighting to the last. Can you determine which blow is necessary and which is not?" Lenin asks him.

The talk is joined by Korobov, a worker, who has just returned from the south where he went to get bread for Petrograd.

Korobov indignantly describes the kulak counter-revolution and grain speculation, and stresses the need for stamping out the kulaks, the saboteurs and the enemies of the Soviet state.

"So that's how it is," Lenin says thoughtfully, and then, feigning doubt, adds:

Boris Shchukin as V. I. Lenin and Nikolai Cherkasov as Maxim Gorky in the film *Lenin in 1918*. 1938

Alexander Borisov as Pavlov and Nikolai Cherkasov as Maxim Gorky
in the film *Academician Ivan Pavlov*. 1949

"But there are people who say that our cruelty is sometimes un-called for."

These words rouse Korobov's wrath. Who dares to accuse Bolsheviks of uncalled-for cruelty when the enemy is trying to strangle the Revolution by starving the people? And he turns to Gorky for support.

"What are you saying, Vladimir Ilyich? Ask Comrade Gorky. He understands it well. He has had some bitter experience himself."

"You go ahead and ask him!" Lenin retorts, glancing ironically at the confused Gorky.

"What's the matter, Vladimir Ilyich?" Korobov is abashed. "Have I said something wrong?"

"No, no. You're right. But we've had a talk about this with a certain comrade, and he finds himself in difficulty," Lenin replies, covering his face and laughing loudly, and one can feel that he is happy about his successful joke.

"I know this comrade. I shall speak to him," Gorky puts in rather confusedly.

The first actor to portray Lenin on the stage in Leningrad was Konstantin Skorobogatov—at the Pushkin Theatre on the twentieth anniversary of the October Revolution. The play was Trenyov's *On the Bank of the Neva*, and Skorobogatov appeared in two scenes, showing Lenin on the way to the Smolny and at the Second Congress of the Soviets. Despite the briefness of the role and the absence of dialogue, he gave an excellent portrayal.

Playing in the stage version of *Lenin in 1918*, Skorobogatov painted a vivid picture of Lenin's temperament which was rooted in confidence in his strength, in the righteousness of his cause and in its victory—in other words, of his "youthful enthusiasm," as Gorky called it. Skorobogatov showed Lenin as a man who had only one aim in life: the victory of the proletarian revolution. Lenin's spiritual qualities were revealed particularly convincingly in the scene with Korobov—the lively and straightforward man he was.

The play is no longer staged, but the Lenin-Gorky fragment has been retained in our recital repertoire. The audiences warmly react to Lenin's thoughts and formulations because they confirm his theses regarding revolutionary developments. How confident, for instance, Lenin is when he replies to Gorky's request for assistance to scientists:

"Have patience. The time will come when our writers and scientists will have everything, when they will be the envy of intellectuals the world over!"

I often pictured Pavlov when I played Gorky. Twelve years later, again as Gorky, I talked with the famous Russian physiologist about Lenin, and this time I visualized the great leader of the working masses.

I have played Gorky on the screen three times, but, unfortunately, each time it was in a mere episode set in the early years of the Revolution, at a time when one could neither pass judgement on his life's work nor fully show what was most characteristic and valuable in his activities. But despite all that, the role, which I had played so many times on the stage and which I sometimes re-create in my public appearances, enriched me. It was a school, so to speak, that showed me the right way to play outstanding Russians. That is why I have dwelt so long on this character, why I have singled it out from among my other roles.

Like many of my colleagues, I have been fortunate to take part in fulfilling the many important tasks in the field of art set us by the people and the Party. One of these was to create true to life portraits of Soviet people on the screen and stage.

I have played my contemporaries in the films *Friends*, *Sixty Days* and *Bon Voyage!* The first, from a script by Nikolai Tikhonov, was about the friendship of the Caucasian peoples, freed from the feudal yoke by the Great October Revolution. I played Beta, a poor Ossetian peasant who had seen nothing but misery as a farm labourer and who was given a new lease on life after the overthrow of tsarism. In *Sixty Days* I was Antonov, a young Soviet scientist who spent all his time in research work. Called up for a short military training course, he could not get accustomed to camp life and at first had a hard time learning how to march. He finally showed his worth at a tactical exercise in which he successfully fulfilled a difficult and responsible assignment. In *Bon Voyage!* I played Captain Levashov, a wise and kind instructor in one of the Nakhimov naval schools.

On the stage, one of my first roles in the Soviet repertoire was that of the chairman of a millionaire collective farm in Alexander Korneichuk's *The Banker*. In Trenyov's *On the Bank of the Neva* I was worker Buranov, and in his character I tried to show the typical traits of a Bolshevik and political organizer of the masses.

In Alexander Afinogenov's *On the Eve*, one of the first plays about the Great Patriotic War, I was Zavyalov, a young agronomist, who volunteers and is sent to the front lines. In this role I strove to paint as vivid a picture as possible of the heroism of our younger generation. I had a small part in Korneichuk's *The Front* in which I played Private Ostapenko, and the task I set myself was to bring out in bold relief the deep faith of ordinary Soviet people in victory over German fascism, the hero's inexhaustible optimism and natural humour.

* * *

We Soviet actors take an active part in public life, often make personal appearances in university auditoriums, army units and workers' clubs and usually have to answer a great many questions.

We are often asked how we work at a role, get into the mental attitudes of our characters and build up their outward features.

I shall try to answer these questions briefly, on the basis of my own experience. I must stress, however, that I do not intend to give a scientific analysis of the art of acting. That has been done, and well, by Stanislavsky and his disciples. My task is to tell the reader about the paths which lead to creative art and to give a general picture of what a Soviet actor is called upon to do.

For an actor, the day he gets a new role is a red-letter day. He is happy, elated, enthusiastic, although he knows that it is by no means easy, in fact very difficult, to create a character. But despite that he is certain that he will succeed.

When the director reads a new play to the cast, their imagination is set at work. The dramatic reading stimulates imagination even more.

As he reads his lines, the actor gets acquainted with the role, determines his relationship to other characters, defines his main task and seeks for means to implement it. At the same time he tries to grasp the underlying idea of the play, compares the situations with life and places himself not only in the position of the character he must play, but in that of all the other characters. Proceeding from the general task, the actor defines the thoughts he has to carry to the audience.

In the first stage of the rehearsals the actor builds up his confidence in his abilities. He never parts with the role he is to play: he falls asleep thinking of it, often dreams about it and thinks of it the moment he wakes up. The character lives in the actor's imagination, growing, developing and maturing, and it is in this process that superfluities are weeded out. It is in this period that the actor gets a better understanding of the play, its underlying idea, its leit-motif or, as Stanislavsky calls it, its "through action," and that he studies the background and the period.

Then there comes a time—and that happens with everyone—when the actor grows disappointed and begins to doubt his abilities. In such cases an experienced director comes to the actor's assistance, defines his tasks more clearly, shows him the ways to achieve his goal. His imagination revived, the actor regains confidence in himself and belief in his final success.

In this difficult creative search even minor, seemingly insignificant details are at times apt to bring the actor closer to the character he is portraying. Sometimes, when the character is not clear enough to the actor, the director may suggest that he rehearse in costume and make-up, and use properties—and this frequently helps the actor to get into the "feel" of his role, provided, of course, he has determined its core.

Working on his role, the actor must be thoroughly convinced that every one of his reactions is well motivated, so that his gestures and movements are in keeping with the character and absolutely life-like.

Eventually there comes a moment when the actor feels an urge to show his work on the character to his friends, relatives and even acquaintances to test their reaction and see how successful he has been in mastering the role.

If I were asked how I work on my role outside the theatre, I would answer that, first of all, I keep placing myself in the position of the character I am to play, and to test whether or not my characterization is a true one, I go out among people. Thus I have scores of spectators before the première of a play or release of a film.

One day after a première I asked a friend of mine, whom I had pestered a lot about my role, whether he liked the play.

"I liked the play and I liked you, too," he answered, "although, I must say, I had expected more of you, especially after our last meeting when you 'played' the role much better than on the stage."

Remarks like that are of tremendous assistance: they show the actor why his acting leaves the spectators cool and help him to play his role more colourfully, clearly and expressively.

An actor should exercise his imagination as much as possible. It is good for him to be constantly in a state of light creative excitability, and it is in this state of excitability that the outlines of his new role are born.

When I was offered the role of Vladimir Stasov in *Moussorgsky,* I was busy playing the title role in *Alexander Popov* and Captain Levashov in *Bon Voyage!* and at the same time doing Ivan the Terrible and Michurin on the stage. But although I thought constantly of these roles, it was Stasov who was on my mind most of the time, and very often, and unexpectedly, I would make some characteristic gesture. In such cases I would exclaim:

"Hold everything! That's Stasov!"

It is enough for an actor to concentrate on some character in a play or film scenario and to interest himself in it, to begin building up the role—especially if he is keen on playing it on the stage or screen.

For instance, working at the Lenfilm Studios in the two pictures I mentioned above, I often thought of Vladimir Mayakovsky whom I longed to play on the screen. The character of the poet had captured my imagination, and I thought of him all the time. Returning home at night from the studio I would take a volume of his poems and imagine that he was there in the room with me. As a member of the Soviet Peace Committee I once addressed a mass meeting in the Palace Square in Leningrad. As I began to speak, I suddenly imagined, for a fleeting moment, I was Mayakovsky whose fiery verse about international peace and friendship revived in my mind.

I cited this incident to show how "possessed" an actor can become, how easily excitable he is when he thinks of a new role and how he takes every opportunity to build up this role.

"When I look at you now, I see you're a healthy, sane person, and yet you played such a degenerate in *Peter I.* How did you manage that?" a young stalwart soldier asked me at one of my personal appearances.

There can be only one answer to that: an actor must know how to play an unusually courageous man and an ailing person, a hero and a villain, a young man and an old man, a wise man and a fool—that is his profession.

In theoretical literature this is called "incarnation." I am one of the champions of the method of "incarnation," and I must say that it has invariably helped me both on the stage and screen.

"Incarnation" is never a question of outer form and make-up, but one of inner experiences and feelings. "Incarnation" is the re-creation on the stage of the hero's inner world, his environment and background, his individual qualities, and qualities that are typical of his social milieu. Outer form can be interesting and true to life only if it harmonizes with the inner content of the character.

An actor should try to lose himself in the personality of the character he plays. He should not play himself but the character, and make his portrayal as true to life as possible both spiritually and physically.

In *Baltic Deputy*, for instance, I played a man 43 years my senior. I had to visualize and make my own his many peculiarities, among them his manner of walking—he had a senile, yet original, light and fast gait. I had to convince the audience that it was not Cherkasov they were seeing, but an aged and respected scientist, and after much effort and rehearsal I succeeded in moving and gesticulating in the manner of my character. The spectators are not concerned with the effort and time it cost me to achieve that, they do not care that my own gait is poles apart from that of Polezhayev. What they have to be convinced of is that Polezhayev's manner of walking is natural and true to life. Moreover, in working out this gait I had to harmonize it with his conduct, with all his movements and gestures, even with his voice.

To "incarnate" a role is the professional duty of every actor, and it requires that he master the technique of acting, the technique of "living" the role.

I liked to play roles in which costume and make-up helped me towards getting the feeling of the character. My movements and gestures changed accordingly as soon as I donned the beard and jacket of an old scientist, the wig, armour and cape of a thirteenth-century prince, the regal attire of a tsar, the broad-brimmed hat and spectacles of an absent-minded geographer. I could not picture myself in a role without heavy make-up and in modern clothes.

And while in my younger days I played mostly old men or men with beards (when I did play young men it was always men with sharply defined characteristic features), in my recent roles on the stage and screen I have played without any such make-up. It was unusual and difficult at first, and I felt sort of unprotected.

Learning that I had been offered a modern role, a director friend of mine advised me against it.

"Go ahead and play Popov, if you want to, but don't touch Captain Levashov," he said. "It's not your kind of a role, you'll fail."

But I have since played many modern roles and hope I shall be offered many more on the screen and especially on the stage. Among these roles are Zavyalov in *On the Eve*, film producer Gromov in *Spring* and Captain Levashov in *Bon Voyage!*

In these roles I did not need false beards, moustaches or any heavy make-up. Nevertheless, I remained true to the law of "incarnation" whose main principle—discovery and portrayal of the character's emotions—applies to these roles too. The young scientist Zavyalov, the film producer Gromov and Captain Levashov are men completely different in type and character.

The method of "incarnation," which I adopted watching the performances of outstanding Russian actors and synthesizing my own experiences, has fully justified itself and proved most fruitful.

Speaking of the process of "incarnation," there is one other thing I would like to say.

One might think that playing Ivan the Terrible in *The Great Tsar* or Varlaam in *Boris Godunov* an actor should transplant himself into the past and, to a certain degree, stop being himself. It is even claimed that many pre-revolutionary actors playing historical roles used to become so accustomed to their historical environments that they found it difficult to return to their normal milieu.

Of myself I can only say that I have never experienced that. On the contrary, the more intensely my mind of a Soviet actor worked, the clearer I pictured the everyday realities, the more confident I felt attired as Ivan the Terrible or Alexander Nevsky.

In my opinion, there can be no question of identifying the process of "incarnation" with some miraculous séance of autosuggestion. No matter how much I try to convince myself that I am Ivan the Terrible, I shall not succeed. The process of "incarnation" is much more complex, and its main motive power is the actor's consciousness. This being the case, the actor's consciousness must be sound so as to enhance his capacity for analysis and synthesis. I think there is also another conclusion one can draw: the more profoundly our actors understand our socialist realities, the better they can portray historical characters.

To prove the correctness of this conclusion it will suffice to cite the examples of such outstanding Soviet actors as Boris Shchukin and Boris Dobronravov.

As Yegor Bulychev, Shchukin gave a superb portrayal of a "civilized merchant" of pre-revolutionary Russia. Historically speaking, the portrayal was absolutely true to life. Bulychev, as Shchukin played him, was the very embodiment of his epoch and class—here was an historical portrait in the very best sense of this word. And yet it was not this that brought the actor his brilliant success. As I see it, Shchukin

As Beta in the film *Friends*. 1937

Nikolai Cherkasov with Lyubov Orlova
in the film *Spring*. 1947

As Captain Levashov in the film *Bon Voyage!* 1949

Nikolai Cherkasov as Antonov in *Sixty Days*. 1941

scored because while playing Bulychev, he was not afraid to reveal himself—a clever, observant and thoughtful Soviet citizen. Shchukin's insight helped him to bring out the characteristic features of his hero, and that was the main reason for his popularity with Soviet theatregoers.

I remember there was once a lively controversy as to whether it is possible to portray one's "attitude" to the role. The answer, and a categorical one at that, is given by our theatrical art: as a matter of fact, it is precisely the actor's attitude to the role that makes it possible for him to create a character; an artist can create lifelike images only if he keeps in step with life.

Dobronravov gave an extremely sincere and powerful performance as Voinitsky in *Uncle Vanya*. Like Shchukin in the role of Bulychev, he was Voinitsky with all features inherent in a man of the Chekhov period. And yet despite this, or rather because of this, the audiences always felt that the man who was revealing the soul of Chekhov's hero was their contemporary, an actor enriched by Soviet reality, an actor who shared their thoughts and conceptions.

It would be difficult to explain how Boris Shchukin, Nikolai Khmelyov, Boris Dobronravov and other Soviet actors focussed the audiences' attention. But I am convinced that the spectators not only deeply appreciated their wonderful ability to "incarnate" roles, but also their ability to remain themselves in a certain way and at certain times. Frankly speaking, it could not be otherwise: in the theatre, just as in every other field of art, the spectators want to see and hear the artist himself. That is why the Soviet actor—whatever his role or range of characterizations—must tirelessly learn from life, master the characters of his contemporaries and enhance his world outlook. If the actor works to perfect himself, then there are no, and cannot be any, extraordinary roles that do not bring tangible creative results.

The great stage masters Stanislavsky and Nemirovich-Danchenko developed and enhanced the best traditions of the Russian realistic theatrical school. They evolved an excellent system of training patriotic and artistic feelings in an actor, of enabling him to interpret all the wealth of man's thoughts and feelings. They played no little role in the radical reformation of theatrical art, and that also had a beneficent influence on the development of Soviet film industry.

Soviet stage or screen actors cannot but feel the generous influence of the Moscow Art Theatre and its founders.

I am deeply grateful for the knowledge I acquired when working in films with such talented Moscow Art Theatre performers as Alla Tarasova, Mikhail Tarkhanov, Vasily Toporkov and Boris Livanov. Our association helped me to master acting technique and determined my artistic orientation.

I shall always be thankful to Boris Livanov for his advice on the set of *Baltic Deputy*.

I was rehearsing the scene of the meeting of the counter-revolutionary intelligentsia. It showed Vorobyov, Polezhayev's former pupil and assistant turned saboteur, sweeping the professor's manuscript, which he had stolen from the printing-shop, off the table.

I was supposed to fall on my knees, and start picking up the pages, almost weeping with grief. Polezhayev, according to the script, was sorry for himself, and tears welled up in his eyes; he was on the verge of fainting. I was dissatisfied with myself, for I just could not get the thing well done.

"Don't overdo that pity act! Put more vim into your acting! Let the *spectators* pity you!" shouted Livanov, playing Bocharov, a young Bolshevik and Polezhayev's favourite student.

I heeded his advice and changed my tears for a smile, as if apologizing to those present for causing them so much trouble—lifting me on to a chair and getting me a glass of water to calm myself. Smiling guiltily, my Polezhayev repeatedly murmured an impromptu phrase: "Just look what's happened...."

Thus, Livanov's advice reminded me of Stanislavsky's "reverse colour" method. If this scene were to be shown separately, it would look as if Professor Polezhayev was apologizing for something he had done. In the film, however, it creates a deep and fully justified impression.

Playing Yegor Bulychev, Shchukin used this method with excellent results.

Bulychev was a dying man, but Shchukin did not for a moment allow the audience to suspect that. That is why when Bulychev was reminded of his ailment, it hurt one to hear this said of a man who looked so healthy, so full-blooded and lively. It goes without saying that the last act, and especially the scene of his death, extremely tense and tragic, created an unforgettable impression.

At about the same time I saw Bulychev played by another well-known actor, Nikolai Monakhov. His interpretation of the role was diametrically different. Monakhov repeatedly reminded the audience that Bulychev was a sick man. He actually portrayed the ailment, Bulychev's resignation to his doom, not his struggle against the disease and for life. And the result was that instead of exciting the spectators, he only tired them. I remember how artistically he would touch the aching place. Shchukin never did that. He would approach the stove, embrace it and warm the ailing spot. Monakhov portrayed the ailment, Shchukin resistance to this ailment; Monakhov played the theme, while Shchukin laid stress on action.

The theme should not be played, although sometimes we ignore this fact. An actor should not play up the result of action and anticipate the climax from the very first scene. On the contrary, if he is fully to *live* the role, if he is to develop it logically, he must not think of what is to take place or of how the play is to end, but go through the experiences and action as if he did not know what was ahead.

One is often asked what it is harder to play: good or bad characters.

Soviet playwrights have created many heroes, but sometimes they are less colourful and more schematic than the villains. For that reason it is hard indeed to play good characters, to bring out their inner world and to present them true to life—hard even though such roles are attractive.

In a good character one can always find certain characteristic features which permit to bring out the hero's character in bolder relief, to do away with sketchiness and colourless outlines.

In my opinion, my best stage roles after the war are those of Ivan the Terrible in *The Great Tsar* and Michurin in *Life in Bloom*.

The role of Ivan the Terrible on the stage was a sort of continuation of my work in the film. Belinsky had once called Ivan the Terrible an energetic, profound and gigantic soul, and it was on these words that the play was based.

The month I was given to rehearse the role (the rest of the cast had six months to master theirs) passed very quickly. The première, the Pushkin Theatre's first on its return to Leningrad, was a festive occasion, and the performers rose to it by scoring a singular success. The difficult role of Prince Vasily Shuisky was superbly played by Valentin Yantsat. Yuri Tolubeyev made a convincing Boris Godunov. A very colourful portrayal was given by Alexander Borisov who, contrary to accepted concepts but fully in keeping with the play, presented Tsarevich Fyodor Ivanovich as a clever and cautious man hiding behind a mask of sanctimoniousness. The festive atmosphere of the première and confidence in the success of the play were stimulating, and I went on resolved to succeed, though somewhat perturbed by the thought that I might slip on the role. This will to succeed helped me to overcome all difficulties.

One of my most favourite modern roles is that of Michurin.

The famous naturalist had captured my imagination by his devotion to the task he had set himself in life and by the ardour, patience and perseverance with which he probed Nature's mysteries. Day after day, battling against difficulties, without rest and without allowing anything to distract him, Michurin worked on his miniature garden plots, raising the harvests of the socialist tomorrow.

"Time is short, and the flowers are calling," he says in *Life in Bloom*, adding, "I'm serving the future."

What I had to show was his restless soul, a soul full of life and passion, the soul of a man whose cherished dream impelled him to work for the good of mankind. I saw his image clearly in his lofty aims in life and in his relations with people.

When I accepted the role, some of my friends said they were afraid

* * *

I might pattern Michurin after Polezhayev—both had similar scientific interests at heart, both were naturalists.

Personally, I did not share these fears. I would have been a poor actor indeed if I could not distinguish the core of Polezhayev's role from that of Michurin's. A militant scientist and a democrat, a professor of Moscow and St. Petersburg universities, a recipient of honorary degrees at Oxford and Cambridge universities, Professor Polezhayev—like his prototype, Timiryazev—used his profession to propagate materialism. The environments in which Michurin lived and the character of his scientific work were quite different from those of Professor Polezhayev. Michurin, the great scientist and materialist, spent his life—to use his own words—"sitting on a garden plot in the backward little town of Kozlov." In one of the scenes of the play he puts it even more clearly: "My place is not on a tribune, it's on a garden plot!" Michurin and Polezhayev were men of different characters, different biographies, different human qualities. But they shared the same desire: to make Nature serve Man.

Correct determination of the "core" of the role is just the first step towards its "incarnation." One must show the concrete motives underlying the hero's actions, the real reasons that induce him to act as he does. And while I saw these motives clearly in Michurin's post-revolutionary activities, much in the pre-revolutionary period, i.e., in the first half of the play, remained vague.

This is where Alexander Dovzhenko, the author, came to my aid. Although busy filming Michurin, he found time to come to Leningrad to rewrite certain sequences at the request of the producer and the leading players.

When he decided to write the play, Dovzhenko told me, he studied Michurin's life and went to Kozlov. There, to his surprise, he learned that in his younger days the famous naturalist was known as "Ivan the Mad."

"Mad" in the sense of "persevering," "possessed" and "zealous" became one of the most important elements in my characterization of young Michurin.

He was "mad" because he was poor and this poverty fettered his plans, because he was surrounded by routine and religious obscurantism, because the government would not recognize his work or come to his assistance. He was "possessed" with the idea of a naturalist and innovator and "mad" at the very thought that his experiments, requiring as they did much time and effort, might remain unfinished. Such was the characterization we gave the Michurin of the pre-revolutionary period, and I was grateful indeed to Dovzhenko for his timely assistance.

Dovzhenko wanted to show all the landmarks in his life and struggle, and to do that he had to cover the second forty years of the famous naturalist's life. The task I faced was truly unusual: in four hours of stage action I had to live forty years.

That is quite a period, and naturally there were changes in the thoughts, feelings and character of the hero, particularly since this period was bisected by such an historically momentous event as the Great October Socialist Revolution.

These changes, particularly in his character, required more than just all-round knowledge of his life and work. Before the very eyes of the spectators Michurin grows old, turns grey, bends with age. I had to convey all that, and convincingly. At the same time I had to show that his firm belief in his idea was giving him moral strength and keeping up his militant spirit.

In mastering the role, I was greatly assisted by régisseur Leonid Vivien and my colleagues. Natalia Rashevskaya, Alexander Borisov, Boris Zhukovsky and Yuri Tolubeyev, all of whom had important parts in the play. Tolubeyev gave a wonderfully simple and yet forceful performance as Terenti, Michurin's faithful assistant and—to use the famous naturalist's own words—"an unaccomplished Russian scientist!" We showed them as friendly enemies, always quarrelling and bickering, and if one saw these scenes separately one might think they hated each other, although in reality they were close friends. Borisov made a very charming Mikhail Ivanovich Kalinin, who was pesented not only as head of the Soviet state, but also as a man who dreamed of the future, of the happy life in communist society.

After the première, on the thirtieth anniversary of the October Revolution, I was in my dressing-room taking off the make-up when the telephone rang. The caller said he was one of Michurin's assistants and would be grateful if I saw him. Expecting criticism and afraid that it would make me lose confidence in the role I had just created, I tried to avoid meeting him. But he was insistent, and I had to give in. Recalling the old maxim, "attack is the best form of defence," I opened up with my guns the moment he walked in.

"Please bear in mind that I did not know Michurin personally, just as I was not acquainted with Alexander Nevsky, Tsarevich Alexei and Ivan the Terrible, so I can't claim I'm the living image of Michurin, ' I said, hastily rubbing off my make-up.

"I can't believe that!" my guest interjected. "When I saw you on the stage, I was impressed by the way you re-created some of Michurin's characteristic features, his choppy and sharp manner of speech, his whole character. I was sure you knew him."

It took me a long time to convince him that I had never set eyes on Michurin. He had worked with Michurin for many years, remembered him well and wondered how I had succeeded in achieving such close resemblance. I asked him which scene had impressed him most, and he said it was that in which Michurin spoke of his faith in Lenin's cause, in the future of the country for whose happiness Lenin lived and fought. In this scene there were none, and could not be any, of the so-called Michurin intonations and gestures, but it did reveal his thoughts, convictions and aim in life. I was always excited while reciting this monologue. Probably my excitement communicated itself to the audience, and having compelled it to believe in my Michurin, I convinced it that the outer form and peculiarities of my character were correct. After that it was clear why I had succeeded in convincing a man who had known Michurin so well.

I was already a mature actor when I played Michurin and naturally was less concerned with details and the re-creation of the physical features of the great scientist than when I first played Gorky on the screen. Some of the traits of Michurin's character were the fruit of my imagination—the imagination of an actor and artist, the result of my close study of his life and fate, of my admiration of his spiritual qualities. That, perhaps, explains why my stage portrait was so faithful.

It was a pleasure to play in *Life in Bloom*, and I consider the role one of my best on the stage.

Of my recent screen roles I should like to dwell upon the part of Captain Levashov in *Bon Voyage!*, Alexander Popov in the film of that name, and Vladimir Stasov in *Moussorgsky*.

Bon Voyage! was one of the first films about the Nakhimov schools where future Soviet naval officers get their education.

The lofty idea of the film, produced chiefly for young audiences, captured my imagination and gave me an opportunity to dedicate my efforts to our Navy and its wonderful men, to portray a wise instructor—a Party member and a disciplined officer, entrusted with training future commanders.

In the script, however, the role was not sufficiently clear and characteristic, and to make it more vivid and true to life, it was necessary to find the "key" to the role, to determine its "core."

I had associated quite a lot with seamen, especially in the early years of the Revolution, and was friends with many. Having agreed to play Captain Levashov, I decided to draw upon my impressions and observations for the material with which to mould my hero. But then Levashov was an instructor at a Nakhimov school, and since I had never been inside one, my impressions and observations proved useless. So I turned to literature—novels, memoirs and notes, but here too I could find no material to help me to fashion the character, although I read everything I could find, including an account of the Tsushima Battle in which Russian sailors had displayed such wonderful tenacity, courage and valour. These excellent traditions of the Russian Navy, which Soviet sailors have inherited, helped me in my work on the role, but could not determine its "core." The alternative was to meet instructors of Nakhimov schools.

As Ivan the Terrible in the play *The Great Tsar*. 1945

As Ivan the Terrible. 1945

I thought a lot, naturally, of Levashov's attitude towards his pupils and of their relations.

It seemed to me that his love for the youngsters—in this case orphans, whose parents had perished in the war—ought to be expressed through the medium of kindness, friendly smiles and paternal solicitude. But that would have inevitably led to false sentimental intonations.

I therefore thought it would be better to play Levashov as a man who does not smile, who is outwardly gruff and something of a mystery for the spectators and even for his associates.

I wanted the spectators to be puzzled right from the time he meets his future pupils, to make them ask questions: "Why is Levashov so morose, so strict and so demanding? Doesn't he like children? Is he dissatisfied with his job? Perhaps he lost his children during the war and finds the sight of happy youngsters unbearable?"

But Levashov does love children. That is revealed as the film unfolds. He is an efficient instructor. In my opinion it was more natural to have him serious and strict, to let him smile only a few times in front of his pupils.

Just before the film went into production I read a newspaper article headlined *The Notes of an Officer*. Its author, instructor at a Suvorov military school, wrote of his experiences and gave a vivid description of life in such institutes and of relations between instructors and their pupils. Among his characters were two officers. Both of them were respected by their colleagues and loved by their pupils. Both were instructors of excellent reputation, though using diametrically different methods of education. One of them advocated unconditional obedience and a purely military attitude to the pupils. The other held that the children were orphans, that they did not know what a caress was and that they should therefore be treated kindly and tenderly. The conclusion that the author reaches is that the correct system of education should take both these approaches into consideration, that instructors should be moderately exacting and strict and at the same time kind and tender so as not to deprive pupils of the joys of childhood.

The author reached this conclusion on the basis of his work and experience as an instructor; mine was the result of an analysis of the ideological and educational value of the role, and I was extremely happy that my conclusion was fully confirmed by an experienced instructor.

That is why Captain Levashov was, in a certain measure, the embodiment of that ideal type of instructor described in *The Notes of an Officer*.

All through the film I tried to show Levashov as an exacting officer who loves his pupils well and wisely. He understands the psychology of children and everything he does is motivated by his solicitude for the youngsters the state has placed in his care. The warm reception given the film by instructors and pupils showed that my portrayal of Captain Levashov was correct.

My role in *Alexander Popov,* which was more than just a biographical film, was extremely difficult.

The story, laid in Kronstadt at the end of the last century, describes how Popov, a lecturer at an officers' mine school, assisted by Rybkin, overcomes numerous difficulties before he succeeds in wirelessing messages—first to a receiver one metre away, then five, ten, hundred metres—how the first antenna in the world was made, how radio was first used to save people's lives. Our task was to make clear to the cinema audiences the technical aspects of Popov's momentous invention, in other words, to produce an historical, scientific and educational feature, all rolled in one.

Playing Popov seemed an excessively difficult job, particularly since the scenario was anything but perfect. In my effort to present a true picture of the great scientist, I turned to every source available and interviewed his contemporaries.

"What was Popov like?" I asked Professor M. A. Shatelen, one of the oldest Leningrad scientists and a friend of the inventor.

"Nothing extraordinary."

"What do you mean?"

"He was just an ordinary man," came the reply.

The more I learned about Popov, the more I came to like him and the more I was convinced that he was a very modest, tactful man without any outstanding characteristics. He had no sharply defined traits inherent in other great men—he was neither restive like Pavlov nor temperamental like Timiryazev—no traits that could be used to paint a colourful picture. We spent a lot of time wondering how best to characterize Popov, how to describe his life and work in an interesting way.

The picture was to feature the apparatus made personally by the inventor, and after a close inspection I came to the conclusion that his were really skilful fingers.

Popov loved to make various apparatus, technical gadgets and even toys for his children, like rattles and self-propelled cannon. He needed filings for his experiments and he obtained them from aluminium pots, using a tool of his own making. I wanted very much to show Popov's skilful fingers in action—fingers that were always doing something, the nimble fingers which made all the technical apparatus he needed. We thought at first of filming an episode about this passion of his, but then gave up the idea lest it should detract from the general characterization of the great inventor and the tragedy of his life. Perhaps I failed to show his skilful fingers as I had intended to, but the very thought of them—a thought that never left me—enabled me to create more fully his image and character.

I tried to show Popov as a wise, wilful and far-sighted scientist, as a genius who had given the world a wonderful discovery. The main thing, as I saw it, was to stress his ardent faith in the feasibility of using electro-magnetic waves, despite all sceptical claims to the contrary, for the good of mankind. His tragedy was that he was given no assistance whatever by the tsarist government.

I fell in love with Popov and with the role. In all my previous appearances on the stage and screen I had dynamic roles, roles that gave me ample scope to make use of my plastic and intonational capacities. In *Alexander Popov* I had to rein in these capacities and build up the role on the basis of the dynamic thought of the great inventor.

It was while playing Popov that I was offered the role of Vladimir Stasov in *Moussorgsky*.

The offer was more than welcome. After playing the modest, unobtrusive and collected Popov I was eager to tackle a role in which I could make full use of my plastic and especially vocal capacities, for Stasov was well known as "Vladimir the Loud."

His colourful figure, his frankness and conviviality, his extraordinary optimism and faith in the might of Russian national art, his fervent patriotism which inspired him to rally talented Russian musicians and artists—all this afforded a wonderful opportunity to create an artistically rich character.

I read Gorky's reminiscences of Stasov, and his penetrating analysis gave me a clear picture of the well-known critic. "Art was his passion, religion and god," Gorky wrote, "he always seemed drunk with love of art. Listening to his impromptu speeches, one could not help thinking that he was anticipating major developments in art, that he was on the eve of creating major literary, musical and artistic works, that he was always looking forward to some big holiday with the eagerness of a child.... Stasov was a tall grey-haired child with a big and kind heart. He had seen much and knew much, he loved life and stimulated the love of life in others." The key to the role lay in the words Gorky said after Stasov's death: "Here was a man who had done everything he could."

The film, showing the struggle waged by a group of patriots against cosmopolitans in the sphere of national realistic art, promised to be an outstanding achievement. The earnest of that was the excellent scenario, the talented portrayal of Moussorgsky by Alexander Borisov and the expert choice of actors for the roles of other famous Russian composers.

I shall return to my role of Stasov in *Moussorgsky* and dwell on my portrayal of the well-known critic in the film *Rimsky-Korsakov* in another chapter in which I shall describe how a film actor works on his roles.

As I come to the close of this chapter I should like to speak of an argument that has been going on among actors for a great many years, the argument of whether in portraying a character the actor should proceed from inner content to outer form, or vice versa.

I am convinced that whatever may be the method the actor uses, it is in his character and nature to think in images, and for that reason outer form with him is inevitably linked with inner content.

In practice, we may pay more attention to any of these two aspects, and I personally think that both ways are constructive.

Technologically, the meaning of inner content could be defined as "what to play" and the meaning of outer form as "how to play."

In the theatre with its protracted rehearsals "what to play" is the more important question and leads through the process of dramatic readings and rehearsals to the question of "how to play."

In the films where rehearsals, as a rule, are held immediately before the actual filming, the actor should have a clear picture of what his character looks like from the very first. Therefore, the question "how" is the more important, blending with "what" as the actor prepares to act before the cameras.

In an effort to be clear, I have divided these concepts and described them separately. A more profound analysis will show that penetration of inner content is impossible without a search for outer form. That is why a stage actor seeks for concrete outer forms in inner content, and, conversely, a film actor discovers inner content in the process of his search for outer form.

The specific character of film work demands that the actor should be able, from the very first day, to embody his role, whereas in the theatre the demand is that the actor should not hurry in determining his outer form.

THE STAGE ACTOR'S TECHNIQUE

In acting, as in any other art, technique makes for perfection in form, and its mastery is therefore of the greatest importance. It is the framework on which the actor builds his role, the firm foundation on which he can always depend when in difficulty.

Stanislavsky teaches that the actor should be conscious of the principal idea behind the character he portrays all through the performance, regarding this as his supreme task. Technique is the actor's scientific equipment, and it will help him to cope with this important task.

Talent, of course, is essential; but the creative possibilities inherent in talent can never be fully expressed without a consummate technique.

Each of the many theatrical arts has evolved a technique of its own. I shall touch briefly upon the main problems of technique in those fields in which I had myself worked. These range from the opera and ballet to vaudeville and the circus, from pantomime and classical comedy to psychological drama and historical tragedy.

My own experience with Don Quixote shows how different these problems are. I have played Cervantes's hero four times. The first time it was in Massenet's opera, doubling for Chaliapin in the windmill scene, in which I had to ride across the rear part of the stage on a white steed. Then I impersonated Don Quixote in the ballet by Minkous, doing the part in pantomime. My third appearance was at the Young Spectators' Theatre in the musical comedy version. And finally, I led the cast in Bulgakov's dramatization of Cervantes's novel at the Pushkin Theatre. In this play a deep psychological study of the character was combined with grotesque and a touch of the eccentric. Hence in each instance I had to fall back on a distinctive technique best suited to the genre of the performance.

It was at the Mariinsky Theatre that I first became absorbed in problems of technique. I was so entranced by the music in the love-scene in *Prince Igor* that I did not even notice the unnatural behaviour of the lovers: they did not even look at each other. Fearful of falling out with the orchestra, they kept their eyes glued to the conductor's baton; at times they even nodded and swayed to the rhythm of the music. Needless to say, in the opera, where music is all-important, the actor must watch the conductor's baton, and he therefore finds it more difficult to act than in drama. But the opera singer who has perfect command of technique is never at a disadvantage and acts realistically and convincingly.

Our greatest singers, such as Ivan Yershov and Feodor Chaliapin, were also our greatest actors. They were able to get away from the conventional opera, and even in the most difficult scenes, from the musical pcint of view, their acting carried conviction.

A striking example of natural and realistic acting was Chaliapin's exit in the last scene of the third act in *Khovanshchina*. Chaliapin sang the part of Dosifei. Standing quite close to the footlights, with a beautiful sweeping gesture he put his arm around Marfa. Then turning away from the orchestra, he walked slowly off with her to the rear of the stage, singing with deep emotion the closing lines of their duet: "Be patient, dear, go on loving, dear, and let bygones be bygones. . . ."

His voice, soft, beautifully modulated and harmonizing perfectly with the orchestra, carried to the crowded wings, and to every corner of the packed house. Even the last notes, sung pianissimo at the back of the stage, were distinctly audible everywhere.

Chaliapin's exit made a powerful impression. It was achieved by the rare expressiveness of his intonations, the sculptural quality of the image he created, the singular grace with which he could wear the flowing dissenter's robe, and above all by the realism of his acting. He would never have been able to achieve such effectiveness, had he not a splendid command of the opera actor's technique.

A knowledge of technique makes the talented actor extremely resourceful. It gives wings to his imagination. On the other hand, no amount of technique will do any good when the actor is a mere craftsman.

My early stage experience is connected with pantomime acting in the ballet. Eager to learn everything I could, I watched closely the performance of the great masters of mime in the Petrograd ballet.

But I soon realized that the language of pantomime, born of conventional gestures, evolved through the efforts of generations of choreographers, had grown antiquated and fell short of the requirements of realistic ballet. Of course, there was some "logic" to the gestures. For example, bending yourself back a little, raising your hand, then lowering it and pointing the forefinger at your partner meant "thou." "You" was conveyed by similar gestures, except that the hand was first lowered and then raised and the curtsy was more deferential. When the dancer's movements were sharply defined, the distinction between the two salutations was quite obvious. But in most cases the gestures conveyed nothing to the audience at all. The language of pantomime had grown encrusted with clichés and was even ridiculous at times. To translate into this language "I saw you in my dreams yesterday," for example, one had to go through the following motions: first point to oneself, meaning "I," next make a few circular motions with the fingers over the eyes for "saw," then raise one's hand with a pointed forefinger and make a bow to indicate "you," point the thumb over the right shoulder near the ear to mean "yesterday," and finally lean one's left cheek on clasped hands and lower one's lids for "in my dreams." Such gestures went over the heads of even the most sophisticated ballet lovers, let alone the general public. They formed part of an obsolete dance lexicon which stood in the way of the creation of the new Soviet ballet.

The time had come to renovate the art of ballet pantomime, and with all our youthful fervour we, the young members of the Mariinsky Theatre, attacked the clichés and canons of the old ballet. We fought for attitudes and gestures that would be more understandable, realistic and convincing. To what extent we succeeded in overthrowing the old and bringing in the new at that time is difficult to say.

But Soviet choreographers have long since broken away from the conventional forms and attitudes of the old ballet. They have abandoned the old stereotypes, substituted them by realistic acting and thus developed a new technique of ballet pantomime.

I was cast in a good many mime parts at the Leningrad ballet theatre because it was a tradition there to cast dramatic actors in these parts. I impersonated Don Quixote at ballerina Lyukom's jubilee performance and at a memorial performance in honour of Petipa, the great choreographer. I played King Florestan in *The Sleeping Beauty* in which Ulanova and Semyonova danced. In these parts my

As Michurin in the play *Life in Bloom.* 1947

Nikolai Cherkasov with Yuri Tolubeyev as Terenti
in *Life in Bloom*. 1947

Nikolai Cherkasov with Boris Zhukovsky as Professor Kartashov in *Life in Bloom.* 1947

Nikolai Cherkasov in the title role in the film
Alexander Popov. 1950

movements and gestures were restrained and realistic, essentially of a plastic quality, faithful to the rhythm of the music.

I strove at the same time to make my portrayals poignant and vivid. To do this I needed colour, and I used elements of the grotesque or the eccentric.

In those early days of my career, when I was mastering technique, I gave particularly much thought to the eccentric element in acting.

When we use the word eccentric in relation to human behaviour, we mean a departure from the normal, an absence of logic in our actions, and asymmetry in our movements. Eccentric acting when it is done merely for effect is just another expression of formalism. But when it pursues the definite aim of enhancing a portrayal and stressing idiosyncrasies, it is extremely useful and its technique must be studied.

In classical comedy, drama and even tragedy, the actor frequently resorts to eccentric gestures and attitudes, particularly in scenes showing madness or other forms of mental derangement. In such scenes it is well to mould the image in asymmetric rather than symmetric lines. That comedy should abound in examples of eccentric acting is quite understandable. But in drama, too, and particularly in historical plays, the actor finds eccentric elements helpful in portraying complex emotions. In one of his most successful roles, as Generalissimo Suvorov, Skorobogatov here and there gives a touch of the eccentric to his characterization. Its usage is fully justified in the camp scenes showing the general among his men. But the actor also introduces it in psychological scenes.

In the ball-room scene, in Prince Potyomkin's palace, when General Kleinrogge presents his nephew to Suvorov and asks him to take the young man as his secretary, the famous generalissimo replies: "Your nephew as my secretary, you say? Well, upon my word!" And he punctuates these words with a funny, abrupt, acrobatic movement of the whole body which is in line with the portrait and gives the scene the finishing touch it requires.

An example of bold and at the same time subtle use of eccentric touches in tragedy is the mad scene in the last act of Lermontov's

Masquerade. In this scene, Arbenin, played by Yuri Yuriev, suffering intensely because of Nina's death, appears holding a candle at the rear of the stage. After a brief soliloquy, his gaze falls on The Stranger and Zvezdich. They denounce him, and the effect of their words is plainly shown on his face. We see the turmoil that possesses his soul and the attempt he makes to hide his true feelings from those around him. Then quite unexpectedly and, as it seems, out of keeping with his previous manner of acting, he passes to a sharply asymmetrical portrayal. His knees grow jerky, he acquires a stoop and suddenly looks old. The angular jittery appearance of his figure suggests at once a mind unhinged. He looks pitiable and ludicrous and fearful all at the same time. In this state, his voice grown shrill, he speaks to his persecutors:

> Ah, a plot? Good.... I'm in your hands.
> Who dares prevent you from carrying it out!
> . . . .
> The thing's well conceived indeed.
> Yet you know not what the outcome will be!

And when The Stranger, having tasted the sweetness of revenge but unable to make the mad Arbenin understand him, exclaims, "And this proud mind, too, has broken down today," the words do not come as a surprise to the spectator; Arbenin's tragic end was suggested at the very first encounter with The Stranger. Yuriev's performance in this scene hallmarks him as a great actor. He makes ample use of eccentric elements which do not seem incongruous with the classic verse of the drama and the "dinner jacket" stiffness of the role.

I have found eccentric touches essential in re-creating such characters as Varlaam in *Boris Godunov* or Don Quixote, and extremely effective in psychological scenes, also in such tragic roles as Ivan the Terrible—in the scene where the tsar stands at the coffin of the son he had killed. He hears the chorus singing backstage and is so strongly impressed that his mind begins to wander. And here I change from a pose of regal dignity to one which is asymmetric, angular and undignified. The new pose may, for a fraction of a second, appear ludicrous to the audience but I have never heard a laugh in the theatre during its performance. Quite the contrary, I felt, if anything, the growing tensity of the audience.

Playing Michurin (*Life in Bloom*) I resorted to eccentric touches to show Michurin as an aged and feeble man in the final scenes of the play. A sculptor friend of mine told me after the play's first night that my face, especially the mouth, was extremely expressive in these scenes. But when he asked me how I had achieved this, I was at a loss to answer, for it had come quite natural as a development of the general portrait—the bent, shaky legs, the stooping shoulders, the slightly drooping head. I knew, however, that a touch of the eccentric in the gait, movements, gestures, in the inflections of the voice, did much to enhance my portrayal of the naturalist and stress the newly acquired traits and foibles that come with old age.

My acting experience in performances of a synthetic nature—at the Young Spectators' Theatre, in the operetta and in the opera—has proved of great benefit to me in my later career and in a further study of technique.

I learned how flexible technique is and how versatile the actor must be. In operetta, for example, the actor, apart from thinking of his role along dramatic lines, must be aware of the musical images. Thus, although his tasks are the same as those of the dramatic actor, they are rendered more complex by the singing, music and dancing elements that go to make up the role.

In drama, the actor often changes his technique and manner to suit the style of each particular play. This requires an adaptability which comes with experience. Sometimes playing one and the same part over again will greatly enrich the actor's technique.

When I joined the Pushkin Theatre, my technique was becoming more and more firmly rooted in the Stanislavsky method—thanks to my association in the making of films with producers and actors of the Moscow Art Theatre. This helped me to get rid of some of my shortcomings. One of them was over-emphasis of outer effect which led to overacting, particularly in comedy, where the actor is tempted to go to any length to win an extra laugh from the audience.

Comedy requires a technique all its own. Comic situations also require a sincerity and clarity of idea or they won't get over. This, alas, is sometimes forgotten, and the underlying ideas of some of our comedies are all too vague. In comedy, the actor must believe implicitly in the situation in which he finds himself, no matter how improbable it may be. He must be wholly absorbed in what he does and do it in all earnestness.

Of the comic parts I played as a mature actor, the one that appealed most to me was that of Lelio in Carlo Goldoni's classic comedy *The Liar*.

Goldoni's Lelio, the incorrigible fibber and "dashing cavalier," is a vivid personality, a young man of versatile traits. He possesses great imagination. He is resolute and brave, even devil-may-care at times. He is full of the joy of living. He is hot-headed but amazingly resourceful.

In its production of this play our company was eager to reflect the many improvements which the Italian dramatist wished to bring to the theatre. I learned of these when I read Goldoni's memoirs—Goldoni waged a struggle for a free people's theatre—and his play *The Comic Theatre* in which he champions lifelike acting.

There were many technical difficulties connected with the role. One was "shrinking" in size—I was too tall for the part. Another was playing in a rapid tempo: Lelio was a deft and spry young man. Then, like all cloak-and-sword plays with their fencing and endless ceremonial bows, *The Liar* required a grace of movement which it took me some time to achieve. Once I mastered the outer features, the characterization took its natural course. I began to act with great sincerity. Everything Lelio did and said I accepted in good faith. I worked hard at getting the correct voice inflections in Lelio's speech, and so was able to make his most boastful monologues ring sincere, and even lend them a certain dignity. I must mention here that Malyutin, my partner in a good many of the scenes, helped me considerably to build up my character.

The Liar is a comedy of the type in which the actor must, in many of the situations, establish direct contact with the audience, such as in the interludes where he complains of his misfortunes, seeks sympathy, divulges secrets, or familiarizes the spectator with the further course of events. In such instances I always made it a point to pick some person in the audience to whom I spoke directly. I tried to speak simply and to put sincerity into my words, choosing our best elocutionists as my models.

Only after endless rehearsing, after playing the part many times before audiences and performing fragments from the play on the variety stage did I succeed in attaining the spontaneity of dialogue and movement which is typical of the comedy of Goldoni's time.

The part of Osip in Gogol's *Inspector-General* required quite a different technique, incidentally a slowness of gesture and rhythm. Osip is a sharp-witted roguish fellow, a serf spoilt by life in the Russian capital. He is really no less a knave than his master and frets against the latter only because he keeps him hungry most of the time. He disapproves only of those actions of his master's which are likely to bring them both to harm.

The monologue in which Gogol gives a pen portrait of Khlestakov just before he makes his appearance is the most difficult place in Osip's role. In rehearsing this monologue I worked out a certain technique. I would find some person or some object to focus my attention on, and sometimes I would be addressing myself. Thus, when railing against fate I addressed an imaginary listener, when arguing or dreaming aloud I addressed myself, and when the monologue called for me to vent my anger on my master, I imagined some object to be him.

At the beginning of the monologue when Osip exclaims: "Devil take it, I'm hungry," he is bitter against his lot and addresses an imaginary listener. "I'm tired of this sort of life. It was better in the country...." There and then he starts an argument with himself—"No! It's better in St. Petersburg, no one'll deny that." Osip falls into reminiscing about life in the capital. This part of his monologue may be termed "dreaming aloud": "The old officer's old lady drops in...."

You never walk but hire a cab and take it as easy as your master...."
And then addressing himself to a stool as though it were his own
master, he shouts: "If your old father only knew what you're up to,
he would...."

It took me a long time before I had polished up all these parts
of the monologue, which I saw as distinctly different fragments, and
achieved the desired effect.

The trouble with a good many comedy actors is that they "point up"
bits of action artificially just for the sake of getting an extra laugh.
They do this at the expense of the thought behind the action, the idea
of the play, the style of the period, and thus err against truth and logic.
I myself was guilty of this more than once, the laughs of the audience
going to my head.

A role of great psychological depth is rooted in emotional technique,
in the capturing of the spirit, with outer movement and good voice
being mere accoutrements of the part. It requires great repression. The
actor should depend upon a single movement, a shrug of the shoulders
or a mere nod to evoke a response from the audience. A pause, too,
can be very effective. In such parts the actor aims at simplicity and
complete fusion of his own personality with that of the character he
plays.

It goes without saying that mastery of the mechanics of emotion
which will help the actor to best project the inner traits of the character is essential not only in psychological roles but in all dramatic
acting.

The actor must always strive to create a lifelike atmosphere on the
stage, and think of acting as a give-and-take process among players.
It is just as important for the actor to listen to the lines of his partners
as it is for him to speak his own.

In *Inspector-General* there is a scene where Khlestakov receives
some merchants who bring him sugar, bread and viands. The director
suggested that one of the merchants hold two plucked geese, their
heads dangling. When the merchants appear, the geese at once catch
the attention of Osip, Khlestakov's manservant, and he stares at them,
his mind made up to snatch them.

Throughout this long scene, I stood without stirring, gazing in fascination at what I hoped would soon be my booty.

And yet at the première increasing peals of laughter came from the audience, and I realized that I was taking the scene away from Khlestakov. So I toned down on my acting considerably. This incident taught me an important lesson: on the stage one must be careful not to steal the scene from one's acting partner.

There was another lesson too: the actor must not follow blindly his predecessors—actors who had played the same part before him. I made that mistake. I followed the Varlamov tradition and showed Osip as a fat man with a pot-belly. I copied Varlamov's make-up and wore a good deal of padding which hampered my movements. The figure of Osip clashed too much with my own appearance. I felt there was something artificial in my set-up. I just could not step freely into the role. Gradually I began to remove one padding after another but still the true mental state of my character evaded me.

Afterwards, in 1952, when the centenary of Gogol's death was commemorated in our country and the Pushkin Theatre revived *Inspector-General*, I played the part quite differently. And it is with a feeling of exhilaration that I recall the rehearsals directed by Vivien— particularly in the principal scenes with the mayor (Tolubeyev) and with Khlestakov (Freindlikh).

When I come on the stage I remember the advice of our great actors and imagine that I am completely ignorant of the plot. I make believe that every scene, every line takes me unawares. This makes the dialogue flow easily and naturally. In some instances I even repeat softly to myself the words spoken by my partner, the better to be convinced that I am hearing them for the first time.

To hold the attention of the audience, to convey to it the mental and emotional state of the character he portrays, the actor makes use of various means. He uses the power of words, vocal technique with its wealth of tone, as well as gestures, movement, tempo and pauses.

In working on the lines and the meaning behind them, the actor should try to enunciate each word clearly.

I used to stammer in my childhood, and to this day have not completely overcome this impediment. This is one of the reasons why I take special pains with my diction. I have made it a practice to repeat at home a hundred or more times words or phrases containing vowel or consonant combinations difficult to enunciate.

It is truly a pleasure to listen to the actor who is able to make the words he utters sparkle like precious gems.

Of course, this does not mean that the actor should give emotional colouring to each word in the sentence; only the main words, the thought-carrying words must "sparkle." A tendency to "play up" words for effect will only result in obscuring the meaning. The actor is often tempted to do this with beautiful-sounding words. He should overcome this temptation if he wishes to bring home to the audience the principal thought behind every bit of the text. In *The Great Tsar* I was up against many speech difficulties. The play is written in blank verse and abounds in lengthy monologues by Ivan the Terrible. These contain many sixteenth-century words long grown obsolete. I worked hardest at places of high tonal pitch and those most emotionally vibrant to get variety and colour in my voice. I hoped that my diction in this long play would at least come up to professional standards.

In blank verse there is one great danger for the actor. It tends to make him adopt a declamatory style which blurs the meaning behind the words. To avoid falling into this error I worked for hours at every bit of text.

First of all I tried to give full value to the thoughts behind each line and to make my words ring strong and authoritative as befitted the august personage I played.

I had to build towards a climax, as, for example, in the fifth scene of the play in which Ivan the Terrible meets with Chernets. At the end of the scene the tsar turns his back to Chernets, walks to the throne and after some pauses, with hardly a glance, flings at him the closing lines of his monologue.

A shift of scene and changes in the tempo of action make the actor alter the rhythm of his own movements and change the tone. In inti-

As Osip in Gogol's *Inspector-General*. 1936

Vladimir Voronov as Harlequin and Nikolai Cherkasov as Lelio in *The Liar*. 1940

mate scenes there are no metallic notes, but an appealing softness and subdued tones. Changing his intonations to suit the scene, the actor at the same time sees to it that his diction is good and all sounds pure and clear. His voice must never be monotonous. Different qualities within the pitch and range and tone subtleties are essential to express the emotional state.

When I played Polezhayev I spoke in a high-pitched voice, at times rising to a falsetto. A crude, metallic, lush ring was needed when I played Varlaam. Soft, velvety, at times sing-song tones went into the making of Don Quixote's voice. I had to speak in a low, chest voice, sometimes hoarse, for Ivan the Terrible.

Voice problems of a peculiar nature confronted me when I rehearsed the part of Michurin, as the action of the play covers a period of forty years of the hero's life. I had to show the changes that the voice underwent with age. At the end of the play, for example, when Michurin is shown an old man, his voice loses a good deal of its force and grows thinner.

Gestures also help the actor to build up his character. In tragic parts the actor should be careful not to "gesture." He should use gestures sparingly, only to lend greater emphasis to an important thought (excepting ritual gestures which are common in historical dramas).

During the rehearsal period, the actor is continually tempted to use gesture—as a substitute for thought and feeling.

It is most effective to mould the portrait of the character in severe sculptural lines. Unsparing "gesturing" only weakens the impression. It is told that many eminent actors, among them Monakhov, would sew their sleeves to their coats to avoid too frequent use of gesture. Nikolai Khmelyov of the Moscow Art Theatre created streamlined, well-sculptured portraits that helped his acting to carry great conviction. In Chekhov's *Three Sisters* in the Moscow Art Theatre, Livanov plays the part of the inscrutable Solyony and needs but a few gestures to draw the attention of the audience to himself.

Playing tragedy requires a plastic expressiveness all its own, broad, sparing gestures, tense dramatic pauses, sculptural lines in the run of the scenes, an elevated spirit, and a rejection of the trivial.

In *Don Quixote* my gestures were influenced by the lofty thoughts, as well as by the costumes worn by this "knight of a rueful countenance."

Don Quixote's tall, lean figure could not but be extremely lithe, yet when he found himself in a difficult position it grew clumsy and ludicrous. During the rehearsals I involuntarily gesticulated too much, particularly in some of the monologues. This only resulted in making my portrayal trite. The régisseur tried to restrain me, and it took a long time before I toned down my gesturing. Too many gestures tend to disintegrate the portrait the actor is trying to create.

The style, customs and dress of the period determined to a good measure my gestures as Ivan the Terrible. They had to be in keeping with the heavy brocade garments he wore, with the sceptre and orb, the scrolls he held, the solid gold and silver goblets he drank from. Manliness and majesty of bearing required gestures that were restrained yet monumental. In many of the scenes to achieve a sculpturesque effect I assumed certain attitudes and retained them for a short space of time. Poses and attitude, like gestures, must be in harmony with the period and costumes. For example, as Peter I, I would now and then cross my legs when sitting. Such a pose was impossible in *The Great Tsar*, if only because of the long robe Ivan the Terrible wore.

When playing an historical character the actor goes to paintings, prints and other materials for his gestures and poses. When I played Professor Polezhayev, a scientist accustomed to books and the laboratory, I knew I had to give the impression of smooth hands and graceful gestures, but Michurin, a practical scientist, had hands that were rough and sinewy.

From his early days the actor comes to realize that effective and convincing handling of properties is of utmost importance. This makes the actor's movements and actions more lifelike. When wearing or handling imitation objects, the actor, if the play requires it, must create the illusion that they are real and heavy, hot or cold, clammy or prickly. He must drink out of empty goblets and feel wine coursing through his veins. In his manner of handling such objects as the tsar's sceptre and orb, the bishop's crozier and rosary, the policeman's club and handcuffs—the actor reveals the character he represents. For fencing scenes or scenes requiring the use of pistols, etc., the actor must train and become perfectly adept at the use of these weapons. It required long practice before, as Ivan the Terrible, I could fling my staff some inches away from Kirilovna lying on the floor to produce an impression of striking her. A. Kozlova, who played the part of Kirilovna, usually closed her eyes and conveyed very well the fear that possessed her.

The actor's manipulation of hand properties, such as a cigarette case, a cigarette and matches, bank-notes, a wallet, a book and pencil, paper and pen, may go a long way to disclosing certain sides of the character he impersonates.

We often speak of two types of rhythm—inner rhythm and surface rhythm. A slowing-down or a quickening of the inner rhythm does not necessarily lead to static or dynamic action, nor to corresponding changes in speech. White heat in inner rhythm may be conveyed by slow and measured dialogue. Inner calm may be rendered by brisk movements and snappy speech.

Different inner and surface rhythms often exist in complete harmony, helping to bring out more sharply the idea behind the scene and to heighten the emotional atmosphere in the auditorium. As Krogstadtes in Ibsen's A Doll's House, I remember asking Nora: "Was it really your father who signed the promissory note?" I said this, rising slowly from the chair, and held the note out to her. There was a short pause. Nora, played by Y. Karyakina, strode across the proscenium, turned slowly around and with a proud, somewhat challenging toss of her head replied: "No, it was I." Figuratively speaking, the inner rhythm rose to 104° but the surface rhythm was far below 100°.

A dramatic pause can be used by the actor with great effect. There are two types of dramatic pauses: one involving movement and action on the stage and lasting two, three or four minutes, and a brief one during which all action and movement ceases.

At the close of the audience scene in *The Great Tsar* there is a good example of effective use of the long pause. The Polish ambassador leaves; all wait in silence for the tsar to take a decision. Ivan the Terrible slowly hands his sceptre to his son who is sitting close by, and a few moments later his orb and crown. He sits slightly hunched for a moment, then rises abruptly, tries to take a step forward but suddenly clasps his heart. His son comes to his side to support him. For a few seconds the tsar stands frozen in this pose. With a gesture he declines his son's support, then slowly descends the throne steps and walks across the hall. The nobles approach him. He waves them aside and walks off in the opposite direction. Suddenly he clutches his head, drops on to a bench and remains petrified in that position while one of the nobles begins his monologue. It was after many rehearsals that this long pause and the mises-en-scène that go with it were introduced. It fits in naturally with the main idea of the scene and helps to bring out the relationships between the various characters.

The same play offers a good example of a short pause. When Shuisky tells Ivan the Terrible of the plot against him and names its ringleaders, the tsar, sitting motionless in stern silence, averts his gaze, then turns first his head, then his body and keeps that pose for a few seconds. The pause closes with a gesture, actually a signal showing a change of mood. "There is reason in what you say...." Ivan the Terrible speaks his lines in a low, muffled voice.

Dramatic pauses, brief or long, emphasize important thoughts and are calculated to keep the spectators in suspense.

One of the scenes in *Boris Godunov* is laid in a tavern on the Lithuanian frontier. Among those present in the tavern is Grishka Otrepiev (Pseudo-Dmitri). There is a price on his head. The bailiffs have fallen on his scent and tracked him down. Otrepiev, who is the only literate person there, reads the tsar's order, changing the description to fit Varlaam. All eyes are turned on the latter. Varlaam looks aghast at the bailiffs, then averts his gaze and with affected indifference examines the walls and ceiling of the tavern. A moment later he turns abruptly to face his would-be pursuers, pulls his stomach in, brings his legs under him, as though gathering himself up into a ball and making ready to pounce on them. In a flash he flings up his hands with long, outstretched, crooked fingers and lets out incoherent hissing sounds to frighten those present. The horror-struck bailiffs are ordered by their chief to seize Varlaam. This is an extremely eloquent pause of suspense which closes with a comic touch relieving the tension in the auditorium.

What happiness it is for an actor to be able to sway his audience, to move it to tears or joy, to keep it breathless. In the scene in which Ivan the Terrible, his mind unhinged, speaks to his dead son, I always feel the tense silence in the auditorium, although I am quite far from the proscenium. In a half-whisper I utter the words: "What sad remorse that in hot blood I had cast the staff at you. Have I really killed you?"

I place my hand slowly upon the dead tsarevich's forehead. Then I tear it away and run impetuously to the footlights, shrieking:

"Yes, I have!"

At this juncture my ear would invariably catch a strange creaking sound coming from the darkened auditorium. At the first performances I was greatly puzzled by this sound. But the mystery was soon cleared up by a theatre worker who sat among the audience. It appeared that at the beginning of this highly dramatic scene the spectators would lean forward, but when Ivan the Terrible rushed to the front of the stage, they invariably flung themselves back in their seats. It was this that caused the creaking sound.

The actor will find that with complete mastery of the technique of his craft comes perfect self-control. That is something I always admired in Chaliapin, even back in the early days of my career when my ideas about the actor's equipment were still very vague. I can't help remembering something that happened just before the curtain rose, when the orchestra had already struck up the overture to *Ruslan and Lyudmila*. Chaliapin was singing the part of Farlaf. He came on the stage and before taking his place at the table, as the scene required, noticed his boots were not strapped properly. He tried to adjust the straps himself, but failed and went backstage in search of the costumier. I stood behind Lyudmila holding a torch. The overture was drawing to a close and I was getting more and more jittery—what if Chaliapin should be late? But he wasn't. He came cool and collected, and took his seat at the table a moment before the curtain rose. It was an amazing example of self-control.

Lack of self-control or collectedness may bring failure to the actor as one of my own early experiences in the play *Uncle Vanya* shows. When the Pushkin Theatre was producing this play I was assigned to understudy the actor who played Astrov. I thought I could manage the part quite well, since I had already played it rather successfully in my student days with no experience and no real knowledge of technique to fall back upon. It was my first attempt at portraying a realistic part.

For a full half-year I zealously worked on the role. But due to certain circumstances we had very few rehearsals and only one full-dress rehearsal. Hence, when I came on the stage I had a feeling I was not entirely established in the role. Self-control slipped away from me. I regained it only in the fourth act. And only then did my acting carry conviction.

Psychological roles are built around inner emotions and require great collectedness. This comes after continual rehearsals and a full mastery of the technical sides of the part. When the actor is collected his creative imagination works well. He gains that great asset—self-control.

That the leading actor will be at an advantage if the supporting cast is weak is a fallacy long overthrown. Yet some régisseurs imagine that one or two good actors will ensure the success of a performance even if the rest of the cast is second-rate. Acting is a give-and-take proposition. And like the chess player, the actor will play all the better if his partner is expert at the game. A good and really talented actor finds that when the supporting cast is a match for him, he draws force and inspiration from a creative alliance with his fellow-actors.

In discussing the actor's technique I should like to say a few words about theatre plays on the air. Regular "Theatre at the Microphone" broadcasts are extremely popular with Soviet listeners. They bring to radio listeners the best productions performed by our leading companies.

Sometimes plays are broadcast direct from the theatre. But in most cases they are rehearsed especially for the radio and transmitted from radio studios. In this case most actors use the same technique as on the stage. This seems wrong to me. Performing in front of the microphone requires a technique all its own. Radio versions of plays, when rehearsed at the studio, are always more convincing and have a greater appeal for radio listeners than plays broadcast directly from the theatre.

The actor who performs for the radio must pay particular attention to the delivery of monologues. Apart from conveying to his listeners the force and emotion behind his lines, the actor must above all convince his audience that he is "soliloquizing," or uttering his thoughts aloud to himself.

In his début before the microphone, the actor is usually extremely nervous—actors are known to have stumbled over their lines, this greatly aggravating their state of nervousness. The very atmosphere of the radio studio and then, of course, the realization that millions are listening in affect the actor.

Thus, my fellow-actors and I have had to rid ourselves of many stage stereotypes to make our dialogues and particularly our monologues sound real and convincing to radio audiences. The guidance of exacting and talented radio-play directors was a great help to us.

Acting before the microphone has one peculiar advantage for the actor. He needn't worry whether or not he resembles the character he portrays. The actor does not have to be tall or have regal bearing to play Peter I. But he must have a rich, low voice trained to command. A tall, heavily built actor can easily impersonate the short Sancho Panza or the slender Khlestakov provided he has a good voice and a feeling for the part.

Of my own performances before the microphone I have a particularly vivid recollection of the part of a short, frail man with a thin squeaky voice that I played in a one-act play by Turgenev. It would be hardly possible to imagine a character so different in every respect, especially in appearance, from myself. It took many long rehearsals, attentive listening to their recordings, and much coaching from the radio-play director before I could step into the part.

The actor is often called upon to appear in variety programmes. Here, too, he must acquire a specific technique.

As a rule, the actor performs in variety programmes without make-up or costume, without the benefit of scenery or sets. He is allowed 10 or 15 minutes for a recitation, a small sketch, or the performance of a fragment from a play. In this short period of time whatever he brings to the stage must be complete in itself, must have polish and finish. All this requires the study of technique adaptable to the variety stage and demands a maximum of expressiveness by means of gesture and movement, emphatic or subdued, depending on the main idea of the play.

A good deal of thought must be given to selection of fragments or pieces for the variety stage. A scene that is complete in itself is preferable to anything sketchy. The actor should always remember that the variety makes different demands on him than the theatre. And that means he should act differently. There can be no gradual unfolding of the personality of the character. It must be clearly shown at once.

Variety programmes often feature ballet dances of dazzling technique, recitals by first-class musicians, circus performers that take your breath away. The dramatic actor who appears after a number that has brought the house down must possess a wonderful technique and great powers to match his art against that of the virtuoso.

Variety attracts a great many stage actors. Vasily Kachalov, one of the Moscow Art Theatre's greatest actors, was a popular figure on the Soviet variety stage. His readings from Russian classics and Soviet literature, and his recitals of monologues, fragments from plays and dialogues, won him thousands of admirers. I had the good fortune to appear with him in the same programme several times and his advice has been invaluable.

I have always found readings on the variety stage, at public meetings and particularly to radio audiences extremely gratifying. I have recited many poems by Pushkin and fables by Krylov. When I began

F. Gorokhov as Misail, N. Cherkasov as Varlaam, A. Kozlova as the proprietress of the tavern in *Boris Godunov*. 1947

As Peter I. 1938

working on a portrayal of Vladimir Mayakovsky, I asked V. A. Kata-nyan to write a series of short stories about the great poet so that I could render them to the public. He depicted Mayakovsky talking to his readers and listeners, reading his poems to them, telling them of his travels and plans. Readings on the variety stage and radio broad casts have given me the opportunity of reaching far bigger audiences than acting in the theatre.

I have given many readings of Don Quixote's parting words to Sancho Panza. While reciting this monologue I tried very hard to create the impression that the faithful squire was there at my side. I spoke as though he was actually there with me. I have learned this trick well from my work in films where the actor often has to speak his lines to someone who is not there—in close-ups, for instance. I tried to make my audience see Sancho Panza too, even see his reaction to my words, his very gestures and movements. I spoke my lines, then paused for a moment as though waiting for the thoughts and feelings of the absent Sancho Panza to register in my mind and in the minds of the audience. It was as if I were asking Sancho Panza, "Well, what do you think about it?" Then, getting a reply from him, I would go on with the monologue.

To succeed in the drama theatre, on the variety stage, in radio broadcasts, etc., the actor must make the audience feel the emotions he is portraying.

Talent and ability are things the actor is born with. But technique is something that is acquired through a tireless daily grind, through experience gained and thoroughly assimilated. Just as the musician must practise every day, so must the dramatic actor constantly work to build up his technique.

Every evening the curtain rises at hundreds of Soviet theatres—theatres with great traditions and theatres born in the Revolution, big theatres in Moscow and small ones that have sprung up in the provinces—and the eyes of hundreds of thousands of spectators are eagerly turned to the stage.

The Soviet audience is one of the most appreciative in the world, and the actor cannot help feeling elated when playing for such an audience. There is a lasting bond between the Soviet actor and the spectator.

The actor helps to educate the people and to develop their artistic taste. The Soviet actor is thus not merely a performer but a citizen and an educator. After the performance he reviews the work of the day, taking special note of his errors, rejoicing in his discoveries, recalling in every detail the public's reaction and all the time straining hard for improvement.

THE ACTOR AND THE MAKE-UP ARTIST

The actor's work brings him almost daily in contact with the make-up man. The latter can so completely change the appearance of the actor as to make him resemble closely the personality he must incarnate.

Make-up and the changes it could work in one's appearance fascinated me when I was quite a child. I delighted in the funny noses and strange paint that made strolling singers and organ-grinders look so very funny. I noticed how the slightest change in the shape of the nose or the line of the eyebrows altered the entire expression of the face.

I was rather good at mimicking and amused my playfellows by making up like the strolling singers we often saw. To do this I would lengthen or flatten my nose by pasting some crushed bread on it and pencil my eyebrows.

But it was on the day of my "début" at the Mariinsky Theatre that I realized how important the art of make-up was. Sitting in front of the mirror, I watched the make-up artist work marvels with my face. The result was startling, and my admiration knew no bounds. The next day I appeared in *Judith* and anticipated the pleasure of again having the make-up artist fuss over me. I decided that this time I would watch him very closely. I was one of the sixty supers chosen to march as Assyrian warriors across the background of the stage. The scene was planned to resemble an Assyrian bas-relief, and we were all to look exactly alike. There was to be no individual make-up.

We were shepherded into a spacious dressing-room on the third floor, ordered to get into brown tights and jerseys and on top of them skirts and a coat of chain mail which gave me quite a thrill to wear. Identically clad, we were ushered into the make-up room and lined up. Several make-up men got busy at once. The first walked down the line with a big box of brown powder and a huge puff, changing the colour of our faces to a dark tan at almost a single stroke. Immediately behind him came another artist carrying a big brush in his right hand and in his left a can of black grease paint that looked very much like shoe polish. One, two—two rapid strokes, and we all had the same kind of moustache. At the side of the second make-up man walked a third and along with him a youthful apprentice with a huge cardboard box full of identical Assyrian beards made of glossy horsehair. The boy leisurely handed the beards to the make-up man who tied them behind our ears. This boy, Ulyanov, became one of our best make-up artists. I met him thirty years later at the Lenfilm Studios where I was playing Stasov in *Moussorgsky*, and we spent many delightful moments recalling the Mariinsky Theatre. Ulyanov is responsible for the players' splendid make-up in *Academician Pavlov*, *Moussorgsky* and many other films.

For the Assyrian scene in *Judith* we were made up in conveyor fashion, the whole procedure taking no more than seven or eight minutes and leaving me greatly disappointed. I was eager to learn the secrets of the art of make-up—how a little touch here and there could change the expression of the eyes, the line of the mouth, the very mould of the face. Naturally, I could learn nothing from the rapid method used in making up the Assyrian warriors. Watching experienced make-up artists at work on individual make-up later on, I gained a good insight into the professional secrets of their art.

I conceived a great respect for the art of the make-up man from my very first days in the theatre. I used to wander into the make-up artists' studio every day, noting how softly the men spoke and how slow and measured their movements were. The place had the air of a laboratory. It would give me quite a thrill to see the make-up men at work.

Later, while I continued playing in pantomime at the Mariinsky Theatre, I began experimenting with make-up myself. I made noses for myself and adjusted them, used pencil and paints to accentuate what I thought would bring out more sharply the features of the character I played.

It was common among us young actors who played minor roles in pantomime to give a good deal of attention to make-up. We were very particular about being made up perfectly, thinking that once we were on the stage we were as much in the eye of the audience as the principal actors. But in reality the audiences care little about how mimes look. Now and then we would be rewarded for the pains we took with our make-up by getting a compliment from the stage manager or his assistants, and that pleased us very much.

Whenever we newcomers thought of make-up in terms of perfection we always associated it with Chaliapin, and in some roles with Yershov. They were our models. Of course, the art of make-up has progressed tremendously since their day. Yet I have never seen any make-up that in effect and authenticity could match that used by Chaliapin. His was always a perfect expression of the personality of the character he portrayed.

Perhaps the fact that Chaliapin was an artist and sculptor besides being a great actor and singer—drawing and modelling were his favourite pastimes—had a good deal to do with his uncanny gift for make-up. Creative aptitudes along such lines have always proved an important asset to actors. Samoilov, Stravinsky, whose direct successor Chaliapin was on the operatic stage, Lensky, an eminent actor, all possessed a talent for drawing and worked on their own make-up.

Chaliapin would often make sketches of himself in different roles. He did them in his dressing-room with a make-up pencil and on any slip of paper that happened to be handy, sometimes on cigarette packets; he even drew on the walls and doors of his dressing-room. Chaliapin's pencil sketch of himself in the part of Dosifei (*Khovanshchina*) hangs to this day in the dressing-room he once used at the Mariinsky. In the adjacent dressing-room hangs a drawing by Yershov of himself in the part of Grishka Kuterma (*The Tale of the Invisible City of Kitezh*). Both sketches are excellent and show how well the two artist-singers had caught the typical features of the characters they impersonated. We young actors, who were their ardent admirers, often visited their dressing-rooms to take a look at those pictures, which had the additional charm of being done in make-up pencils.

To this day make-up has not lost its fascination for me. I love the feel of the first coating of grease paint on my face on the day of the dress rehearsal and see how I gradually grow into the new personality I must act, the personality that becomes more real and tangible with each rehearsal.

Like actors, make-up artists are keen observers of people and surroundings. That is essential for their profession. They study the laws of anatomy, painting and sculpture. You will find their studios stocked with reproductions of the world's greatest paintings, with photographs, caricatures and cartoons. They are always experimenting with new combinations of colour and new make-up, and sharing their secrets with each other.

Some of the Soviet theatre's most talented make-up artists are Y. Gremislavsky, M. Faleyev, S. Makovetsky, S. Alexeyev and A. Bersenyev, to mention only a few. Their work contributes greatly to the high quality of Soviet theatre performances.

There is no limit to the possibilities of make-up or to what it can do to the face of the stage actor and particularly of the film actor. To the make-up artist in the theatre and the cinema the actor's face is a canvas upon which he creates a character. The appearance must harmonize with the personality. A mistake in make-up may completely mar the outward image, in the same way as the slightest interruption in the actor's train of thoughts will make the actor lose touch with the mental state of his character.

Make-up in the cinema is quite different from that on the stage. On the stage, as a rule, the actor's face is not distinctly visible beyond the tenth or twelfth row. On the screen, particularly in close-ups, the face is very well seen by all spectators and facial expression plays an important part in the telling of the story. In the theatre, it sometimes takes the make-up artist no more than an hour to get all the principal characters ready. Screen make-up requires much finer work; greater pains are taken to give every feature its fullest value. Hours are spent on tests. Sometimes it takes weeks before a satisfactory make-up is found and the actor faces the cameras.

In the early days of Soviet film-making too much emphasis was put on type. Directors went hunting for "types." People were often picked to play in films just because they had a striking appearance, good looks or closely resembled some character in the script. The quest for "types" was frustrating the professional actor eager to demonstrate the wide variety of roles he could play. Directors ignored the fact that physical resemblance was nothing if the actor failed to re-create the character from within. In silent pictures even the "stars" were often people with no professional experience, chosen only because they were the type or because they screened well.

There were many funny little incidents connected with the engagement of "character extras." One day, I recall, the make-up man came around to collect his wigs, beards, moustaches, etc. Seeing a bearded man, he pulled at his beard. How he was surprised when it wouldn't come off!

Casting directors to this day prefer real old men, complete with wrinkles, natural beards, etc., for old men's parts. This may be all right for small episodes requiring definite types of old men. But in most cases a young talented actor, skilfully made up, can well tackle an old man's part.

Soviet make-up artists have made important advances in their craft in the last few decades. Their shrewd artistic handling of make-up in biographical and historical films has helped our actors to achieve striking resemblance.

Make-up is a very important factor in helping the actor to assert himself in the new personality he represents. I remember that when we began making *Friends,* a picture in which I played Beta, a poor Ossetian peasant, I could not go on with the part because the make-up was not satisfactory. A. Andzhan was my make-up man and we tried ten different faces before we found the one we needed. With a wig of wild thick hair falling over the eyes, bristling moustaches, unkempt beard and a Caucasian fur cap pulled low over the forehead I thought

I looked just how Beta should, and it helped me to enter more deeply into the part.

Andzhan has been my make-up man on many occasions and I admire him greatly. At times he thought nothing of treating my forehead, nose and jaw in the most devastating manner. As soon as I would get a new role I would go to him, sit down in the make-up chair and we would begin to experiment. He would study carefully every line and curve of my face, passing his hands over my features. And he would end by declaring that my chin was no good for the new part and that it would have to be "removed." Similar remarks would be passed about other features and about my whole head needing a good deal of "reconstruction."

Andzhan has created some splendid make-ups making me resemble as closely as possible the characters I have played in historical films. The factor of resemblance in historical or biographical films is an important one, but it decides nothing. Of course, an actor is not likely to be cast in an historical or biographical film unless his make-up try-outs before the camera are pronounced good. But to carry conviction the actor must enter wholly into the psychology of his character. Make-up bringing out in a perfect mould the new personality will go a long way to ensure success. Yet it is but a mask applied to the face. The mask must be animated from within. To create a mask is the duty of the make-up artist, to make it live is the task of the actor.

There is a naturalness to the make-up created by Andzhan that challenges the closest scrutiny. One day, deciding to put my characterization of Professor Polezhayev to the test, I got into the make-up and walked out into the street. I mixed with the crowds, imitated the gait of an elderly gentleman and was taken for one. I went to see my old friend Mravinsky. His mother, who had known me ever since I was a youngster, opened the door, and, not recognizing me, told me her son was out. This convinced me that the make-up was good. But I must say that it was an arduous job for Andzhan to make me up as Professor Polezhayev. I spent over three hundred hours in the make-up chair during the four months *Baltic Deputy* was in production.

In mass scenes make-up men and their assistants work with remarkable speed. Playing in *Peter I* I saw about 1,500 extras made up in no time as Russian and Swedish soldiers for the Battle of Poltava. The whole procedure was somewhat reminiscent of the en masse treatment of the Assyrian soldiers in *Judith*. In the same way several boy apprentices kept producing moustaches out of cardboard boxes and handing them to the make-up men. Here, however, make-up was applied more carefully. The wigs had to be combed and curled on the heads of the soldiers, and each man required attentive treatment so that he would look natural in close-ups.

To resemble the character he plays, the actor will go to any length—even to marring his personal appearance. When I played Tsarevich Alexei in *Peter I*, I made a study of a good many of his pictures and engravings which had come down to our day, and saw that I had to have a high elongated forehead that bespoke the degenerate. For the stage a wig with a false forehead would have done very nicely. But for the screen, in close-ups particularly, that kind of a wig was no good. The director and make-up artist saw only one way out—to shave part of my head. This I did. But it so happened that at the same time I was playing in *Baltic Deputy*, and as Professor Polezhayev I had been told to grow my hair a little at the back. Thus, at the barbers' shops I came to be regarded as quite a "queer fish" when I insisted on having the front of my head shaved and leaving my hair at the back alone.

Nikolai Simonov, who played Peter I, also had to shave part of his head and the temples. During the shooting of the battle of Poltava, Simonov, as the script required, walked about with several days' stubble on his face (make-up is not of much avail in producing the effect of an unshaven face). But he had to shave the moustache for he wore a false one to resemble Peter I. Of course he cut a strange figure in the street, making people wonder why he was growing a beard and shaving his upper lip.

I remember with what trepidation the make-up artist A. Yermolov began trying out make-ups for Boris Shchukin when he was cast as Lenin in Mosfilm's *Lenin in October*.

Anton Andzhan begins working on the make-up
for Professor Polezhayev

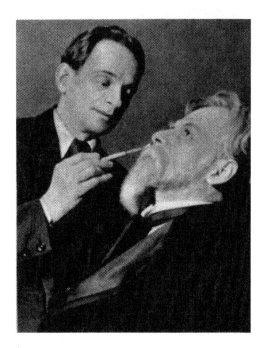

Anton Andzhan putting the finishing touches
to the make-up for Professor Polezhayev

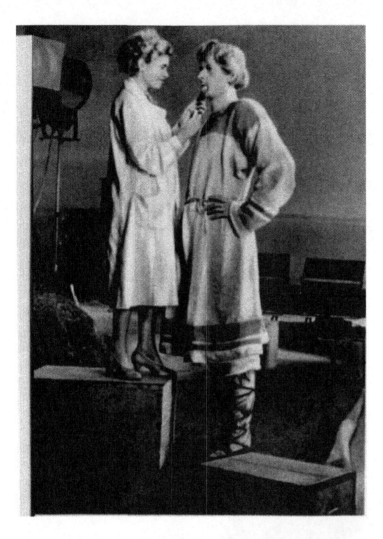

Last-minute adjustment of make-up.
Nikolai Cherkasov as Alexander Nevsky

I played Gorky in this picture and spent five hours a day for three weeks in the make-up chair before we were finally satisfied with the result. It took long hours of building-up with bits of tape to get the right line for the broad cheek-bones, for the wilful chin, the moustache, the eyebrows and the right head contours.

Creating the make-up for Alexander Nevsky was just as difficult. The first tests were all failures: somehow I looked more like a chorus boy from *Prince Igor* than anything else, and nowhere near the great hero. Eisenstein, who always took a keen interest in make-up, made several sketches of what he thought I should look like.

Finally, after much painstaking effort, with Eisenstein himself spending hours over me as I sat in the make-up chair, we achieved success. I looked the part, and the years seemed to have fallen away from me—Alexander Nevsky was not yet twenty-one the time the Battle on the Ice was fought.

Much effort was exerted both by V. Goryunov, the make-up artist, and Eisenstein, before I was made to resemble Ivan the Terrible. Experiments with make-up stretched for six weeks. Our chief difficulty was in showing Ivan the Terrible growing older. At the beginning of the picture he is seventeen and at the end fifty-three. The action takes him through sixteen periods of his rule. Each period required a different make-up. Sixteen sets of make-up were prepared which we numbered— "Make-up No. 1," "Make-up No. 2," etc.

"Make-up No. 1" was the most difficult, for it had to turn me into seventeen-year-old Ivan for the coronation scene. Apart from having to wear a false nose, artificial eyelashes and a wig, I had to smooth the wrinkles on my face. This I did by pasting transparent little bands over my forehead and part of the face. The bands lined out the furrows and were tied tightly at the back of the head. This "youthful" treatment did not make me look seventeen, but it did help me to resemble the young tsar. Every time the bands were removed I thought my wrinkles were increasing in number and growing deeper. I couldn't help feeling alarmed that this rejuvenation of mine might age me prematurely off screen.

It was really fascinating to watch make-up artist Sokolov transform me into Popov, the great inventor of radio. It made me realize how important every detail was to the complete portrait—even adding or removing a few hairs from the beard or moustache altered the effect considerably.

Of the many arts employed in the production of films that of the make-up expert is one of the most important. Before the director starts shooting a scene he expects the make-up man along with the cast, the cameraman and the sound engineer to report that everything is in order. Often there are last-minute adjustments in the make-up.

Actors are expected at all times to be careful not to spoil the make-up. In the "waits" between the shootings they should avoid talking too much and moving facial muscles. The same goes for eating, drinking or smoking.

Working in close cooperation, actors and make-up artists have created many screen and stage portraits of lasting value.

THE SCREEN ACTOR'S TECHNIQUE

Film work makes it possible for the actor to watch himself on the screen and note the places that are flat. When the director tells the actor that he has made a mess of something, he needn't take the director's word for it but should see for himself when the scene is run off for him.

Working in films also enables the actor to get a very complete picture of his looks: neither photographs nor the closest scrutiny in the mirror can compare with the screen in this respect.

But the actor's first meeting with himself on the screen is generally very disappointing. He is surprised to find that his figure and face at certain angles are far from attractive. Most discouraging of all is that he often does not recognize his own voice.

When I first saw myself on the screen I was horrified to find how tall and thin I looked. Nor had I previously suspected that my physical assets ran so low. This feeling of keen disappointment lingered for a long time until I finally grew accustomed to seeing myself as I really was. To this day every time I see my films run off I can't help virtually ogling myself, eager not to miss any let-downs, actual and imaginary, so that I may avoid them the next time.

On the lot the director often asks the actor, "How are you going to do this bit, how are you going to walk up to the camera, how will you make your exit?" In the theatre, on the other hand, the question is always, "What are you going to do?" In film-making the question "What are you going to do?" arises at the very first rehearsals at which the script, the picture as a whole, and the movement and action of certain scenes are discussed. At these early rehearsals the actor already should have a clear idea of "what he must do." When scenes are run through before the camera the actor gives all his attention to the question "How am I going to do this bit?"

Thus when he steps in front of the camera the actor must be ready to do exactly what is required of him and what has been decided upon at the rehearsals. The success of a scene depends on many elements apart from the acting—lighting effects, compositional arrangement, etc. The actor must keep this in mind, get his bearings, avoid the slightest movement or gesture that has not been rehearsed, otherwise he runs the risk of going beyond the camera lines, getting part of his head or hand out of the picture and spoiling the whole scene. Of course minor digressions from what had been decided at previous rehearsals may be quite legitimate from the actor's point of view, may even lend greater emotional value to the scene, but they must not be indulged in to the detriment of the technical plan of the scene worked out jointly by the director and cameraman.

Stanislavsky teaches that muscular tension must correspond to the emotional state of the actor. In films the actor cannot always keep to this golden rule, particularly in sequences where close-ups are intermingled with long shots, and where compositional elements must be given much attention. Here the emotional mood of the moment must be sacrificed to the general emotional reality of the whole scene which the audiences will see when the film has been edited and cut.

Long shots, particularly when they are intermingled with close-ups, require special training. When approaching the camera for a close-up from a distance, the actor must time his movements so as to know exactly where to pause. A mistake of ten inches one way or the other may put the whole scene out of focus and wreck it.

Certain scenes can be "pointed up" in the film medium so that a single movement, a single word may reveal depths of meaning. This reminds me of a scene I did in *Peter I* in which Tsarevich Alexei, learning that his father is seriously ill, weighs with the nobles the possibilities of the tsar's recovery. Suddenly the door is flung open, and Menshikov appears. Alexei rises from his seat, approaches him and anxiously asks: "Dead?"

When we were shooting this scene the camera was stationed at the door through which Menshikov enters, filming first what he saw in the room. As Tsarevich Alexei I walked up to the camera, stopped short at a fixed distance away and, looking a little to the right, had to convey to the audience that I had caught sight of Menshikov. And in the one word "dead" I had to express my innermost thoughts which actually ran something like this: "I believe you come with happy tidings. You come to tell me that my father, that monster of cruelty, is dead, and that at long last I shall ascend the throne! That is what you come to tell me, isn't it?"

After countless rehearsals I succeeded in doing what was expected of me more or less well. The scene was shot three times, then a fourth time with new hints and suggestions from the director and cameraman. At the fourth retake, when I finally came to the word "dead," I felt so fagged out I lost my bearings, stumbled over the word and spoiled the scene.

Hence, too many rehearsals and too many retakes of highly emotional scenes so overtax the actor that he loses control over himself and even forgets his lines. I remember one well-known actor stumbling twice over his lines because of the strain of too many rehearsals.

I have cited these examples to show how important it is for the actor to keep absolutely cool and controlled on the lot no matter how many times he may be asked to redo the scene and repeat his lines. It is very seldom that a scene does not require several retakes.

On the other hand, there are instances when retakes must be re-duced to the minimum, and this places even greater responsibility on the actors and the directors.

Some of the episodes in *Captain Grant's Children* were filmed in the North Caucasus, in the Chegem Gorge. We had a party of mountain-eers build a suspension bridge across the gorge, and the scene we did entailed some very difficult shooting. At first the camera shows the bandit Ayrton setting the bridge on fire. Then its eye travels across the abyss, showing Paganel, Robert Grant and the others running up to the edge of the precipice to watch the blazing bridge crumble down.

The cameraman managed to "shoot" Ayrton just as he was setting the bridge on fire. He also caught us in focus in the shots that followed but he could not get the bridge which unexpectedly crashed before we had reached the edge of the precipice. This spoiled everything. We cursed our luck but could do nothing except stay for another week until a new one was built. The scene was shot over again. But all we had of it was one take.

One of the most trying requirements for the actor is to keep the emo-tion sustained through an episode which for technical reasons cannot be shot at once and is broken up into several sequences filmed months apart.

As I have already described, Alexei's quarrel with Yefrosinya in *Peter I* was a difficult piece in this respect. The shooting of small se-quences of this scene dragged on for several months. Each fragment had to match perfectly. The scene showing Ivan the Terrible's illness apart from being difficult to act was also cut into many bits filmed at long intervals. In this scene, in which the tsar orders the nobles to swear allegiance to the infant Dmitri, his son and heir, I had to keep up the emotion and create the illusion of wholeness.

There are many scenes in which sequences are shot not in their nat-ural order. The end of the scene may be shot first, then the middle and last the beginning. Sometimes outdoor scenes are intermingled with studio shots. The shooting is done pell-mell fashion, and the actor is hard put to it to adjust himself emotionally to the scene.

It is part of the screen actor's technique to develop certain camera habits. One of them is to see that his movements are within the chalked lines marking the camera's focus. And it is hard for the actor when sometimes he does not act for hours yet must remember where he stood last before the camera.

Stage and film actors are often asked how much the continuous strain of reproducing human emotions, particularly in heavy drama, affects their health and nervous system.

It is wrong to think that an actor *lives* the emotions he portrays. If he did he would probably land in a lunatic asylum after the first few performances. As Ivan the Terrible I grieved through ten or twelve takes (not counting the rehearsals) over the illness and death of the tsarina. Playing the part of Tsar Ivan on the stage in *The Great Tsar,* I kill Tsarevich Ivan, my beloved son by my marriage to Tsarina Anastasya, no less than three hundred times (again minus the rehearsals). It is not difficult to imagine what would have happened if I had *lived* these scenes. Actually the actor does not live the emotions he portrays, whether it be great grief, despair, happiness or ecstasy. He only *seems* to live them. We are in a creative state when we act. This state plus our talent and professional knowledge make it possible for us to *create* emotions and to make our audiences really believe that we *live* them. Hence, the actor's emotions are *created* and do not affect his nervous system.

On the other hand, the very process of creating or re-creating feelings on the stage or in films requires great emotional strain and over-taxes the nervous system. For this reason, perhaps, over-sensitiveness is common among the acting profession. Sometimes in following the script the actor is called upon to do things injurious to his health and nerves, and to repeat them many times. There may be scenes and re-takes of scenes in which the actor gets water poured over him or in which he must eat, drink and smoke to excess. A scene requiring of the actor to smoke may seem harmless enough. But when there are many retakes he gets an overdose of nicotine that almost knocks him out, and, of course, neither his physical state nor his nerves are any the better for it.

I played a Whiteguard officer in *Girl Friends,* and in one of the scenes I grab a roast chicken from one of my victims, tear it up greedily and devour it together with my partner. Now, during the first take we ate the chicken with relish; in the retake, too, we tackled it not without pleasure. But when there was another retake we felt an unpleasant heaviness. The scene was shot a fourth time, and what we felt then is not fit to be put down on paper.

But no matter how trying the actor may find some of the scenes he must always remember that the "show must go on." There is a scene in the second part of *Peter I* in which Alexei, confined to a dungeon in the Peter and Paul Fortress, has a cloak flung over his head and is beaten up and strangled by his father's ministers. When we were filming this scene, the director kept shooting one retake after another until I thought I would collapse under the manhandling I was getting from the actors who played the ministers and who were all too eager to make the scene as realistic as possible. At the last retake I received such a stunning blow that I shrieked. Still I managed to see the scene through.

There is a popular belief that actors pose off stage or screen. This is an accusation for which there are no grounds. In pre-revolutionary times the actor who played the "irresistible lover" may have tried to look and act the part in real life, dressing and behaving in a fashion that would attract attention. I believe that such exhibitionism is beneath an actor's calling and intellectual pursuits. Besides, indulging in one's histrionic gifts off stage or screen means unnecessarily spending oneself. The actor should preserve every surge of artistic talent and inspiration for the moment when the curtain rises or when he must step in front of the camera.

Versatility in the human character is limitless. There are all kinds of people, good and bad, brave and cowardly, clever and stupid, handsome and plain, healthy and ill, cheerful and morose, old and young, frank and reserved, open-hearted and treacherous. The formative factors in human character are many. They are background, environment, education, labour habits, social conditions, trade or profession.

I have played people from all walks of life on the stage and screen —factory workers, peasants, soldiers, sailors, army and navy officers, eminent scientists, writers, statesmen and royal personages. A man's station in life, calling or profession certainly leave a stamp on his personality. This the actor must bear well in mind. And the actor should study carefully just how his character's profession affects his personality, habits, his views and his outlook on the future.

It is not necessary, however, to go to extremes. When we were making *Alexander Popov*, one of the assistant directors suggested that I would be more convincing if I learned the Morse code and knew how to assemble a radio set. Then one might as well have recommended to Konstantin Skorobogatov who played Pirogov, the father of Russian surgery, to dissect rabbits and cats so that he would look more convincing as a surgeon. Of course, for the actor to occupy himself in any such manner is entirely superfluous. Yet the actor who plays a surgeon must know how to hold the scalpel if the action calls for its use. More often than not the actor must study the professional habits of the man he plays.

But the importance of such habits should not be exaggerated. Actors who play fliers, cavalrymen, athletes or acrobats generally have someone to double for them in scenes which call for a display of professional skill. In *Alexander Nevsky*, for example, an equestrian doubled for me in the scene where I fight single-handed against several Teutonic Knights. It was a little embarrassing to have the audience burst into applause and attribute to me the prowess and skill I never possessed. Whenever I had occasion to meet with my audiences I always took pains to explain to them how such scenes were filmed and in what shots I had a double.

Doubles are sometimes even used in close-ups. As Billy Bones in *Treasure Island* I grab the edge of a table in a fit of anger and upset it over myself. There was a close-up of the hand clutching the table. My own hand proved too long and thin for the tough Billy, and so an extra was picked for the shot with a sinewy and calloused hand that fitted the character.

Mikhail Kuznetsov as Prince Dolgoruky
and Nikolai Cherkasov as Tsarevich Alexei
in *Peter I*. 1937

As Jacques Paganel in *Captain Grant's Children*. 1936

As Billy Bones in *Treasure Island.* 1937

As Pfaal in *Jan Knukke's Wedding*. 1935

There are singing parts in many pictures. And, of course, an actor who has no voice cannot be expected to do these. Professional singers are frequently employed as doubles. However, whenever possible, the actor prefers to do without replacements. Borisov did all the singing himself when he played Moussorgsky.

In silent pictures much store was set on scouting for types, on photogenic qualities and on the cutting process. Shrewd handling of this process helped the director out of many difficulties, particularly when the acting of non-professionals fell short of expectations.

But in talking pictures it is the gifted professional actor who holds undisputed sway. Non-professionals are now taken on only when strongly marked types are needed for minor episodes. But this is a practice which is becoming less and less common because film directors often have difficulty in teaching non-professional extras to act. Eisenstein, when making *Alexander Nevsky*, spent a lot of time and wasted a good deal of film on a minor scene because an old man picked for a small character part was unable to go through a few movements that would have given no trouble at all to a professional actor. The old man had to hand Alexander Nevsky a goblet of wine, watch him empty it and then, smacking his lips and twisting his moustache, cry out: "Music!"

Another elderly man, picked because of his flowing white beard to play the part of the patriarch in *Peter I,* caused quite a disturbance on the lot. He was afflicted with asthma and his wheezing interfered with the sound engineer's work. When his turn came to step before the camera—the scene he was doing was a very short one—the assistant director begged him to inhale deeply and hold his breath for half a minute. He couldn't, and in the middle of the scene began to wheeze louder than ever. For the same picture we had two other aged extras, looking smart in boyar attire, doing a small bit. It was their business to drop on their knees before Tsarevich Alexei and touch the floor with their foreheads. They did what was required of them splendidly before the camera. But their feeble bodies were weighed down by the heavy brocade costumes and the effort of rising and kneeling repeatedly was too much for them, and so we noticed that all through the long waits between the shootings they remained in a recumbent position.

Sometimes two actors are shown talking on the screen in the most friendly fashion without having been filmed together. The audience does not suspect this because the cutting and editing process creates a perfect illusion of personal contact. There is an important episode in the film *His Excellency* in which two clowns (Rostovtsev and I) perform for the governor (L. Leonidov). I played the scene without once setting eyes on the latter.

My first experience in scenes of this kind takes me back to the time when I was cast as Captain Pfaal—a part requiring burlesque—in *Jan Knukke's Wedding*. I played in a scene with my partner absent and had to fill in the atmosphere by a trick of the imagination. To make such scenes convincing requires a special technique which the film actor must master.

There are scenes in which the actor performs solo. And these perhaps make the greatest demands on his gifts, ability and discretion. In these scenes, to a greater degree than in any others, the actor should be completely oblivious of everything except that he must convey to the audience the feelings and thoughts of the character he portrays.

Our actresses sometimes forget this. They forget that the portrayal of emotion demands the sacrifice of beauty. The audience must be kept from thinking, "How pretty the actress looks when she is suffering," or "What a gorgeous mouth she has, what eyelashes!" I always applaud the actress who completely forgets what she looks like in an emotional scene, even at the expense of marring her personal charm.

In silent films the actor was a far less important figure than he is today. Abundant cutting and editing minimized his role. Close-ups as a rule were left to the end. For these the actor changed his attire, make-up and even the expression of his face. When an actress had to be shown with tears rolling down her cheeks, an onion would be brought close to her eyes or she would smell spirits of ammonia or drops of glycerine would be squeezed out of a tube on her face. Sad music also helped. In sound films, where the importance of the actor has grown immensely, the problem of realistic portrayal has acquired greater significance. Screen acting now requires of the players to be so deeply emotional as to be able to shed real tears. Of course, "genuine" though the players' tears may be, they are not the same as those in real life. A player's tears are merely the result of the ability to capture an emotional state.

Some film players draw tears by recalling their own sad experiences. When they feel the tears coming they signal the cameraman. But since they appear not as a result of an emotion connected with the role but through an outside agency, they are not convincing. I think this method altogether wrong.

I can make tears come to my eyes only when I have entered completely into the emotional state of my character. In *Peter I*, the tsar reproves his son for his misdoings. He does it in a fatherly manner. I tried to enter into Alexei's psychological state, to grasp his reactions. I began crushing bits of candle wax and moulding them into little figures. I thus worked up a feeling of guiltiness and penitence, and real tears flowed down my cheeks.

A scene is usually shot several times, and it is hard to expect the player to shed real tears each time.

I couldn't help admiring Alla Tarasova as Peter's wife for her ability to make real tears come to her eyes at five successive takes.

I recall a scene from *Baltic Deputy*. It shows Professor Polezhayev's birthday and him waiting in vain for his colleagues; he is deeply hurt because they do not appear. He is alone with his wife when the tears choke him. He tries to keep them back. "You must be cold, my dear, I shall fetch your shawl," he says to her and retires to his study. There, fumbling among his instruments, he breaks down.

He sheds the tears of a proud man. I had to convey this to the audience, but for a long time I couldn't make them come. We were shooting the scene at night. Hours went by, and at six o'clock in the morning there still were no tears. Almost in despair, I asked for a pianist to play something. He played fragments from various compositions, and I listened to the music with pleasure. But I was well acquainted with all the pieces, and not one of them could make me cry. At last he struck up Lyadov's "Prelude" which I had never heard before. The music moved me. In the close-up the tears that flowed down my cheeks were real.

When I played the final scene in *Alexander Popov* in which the great inventor addresses the Russian Physico-Chemical Society, I could not help thinking that this splendid Russian died two days after the meeting. There was something tragic about his death and about his whole life in the stifling atmosphere of tsarist Russia. The tears came to my eyes without there being any call for them in the scene. Yet, I think I was justified in shedding them.

Screen art—an art with its own rules and principles which must be thoroughly understood and assimilated by the actor—offers immense opportunities. The spectator sees on the screen what he may never see in real life—Nature's innermost secrets, the latest scientific discoveries, life in all parts of the globe. But the prime mission of film art is to show ordinary people and what they live and struggle for, to portray their feelings and aspirations, their thirst for happiness.

THE ACTOR AND THE CAMERAMAN

In the cinema we find very much the same professional people engaged in creative work as in the theatre—the dramatist or script writer, the director, the actor, the designer, the composer and the make-up artist. But then there is an additional profession, that of the cameraman. The latter ranks high among film-makers. It is his task to put the pictorial quality into the film. He must enhance the mood of the scene by the play of lights. His professional knowledge helps to give a pleasant composition and proper dramatic values. The eye of the camera sees the scene from an angle which is different from that of the human eye. And it is the cameraman who must find the best angle and give proper regard to the general style in which the picture is filmed. But more important than all that must be his deep understanding of the ideological content of the film. All this puts the cameraman on a level with the playwright and director in the making of pictures.

A close creative bond exists between the cameraman and the cast. Actors know full well how much they depend for their success on the cameraman's work. The actor begins to cooperate with the cameraman at the very first tests. The latter is able to tell at once from what angle the actor can be photographed to the best advantage. And it is on the basis of the cameraman's test shots that the question is decided whether or not the actor fits the part.

I have had the good fortune to work with some of our best cameramen who have contributed much to the advancement of their art. And they have helped me greatly in my characterizations.

When the actor performs in a scene at such a distance from the camera which enables him to come into personal contact with his partner he feels quite at ease. It is then very much like being on the stage, and the problems set before him by the director and the cameraman present no difficulty whatever.

A shift to medium shots makes it necessary for the actor to come much closer to the camera. Sometimes the cameraman wishes to rearrange the scene and tells the actor to turn his face to the left or right. The actor then does not see his partner, and carrying on a dialogue with an invisible partner is no easy matter.

Most difficult for the actor are close-ups with dialogues. Here, too, he does not see his partner. He is told to look at a certain point in the camera or off it and imagine that point to be the eyes of the person he is speaking to. It is a great strain for the actor to imagine how the partner he does not see reacts to his words. The cues are generally given by the director who, for technical reasons, cannot always take up the position from which the actor's partner is supposed to speak. And it confuses the actor to get cues from a position he least expects. On the screen, after the cutting process, the scene is so presented that the impression of a perfect dialogue, a give-and-take in thought and movement, is unmarred.

In close-ups the actor often has to take up a very uncomfortable position and remain in it for some time. This happened when we were shooting the scene from *Ivan the Terrible* showing the tsar at the coffin of his dead wife. Eisenstein and cameraman Andrei Moskvin suggested that I get behind the coffin in which the tsarina lay, look at her and speak the line, "Am I right?" Getting no answer I was to lower my head and touch the edge of the oak coffin with my forehead. I thought their suggestion of how the scene should be played interesting and began working on it at once. But we were so cramped for space after I had changed my position to the back of the coffin that the settings were in my way. To move or reconstruct them would have meant spending extra time and money which we could not afford. And so I had to rehearse the scene over and over again and act before the camera with my body in a most uncomfortable position. This, of course, interfered with my acting and made it difficult for me to keep in the emotional state of my character.

More often than not it is the cameraman who is responsible for the uncomfortable poses he makes the actor assume to give a pleasant composition and proper value to the scene. Sometimes he shoots the actor for hours in the same pose until he is satisfied with the result.

When the actor goes through a series of movements in front of the camera he should try to appear as little as possible in positions in which he screens badly. Special tests are made to show the actor from what angles he screens best and what angles he must avoid. But the angles differ depending on roles. For example, when I played Ivan the Terrible, both Eisenstein and Moskvin were convinced that I photographed best in profile, particularly left, and at a quarter angle, but completely overruled full-face shots! Quite the opposite with Mikhail Kuznetsov who played Basmanov. He was photographed full face only.

Audiences frequently display an interest in how actors manage to play double roles. They want to know the technique which enables one and the same actor to speak to himself on the screen.

This is the cameraman's job, and it is quite a tough one. When such scenes have to be shot, he screws the camera's tripod on to the floor to avoid vibration and photographs half of the shot leaving the other half blank. The blank half is filled with action later when the actor changes into the make-up of the other character. Shooting such sequences is a complicated and time-consuming task requiring utmost precision both from the actor and the cameraman.

In *Spring* I played opposite Lyubov Orlova cast in the double role of a scientist and a musical comedy performer. After the camera registered half of a sequence in which Orlova appeared as the scientist, in the other half I was shot with her in the role of the musical comedy actress. I felt terribly cramped in my movements. A chalked line cut up the shot in half. The least movement outside this line meant that part of my body would be excluded from the picture which actually did happen at the fourth retake. I moved my elbow a little too far to the right, and at a run-off of the scene my colleagues and I were not a little surprised to see me on the screen minus the right arm.

It is the cameraman who gets the first look at the scenes when they are run off. And when he reappears on the set from the projection room a silence falls, with all eyes expectantly turned towards him. As a rule he does not break the silence but goes up to the director, takes him by the arm, and the two walk off into the next room. When they return, they share their impressions with the cast, after which the whole company troops to the projection room to see the scenes. The director and cameraman make their selection of what they think is the best take. Preference should be given to the first, in which acting is always more natural. In retakes, on the other hand, the actor is liable to concentrate too much on the technical directions given to him. And what the scene gains in technical effect it may lose in creative inspiration.

There is a scene in *Alexander Popov* where the inventor is shown in a ship's cabin. Towards the end of the scene I found my emotions flagging. Still the first take was fairly decent. The second was much worse. During the third I could not stand the strain of repetition. The shooting was stopped and put off till the next day. I felt quite "in form" on the following day. There were three shootings, all of which promised to be good. But when the takes of the two days were run off on the screen it was the very first one of the day before that was picked. It proved the best.

There are instances when all the takes of a scene are rejected, and the scene must be reshot. In a weak script whole parts of a film have sometimes to be remade.

The actor should never judge by the first few scenes whether or not the film will be a success. Nor do a few brilliantly photographed shots in any way indicate what the final result on the screen is likely to be. Separate scenes may call forth admiration but the whole picture after the cutting process may prove to be dull and fall sadly short of artistic expectations. Often it happens that the first flashes seem flat and uninteresting but clever editing and direction may result in a splendid picture.

When the silent pictures gave way to sound films, another important figure appeared on the lot—the sound engineer. Like the cameraman, he is a creative artist. He blends and mixes the sounds that make up the tonal quality of the picture. He helps the actor to "point up" what is best in the volume and quality of his voice. And the factor of tone is a very important one in pictures.

It is the work of the sound engineer to bring to the screen not only the dialogue of the story but the most complicated sounds—from nature's faintest whisperings to the stirring bars of a symphony orchestra.

Wherever possible sound recording is synchronized with the filming process. But at times, particularly when the film is shot on location, there are many jarring sounds: the rumble of heavy traffic and the hum of passing crowds. In such conditions the sound engineer cannot be expected to do any successful recording. He is compelled to resort to "dubbing."

"Dubbing" is a complicated process. The actor is taken to a dark room. The scenes in which he appears are projected on the screen. He must closely follow the movement and muscles of his face, particularly the movement of his lips, as he reads the lines. After he has rehearsed his lines many times and is at last satisfied that he can make his speech fit in with the articulation and movement shown in the film, the microphone is placed close to him, and the dialogue is recorded.

Sometimes big scenes have to be "dubbed." For example, in *Bon Voyage!* Captain Levashov's long conversation with the cadet Lavrov, taken on the sea-shore—really a monologue by Levashov with the boy putting in a remark here and there—was "dubbed" because there were too many outside noises. There are many reasons why sometimes sound cannot be recorded simultaneously with the photographic action. For instance, on the day we were making a scene in *Moussorgsky*, I was quite hoarse. But the shooting could not be put off, and so the scene was "dubbed" later.

"Dubbing" is sometimes resorted to when the actor's voice is not expressive enough for the part. This happened when we were making *Baltic Deputy*. The actor Melnikov, playing a revolutionary soldier, short and squat, was found to have an extremely high-pitched voice for the part. The director would have nothing short of a bass, and so an actor with a rich low voice was found to "dub" the part.

When "dubbing" a scene, the actor must give himself up wholly to the task in hand. No "dubbing" can be done when the actor is tired. He must be in perfect form not to spoil the scene. For that reason he often closes his eyes and trusts entirely to intuition; looking fixedly at the screen is known to have led to stumbling over words. What helps the actor when he is "dubbing" is the sense he has developed for spacing movement and for rhythm.

There are many instances, too, when songs or music are recorded on the sound track before the photographic image is taken so that they do not conflict with the dialogue.

"Dubbing" permits translation of dialogue into other languages, and this has proved an important factor in popularizing foreign motion pictures in the Soviet Union and our own abroad.

It is a rather strange sensation to see yourself on the screen speaking a foreign language you do not understand. A picture I once made on a Mongolian subject *(Sukhe-Bator)* was "dubbed" in Mongolia. When I heard myself on the screen speaking in a strange, high-pitched Mongolian voice, I was disappointed. But later I realized that the Mongolian actor who "dubbed" for me had brought to the part an air of greater conviction.

In India I saw *Alexander Nevsky* with our Russian cast speaking English. In an epic like *Alexander Nevsky* the dialogue is straightforward without any psychological subtleties. Such films are comparatively easy to "dub." I thought the picture sounded in English very well. Yet I could not help bursting into laughter when I heard the word "Music!" pronounced in English by a rough-looking thirteenth-century Novgorod peasant. The word in Russian was *gulyai*, a folk word approximately meaning "make merry!" but having no equivalent in the English language.

In Paris I had occasion to see *Baltic Deputy* splendidly "dubbed" in French. Apparently the actor who "dubbed" the part of Professor Polezhayev had made a detailed study of the character because he did not miss any of the subtleties of tone in the lines and helped French audiences to grasp the idea behind the characterization. At one of my public appearances I was happy to have the opportunity to thank this French actor for his fine "dubbing."

Soviet films have an important message to carry to the public. The cameraman and the sound engineer have penetrated into all the technical mysteries of film production in close cooperation with the director and the cast. The acting of the cast, the arrangement of mass scenes, the settings, the fine outdoor scenes and even small "props" breathing "period" and "atmosphere"—all these the cameraman and sound engineer weave into the emotional pattern of the picture.

ON THE SET

In previous chapters I touched briefly upon various questions dealing with the work of the actor in films and the assistance he receives from the director, the cameraman and the sound engineer.

In this chapter I shall deal with the shooting process itself. As elsewhere in the book, by way of illustration I wish to fall back on my own experiences and describe the filming of the trial scene in *Moussorgsky* where I played the part of Vladimir Stasov, the well-known critic.

Stasov faces a charge of libel brought against him by a group of critics, who had done their best to run down Russian realistic art and letters. In this scene Stasov turns from accused to accuser by delivering a brilliant speech in defence of his views. This speech climaxed my role.

The filming of this scene was twice postponed for technical reasons. One day I received a call from Lenfilm telling me that the shooting was scheduled for 10 o'clock the next morning and that I must come in two hours ahead of time for costuming and make-up.

I was looking forward with pleasure to the filming of this scene, for I felt that in it I could best show the qualities which made Stasov great—his passionate nature, the ardour which permeated his critical writings, his unswerving faith in the progressive force of Russian democratic art, and his own democratism. We had talked over the scene very thoroughly with the director and I had worked it out independently down to the last detail. Now the time had come to translate into action all that had been gone over at the rehearsals.

I picked up the script and carefully reread the whole courtroom scene. I conjured up the image of the man I was going to play, his somewhat ponderous figure, distinguished bearing, the loose-fitting frock-coat, the mop of hair, the bushy beard, his deep rich voice. When the image was there in my mind I repeated the impassioned lines of Stasov's speech.

While reading the script I remembered that a friend of mine wanted very much to see our work on the lot. I had told him a great deal about *Moussorgsky* and had even shown him a number of stills of Stasov. So I decided to take him along with me to the studios and phoned him. He was on leave and gladly accepted my invitation. We made an appointment to meet outside the Lenfilm Studios.

My friend is a designing engineer, and we got to know each other rather well during some hunting and fishing trips—hunting and fishing are my favourite pastimes. Such trips take me to picturesque spots where I can rest both my body and mind, and regain strength. Moreover, these trips of mine give me an opportunity to mingle with people from all walks of life. I have thus made friends with factory workers, office employees, students and professors, engineers, doctors and men of other professions. The engineer was a close friend of mine and I admired him greatly as a hunter. He was quite an angler too. But besides being a good sportsman, he displayed a keen interest in art. We fished and discussed acting on the stage and screen. I thought it would be nice to acquaint him with our work.

We met at the appointed time and place, and my friend was soon in my dressing-room watching me make up. At ten sharp we made our way to the set and at the entrance ran into Grigori Roshal, the director.

Roshal always treats his cast with great understanding. He makes no mistake about an actor's possibilities, lets him use them to the full, and by his suggestions sets the actor on the right path. Actors like to work with him because of his faith in their abilities. Roshal combines a thorough knowledge of the subject with great powers of imagination. This makes it possible for him to suggest to the actor obvious motivations and to show him some of the finer points connected with them. Roshal is the type of the well-educated and experienced director who is able to fill the many functions that his work calls for.

A film director may be likened to an architect putting up a great big building; he must be able to create a harmonious whole out of many component parts and elements. And when he produces a picture it is primarily upon him that lies the responsibility for making the most of all that goes into synthetic film art.

Roshal met us in his usual cordial way. I introduced my friend and stated my request: would he permit my friend to attend the shooting of the trial scene? He would. The three of us went to the "courtroom." On a slightly elevated platform stood a long table covered with a green cloth and behind it were the judge's bench, the jury box and the box for the prosecutor. A life-size portrait of Alexander II hung on the wall. Over to the right were the benches for the "slandered" critics, and to the left Stasov's bench. Behind the rail were the chairs for visitors. An actor playing a juryman, very smart in a green uniform of the period, sat on the rail, gesturing and speaking animatedly with the extras appearing in the courtroom crowd. They were brightly costumed in the style of the 1870's. Other members of the cast were scattered all over the set.

My friend was surprised to see that the courtroom set had no ceiling. I explained that it was unnecessary since it would not go into the picture. Then I drew his attention to the scaffolding especially erected for the kleig lights. A flood of light from powerful lamps came into the courtroom through the empty space above. *Moussorgsky* was a colour film, hence the abundant lighting.

Alexander Borisov, who played Moussorgsky, approached us. He was on his way to the dressing-room. There was an air of healthy freshness and energy about him. The bulk of the scenes in which he appeared had already been shot, and after they were run off in the projection room it was clear that Borisov had created a convincing portrait of the famous composer. Rejoicing in the success of our comrade and inspired by it, we were all eager to equal his contribution.

"Here's the letter I spoke to you about," Borisov said, handing me a sheet of paper folded in four. It was a copy of Moussorgsky's letter to Stasov for whom the composer had the highest regard. I had not known of its existence—although in preparation for my role I had gone through a good deal of material concerning Stasov—until Borisov mentioned it to me. "You are dear to me," wrote Moussorgsky, "because you have the courage to show up the petty critics who know not when to speak and when to keep silent. I would have felt completely lost without you. No one sees better than you do what my ideas are...." I read these lines with great interest. They gave me further proof of the bond of understanding which existed between the great composer and the eminent critic in their common struggle for democratism in music.

After putting away the letter I got my friend comfortably seated in a place where he could get a good view of a film in the making. Then I suggested that he take a copy of our working script and read carefully the courtroom scene before the shooting began. He agreed gladly but when he saw the thick notebook with the pages all marked off into columns and every detail of the action described, he realized how much trouble it would take reading it, and refused. Still I insisted that he at least scan the script to get an idea of the effort that goes into translating a scene or fragment into action.

Meanwhile, the director conferred with his assistants on the main points of the action and stressed the idea behind the scene. The cameramen and the sound engineer had their own suggestions to make.

This done, the director outlined my scene and settled the questions of lighting effects, sound, colour, etc. After all the elements that go to make the scene had been thoroughly discussed and various suggestions put to the test, the director ran through the whole courtroom scene from beginning to end, i.e., from the moment the indictment is read to Stasov's speech. The field was then taken over by the cameraman, the sound engineer and their many assistants.

There was the usual commotion preceding the taking of a scene. The cameras were brought in, the sound equipment and heavy lights were hauled about and mounted. The sound engineer could be heard shouting orders. Signals were given by the lighting man to his various assistants scattered over the set. The carpenters, taking advantage of the "wait," started hammering away at the sets for another scene. The actors had to raise their voices to hear each other, and that added to the general din.

When I approached my friend he said, almost shouting: "There's enough noise here to kill a person. How can you concentrate on your role?"

I told him I was not thinking of my role as yet. I was making use of the "wait" to relax—preserving my energy for the great battle ahead. The filming of every scene is a battle for the actor from which he must emerge victorious at any cost. His great abilities are his experience and the control he exercises over his mind and body.

My friend was surprised by my high spirits and detached air. I told him the story of a well-known stage actress who had agreed to star in a picture although she had never played in films before. She would begin to concentrate on her part hours before the actual shooting. The first time she had to appear before the camera she spent one and a half hours in her dressing-room thinking of nothing but her role. When she appeared on the set, even the din could not detract her from her part. During the shooting, however, she felt so exhausted that towards the end of the scene she could not grasp what the director wanted of her. For all her acting experience she had made the mistake that few film stars make. Actors used to playing in films know that they must save their energy for the moment when they are called to step before the camera.

Roshal wanted to rehearse my scene with all the lighting effects. It soon appeared that there were many technical points still wanting attention. These were attended to, and the rehearsal continued. A half-hour's break was again announced. My engineer friend and I stepped into the refreshment room. There I told him that we should shoot our scene minus the close-ups. Before the end of the break the make-up man came for a last-minute adjustment of my wig, moustache, beard and a look at my costume. After the break there was a full-dress rehearsal of the fragments we were going to shoot that day.

Finally the director gave orders for the "shooting." And it was only then that I began to really get into the atmosphere of the scene.

The signal was given for everybody to get ready. An absolute hush fell over the set. "Camera! Lights!" The assistant director stepped before the camera. He used a clapper, and the clack was registered on the sound track. The director checked everybody in turn—the cameraman, his assistants, the sound engineer and the actors—to make sure that there would be no hitch anywhere.

It was Stasov's scene, and the camera's eye was focussed on me.

Stasov is the defendant, humiliated but not defeated. There is even a certain cheerfulness in his manner when he thinks of the effect his speech will have on the court.

The shot registered these emotions. Then there was to be a retake necessary in case the original shot proved to be unsatisfactory in some way. Again the lighting was checked and readjusted. The director had additional remarks to make. The sound engineer, too, had some improvements to suggest. There were again last-minute inspections by the make-up man. Then the camera began to grind, and the scene was reshot.

A little later the director, cameraman, sound engineer and lighting men, all decided that the scene would be more effective if shot from an altogether different angle. That required a good deal of preparation on which we spent much time. The scene was shot a third time. Everything went off smoothly, and it looked as though the last take would be the best. Other shots to be taken that day did not include me. But before leaving the studio I wanted a word with the director. There was a break, and I approached him.

"Tomorrow we're shooting Stasov's speech," he told me cheerfully, evidently anticipating the pleasure of working on the climax of the courtroom scene. "Have you had time to think over the points we discussed?"

At our last meeting we had gone over the courtroom speech very carefully. In this speech it was important to show Stasov as an ardent champion of progressive thought. Stasov, according to the accounts of his contemporaries, was never indifferent to the events around him. His manner of speaking was that of the heated polemic who sees great issues at stake and cannot be quick enough at defending them. His speech, as Gorky had put it, was "rapid, coming in quick flashes." It is these distinctive features of Stasov's oratorial gift that I had been working on of late, and I told so to the director.

After that little chat I took my friend to my dressing-room. He was eager to discuss what he had seen at the studio.

"Today is not what I would call a typical day," I told him.

When I had removed my make-up we returned to the set to find the director rehearsing the court verdict scene.

"Doesn't the scene where you make your speech come before the one in which the verdict is pronounced?" asked my companion, somewhat puzzled.

"Yes, it does," I replied, "but due to technical requirements scenes in picture are shot without any regard for sequence."

Meanwhile some of the workmen were moving lights and the sound equipment. Cameras were placed in a different position, and everything was being prepared for the other shots of the courtroom scene. These featured the judge, jury and plaintiffs.

"What I've seen is very interesting," said my friend. "But I don't imagine this has been a particularly successful day for you. You've hardly done any acting, most of the time was spent in preparations."

"But most of our time *is* spent on preparations and technical preparations at that, even when unimportant scenes are shot," I told my friend. "Today we've done exactly what we'd planned to do, so there is no reason to consider the day unsuccessful. There are days when we manage to take scenes running between forty and fifty yards of film and have several retakes. Then there may be days when nothing at all is accomplished.

184

"This is so," I went on, "because the film actor is often at the mercy of circumstances over which he has no control. When scenes are shot on location, for example, actors sometimes have to wait around for hours for the sun to appear. When it does finally break through the clouds, and the signal to start shooting is given, there is general relief. But not for long. Ten, fifteen minutes, and the sun again disappears. When we were making *Alexander Popov* in which many of the scenes are laid on the sea-shore in Kronstadt, we waited around almost a whole week in our costumes and make-up for the sun to come out. Then there were two perfectly wasted days on location when we were filming *Hectic Days*.

"We were doing a scene that was long and difficult from a technical point of view. In this scene Kolya—I played the part—tells Tonya, the heroine of the picture, that he loves her. The scene required of me to go through a series of complicated movements. I had to ride up on horseback to the place where Tonya was sitting on a swing, grab hold of a bough and jump off the horse in peculiar fashion, get on the swing beside her, begin my confession, put my arm around her waist, get slapped, fall off the swing, rise and time my movements so that when I walked off I got hit by the rocking swing. At the rehearsals everything went off smoothly. But when we began shooting the scene we heard the drone of a plane overhead. We had to stop in the middle of the scene. When we got through the scene and started shooting a re-take, two more planes appeared. Again we stopped the shooting. One of our men tried to ring up the aerodrome but in vain. Meanwhile a great big cloud blotted out the sun for something like half an hour. And when the sun came out it had changed its position which made it necessary for us to rearrange the scene and rehearse it over again. The shooting began, and everything seemed to be going fine until the cameraman discovered that the film had run out. The take was spoilt. The camera was recharged, and the same scene was being taken over again when the sound engineer detected a hardly audible buzzing sound. It was made by a bee which kept whirling just over the microphone, and it registered on the sound track. So this take, too, was no good. Meanwhile it was getting on towards 6 o'clock, and the sun had now gone far to the west. When we started shooting the scene over again the sun had got behind a huge poplar, casting a shadow that quite upset everything. The suggestion was made to fell the tree, but the director ordered that its crown be pulled down on a side with a rope. Nor did this do any good, for a passing cloud soon again obscured the sunlight. The next day the weather let us down, and so we actually had not succeeded in taking a single satisfactory shot in two days.

"The taking of every scene, every shot—long, medium or a close-up —is a very arduous task, requiring much energy, patience, skill, talent and time. So you see today's shooting went off well."

That evening I was appearing as Ivan the Terrible in *The Great Tsar* at the Pushkin Theatre. I said good-bye to my engineer friend who promised to come to the studio at noon the next day to watch us continue the shooting of the courtroom scene.

The scenes that were shot the next day were all built around Stasov's speech. The first shot showed Stasov speaking and was taken from the middle of the hall over the heads of the courtroom crowd. I stood facing the judge and the jury, and spoke my lines:

"The men who accuse me are liars...." I had to shift my glance so that it would fall on my "accusers" when I pronounced the next lines: "I can see them flinch at my words."

Several takes were shot. Then the camera was moved a little closer to me, and the same scene was reshot. There was a small break between shots, and I went to my friend with whom I had not yet had a chance to speak.

"It was really amazing the amount of feeling you put into your speech when your accusers weren't there at all," was the first thing he said to me.

"They didn't have to be there. It was my scene—theirs will come later, and they will be filmed listening to my speech without my being present. As for myself, I *imagined* they were there. On the screen, of course, after the film is cut and edited, you will never know that the shots were taken separately."

"Such scenes where you must provide a missing atmosphere must be very difficult to act in," my friend remarked.

"Screen acting is a specific art and, by the way, because the film director in editing the film can work wonders it is sometimes erroneously claimed that he reigns supreme in cinema art. I disagree with this. In my opinion the contribution made by the script writer, the actor and the director, all working in creative cooperation, is of equal importance."

The shooting of the scene was resumed. I stepped before the camera, standing at the same angle as in the previous shots, that is behind the rail cutting off the courtroom crowd from the judge and the jury.

I had to speak the closing lines of my monologue: "The songs of the people have found their way into the treasure store of great music. They bring new vigour. They live in our operas and symphonies. We shall give new wings to these wonderful songs that they may soar, that they may beckon to the great future which will hear a free and happy people sing, their song carrying to all the corners of the globe and bringing joy to all people!" At the last words I was to point at the people in the courtroom and after a brief pause return to my seat.

Before acting the scene the player must go through the movements of the preceding shot. These the camera also records as aids to the "cutter" in editing the film. And sometimes the "duplicate shots" turn out so well that they are given preference over the "original shots" and go into the final release.

As on the day before, the scene was rehearsed over and over again, and after that shot several times.

"You've certainly spent a lot of time shooting just two sequences," was my friend's comment when we found ourselves in my dressing-room and I was removing my make-up.

I explained that apart from the problem of acting there were a dozen problems of a technical nature that had to be effectively dealt with in preparation for the shooting. But though the actor must be able to carry out at a moment's notice all the suggestions that are made, he must never lose sight of his principal task—to convey to the audience the feelings and reactions of the character (as conceived by the script writer, the director and himself) in the concrete atmosphere of the particular scene that is being shot.

"But if so much consideration must be given to technical requirements, how can you keep your mind on the role?"

"The actor, when he makes a picture, never stops thinking about his
character; he 'lives' the character, imagines the situations in which his
character may find himself, even situations which have no bearing on
the script, figures out what the character's reaction might be, gets into
the mental attitude of his part. All this prepares him for almost anything that he might be expected to do before the camera at any time of
night or day."

"Don't you find it annoying to hear the director, cameraman, and
sound engineer give last-minute suggestions just before the take when
you have already stepped into the role?"

"Not at all. I'm used to it. But when some of the suggestions come
after the signal for shooting is given they may make me lose my
bearings."

"And when does the actor begin to step into the character?"

"I don't think there are any hard and fast rules for that. I begin to
concentrate on my role just a few seconds before the signal to shoot is
given, and when the scene is particularly important, long before that.
Have you noticed that before we began taking the last scene the director spoke to me? He refreshed in my memory the action of the scenes
preceding my own which had not yet been shot. He helped to supply
the 'atmosphere,' to create the necessary state of mind. Seeing the scene
as a whole piece, the director keeps check on the actor's mental attitude and helps him to project his characterization within the limits
of the sequence he is doing at the moment."

"It seems to me making a picture is very much like painting many
figures on a huge canvas. There is the idea—that comes first. After the
composition come the details which in the long run are pieced together
to form an integrated whole, right?"

"Exactly, only the painter works alone, whereas the film actor works
in a team, and artistic, technical and musical elements are all blended
together to help him in characterization."

"What is the actor's greatest handicap on the lot?"

"Unpreparedness. The actor always hates to hear the director say to him: 'We've thought up a little additional scene—just a few lines, and we're going to shoot it today along with the scenes we've planned.' Generally, this practice is looked on with disfavour, particularly when the script is satisfactory from every point of view and has been carefully edited by the director. I remember Eisenstein saying to me in jest when we were working on *Ivan the Terrible*, 'Your Majesty, we've added a line.' To one ignorant of the ways of film-making this may mean the actor going up to the table, picking up a pencil and a bit of paper, and putting down a line containing a few words which can be memorized easily. But it actually turned out to be a meaty monologue which, of course, required time to learn. Then I had to go and change my make-up because the new lines were for a sequence in which I was of a different age than in the scene to be taken that day. Since I could not learn the lines at such short notice they were chalked in big letters on a blackboard in front of me. I had to keep looking at the board and at the same time not lose touch with the atmosphere of the scene. Of course, the scene was not well done, but it was essential to enhance an episode, and in this respect it served its purpose. In such instances the director imagines that he can rely on the actor's gifts and adaptability. But distraction causes the actor to fall out with the emotional state he must reproduce and may ruin his performance.

"Not knowing the lines is a terrible handicap. The actor begins to stumble over his words and gets nervous. The director stops the shooting and tries to be sympathetic: 'Never mind, get your bearings, we'll retake the scene.' But then there are times when the director does not show understanding even if he knows the actor could not have possibly learned the new lines. I remember a case when a stage actor, who was not used to the ways of film directors, got his lines rather late and stumbled over them. The director did not hide his annoyance. 'If I had known I would have to put up with such things I would never in my life have come near a studio!' the actor said. He was all wrought up, yet, being a professional actor and knowing that he must go through the scene, he pulled himself together and finally did what was expected of him."

My friend enjoyed his visit to the studio so much that he wished to come the next day too. I told him that we would be doing the same scene only shooting it at a closer range.

Again the actors who played the judge, the jury and the crowd in the trial scene were absent. They were due at the studio at a much later hour. When I spoke I again had to *imagine* they were there and work out a responsiveness to their reactions.

The shots we were doing this time called for movement. I had to be careful not to step outside the chalked lines on the floor which marked the range of the camera. There were certain parts in my speech where I thought it would be effective to lift my hand or raise my head. But I knew that I must not do any of these things or I would be outside the picture. Another reason why I was warned not to raise my head was because it would make my beard protrude in a funny way and spoil the compositional arrangement of the shot. To top it all, the sound engineer told me to strain my voice a little, otherwise the microphone, for technical reasons adjusted at quite a distance from me, would not get its full volume.

All technical directions, trying as they were, had to be obeyed—but first of all, there was obedience to my own mind, so that I could grasp the mental state of my character and strike the correct note in the scene.

The director ran over the action twice before he gave orders for the shooting to start. This made me fall completely into my character's train of thought. I did the scene exactly as we had rehearsed it and kept strictly within the chalked lines on the floor without once looking underfoot. I knew I must not raise my head and I didn't, my big, silvery beard giving me the sensation of being a great weight tied to my chin to keep it down.

When the shooting was over I was quite pleased with myself. The scene which ran to 130 yards of film and required attention to many technical details came off smoothly. But the director said: "Your acting was good, though somewhat cold. Put more feeling in it. Remember you must convey anger and biting sarcasm in Stasov's speech, and the deep faith he had in the genius of the Russian people."

We began retaking the scene. But somehow I failed to step into the part at the required moment and instead of saying "Gentlemen of the jury," I said "Citizens of the jury." I realized at once that I had made a slip and followed up with a mistake in movement and then again faltered over my lines. The director stopped the shooting. That day the heat on the set was unbearable. And I was padded heavily to give the impression of bulk, for Stasov was a heavily-built man. I felt quite exhausted. However, after a short break, I adjusted my make-up, and we went on with the scene.

"Remember your gestures must be well-rounded—no angles, for that would be out of keeping with the general portrait," the director warned me.

As before, the microphone was at quite a distance from me, and the sound engineer repeated his instructions of a short while ago. The cameraman was anxious for me to keep my head at just the angle from which I screened best. Everyone concerned put so much effort into the scene that the final take came off very well. Other bits of the courtroom scene were to be taken after a short break. These included shots showing Moussorgsky, Rimsky-Korsakov and Borodin.

"Patience and self-control are absolutely essential for an actor who goes into pictures," I said to my engineer friend. "The actor constantly develops these two qualities.

"Screen acting must be thought of in terms of hard work. Sometimes the actor puts up with great bodily discomforts. Like other actors, time and again I had to act half-naked in cold weather or, heavily padded, to wait around for hours in intense heat for the shooting to start. I remember sitting around for days in heavy armour, padding and make-up, the thermometer showing over 100° F., and waiting for clouds to appear in the sky, so that the scene in which Ivan the Terrible steps out of his tent could be taken—that was part of the episode showing the capture of Kazan. There is a scene in *Alexander Popov* in which an antenna is put up to help rescue some fishermen carried off on an ice-floe. This scene was shot out on location on frosty days. I was 'locked up' between two huge ventilators and blinded by gusts of 'prop' snow—all to give the impression of a blizzard.

"Add to this the strain of night work, the endless rehearsals, the pains taken over make-up, particularly for a 'character' part, and you will get some idea of the demands that films make on the actor. I spent daily two to three hours in the make-up chair when I played Professor Polezhayev, and over four hours when I played Gorky. Many of us combine work in films with work on the stage. But I must say this for the director and other people who work on the set with the actor, they are always understanding and cooperative, rarely showing annoyance even if the actor slips up sometimes.

"The understanding and comradeship that surround the actor put him at his ease and are conducive to creative effort. When the actor performs before the camera, he feels the eagerness of everyone on the set to convey through him the principal idea behind the picture. The spectators seeing the film hardly suspect that there is a whole army of others who assist the actor in his performance and without whom he would be helpless—the make-up men, costumiers, designers, lighting men, cameramen, sound engineers, their numerous assistants, director's assistants, etc. Then, of course, there are property men, composers, artists, sculptors, all making a very important contribution and helping the actor to succeed in his part. Thus the correlated efforts of many people are behind the actor's work on a picture."

We had walked out of the studio, and I had so warmed up to my subject that I did not even notice how we reached the granite quay of the Neva. In the glow of the setting sun we caught sight of a number of men fishing and eagerly approached to watch them. Soon enough one of the men began pulling up his fishing-tackle, and a fish gleamed at the end of it. It was a chub, and it looked as though it weighed at least five pounds. The rest of the party came to take a look at it and, inspired, returned to their places, casting the lines into the water as far as possible.

"I'd like to see a scene like that on the screen," my friend remarked, and the very thought seemed to give him pleasure.

"It would take at least a full day's work to shoot it," I said, damping my friend's ardour. "It would require about twelve shots. The first shot would show the man casting the line, the second would show it drop-

As Vladimir Stasov in *Moussorgsky*. 1950

A still from *Alexander Popov* with Nikolai Cherkasov
in the title role. 1950

Outdoor shot from *Hectic Days* with Nikolai Cherkasov as Kolya Loshak. 1935

As Stasov in *Moussorgsky.* 1950

ping on the surface of the water, the third a splash where it drops and the ripples in the river, the fourth a close-up of the spoon-bait under the water, the fifth a close-up of the man as he holds the rod, the sixth the fish watching the bait, the seventh the fish swallowing the bait. Then the eighth would be a close-up of the beaming face of the man, the ninth showing the man drawing up the fish towards the bank, the tenth with the fish in the net, the eleventh would be another close-up of the angler, and the twelfth—the man holding the fish by the gills and trying to estimate its weight. Then there may be certain difficulties connected with 'shooting' the fish. You would need two or three fishes of the same size.

"And, by the way, it was in this very place on the bank of the Neva that one of the scenes in *Alexander Popov* was shot. It was the scene in which Popov comes across a little boy who is fishing. So I know from experience how much time and effort it takes to make a little fishing scene, particularly in Leningrad's northern climate where the sun keeps playing hide-and-seek with us."

We parted agreeing to meet again the next morning at the Lenfilm Studios.

My friend was not a little surprised to find that we were shooting Stasov's speech again. This time the director thought we could reduce the action and cut out some shots to make the scene more effective. Going over the scene many times had given me an idea of just how it should be played and as it proved later, my last portrayal was the most convincing.

The scene was shot four times. I had to go through the following series of movements: look into the eyes of my judges, turn to the courtroom crowd, sense its reaction, listen to the applause and shouts, repeat the closing lines of my speech.

"Stasov's monologue lasts no more than five or six minutes on the screen," I told my friend. "Yet it has taken four days to shoot and weeks of arduous work to prepare."

"Yes, I can see to what lengths you film-makers will go to secure perfection. I should think you would prefer the stage. Anyway, it must be more gratifying to act with the audience in front of you."

"In one respect you are right. The stage actor creates an atmosphere on the stage which is directly conveyed to the audience. We feel the reaction of the audience and that in itself is a great stimulus. Every performance on the stage is a sort of jubilee for the actor. But screen acting, too, has its rewards, and its greatest reward is that it reaches out to huge audiences such as the stage can never dream of."

THE ACTOR AND THE PUBLIC

Frequent contact with their audiences is an important feature in Soviet actors' lives.

Looking back on my own life as an actor and reflecting on the various landmarks in my career, I find that contact with my audience has always greatly affected my work.

In the years following the Revolution it was easier for us actors of the younger generation to establish contact with the new audiences—mainly workers and Red Army men—that flocked to the theatres than for actors of the old generation. Even the biggest artists at the Mariinsky, and those who regarded the new proletarian spectator with the greatest sympathy, among them the well-known singer Ivan Yershov, did not know how to approach the new audience. They did not know how to reach out across the footlights, how to break through the wall which in former days kept the actor isolated from the public.

Later, when I joined the Pushkin Theatre, I learned of a practice long in existence among actors of the old generation which enabled them to find out how audiences reacted to their performances, particularly in new roles. This was getting some theatre employee, a "particular friend," generally an usher or a cloak-room attendant, to "sound" spectators.

No doubt that some of the remarks gleaned from among the audience by such "observers," some of whom had long been employed in the theatre and were not bad judges of the audience's reactions, were of benefit to the actor. Often in this way the actor was able to make note of his slips and let-downs.

But this indirect way of "sounding" the audience is a far cry from the many forms of living contact between actor and audience that have become one of the peculiar traits of the Soviet Theatre—a theatre that is organically linked with the people.

It was after joining the Young Spectators' Theatre that I first found myself in the typical Soviet atmosphere in which the actor steps across the footlights to become friends with the audience. The company playing to juvenile audiences catered to the interests of its public, arranged get-togethers between actors and spectators and on the basis of its audience's reactions worked on solutions for its artistic problems. Actors were extremely attentive to the criticism and wishes of their youthful audiences. I found that I was being schooled in the art of establishing and maintaining contact with the spectators, and though the audience in a children's theatre is a specific one, I am very grateful for what I have learned.

Later, when I worked in vaudeville where somehow the relations between the performer and the public were distant, I felt sorely the lack of such contact. Therefore I was quite happy to get an engagement with the Comedy Theatre which performed mainly at culture centres and workers' clubs in Leningrad's suburbs. The theatre often called conferences at which our audiences would discuss its performances. There was an almost permanent contact with the public. This helped me to understand more clearly what the tasks of the Soviet actor were at that particular period, the period of the First Five-Year Plan.

When I finally came to work for the Pushkin Theatre, I was firmly convinced that I must strive harder than ever to be close to my audience, to make friends with it, to listen to its criticism, to know its wishes. In a word, audiences had much to teach me, and I could draw a new vitality by being in constant touch with them.

Every Soviet actor will tell you proudly of the many interesting get-togethers he has had with his audiences. And every Soviet actor has had useful critical letters and notes sent by spectators.

Close contact with the audience is a help to the actor in projecting his art. In this respect I have found my work in films of great use.

When *Baltic Deputy* was released, fan mail and even wires came streaming in. I received a wire from a group of Komsomol members in the Donbas. It read: "*Baltic Deputy* is a great hit with Donbas film-goers. Please send our youth paper *Donbas Komsomolets* an account of how film was made and your work on leading role." Later I established a correspondence with this group of young people.

I made many personal appearances together with the producers and the script writer when *Baltic Deputy* was showing. Our audiences asked many questions and raised some criticism which I think was justified in most cases.

It was because of its patriotic appeal and noble sentiments that the film had so completely won the hearts of Soviet audiences. As we watched the spectators we saw that every bit of the picture found a response, not a single subtlety was lost. This was extremely gratifying. And our conferences with the public helped us in our own development as artists.

The writer Alexei Tolstoi made a speech at the Anglo-Soviet Peace and Friendship Congress, held in London in the spring of 1937. "The greater art is, the truer and deeper it is, the fuller will be the response it gets from the masses," he said. "Heroic sentiment, goodness and optimism—that is what our mass audiences want to see on the screen. It is characteristic and significant that we are now passing from an outward projection of heroic sentiment in our pictures to a portrayal that is deep in the mind and heart. The path of our screen art is from outer to inner movement, from the contemplation of experience to the living of it; that is the path to real art. Before leaving my country I saw a new Soviet film *Baltic Deputy*. It is based on an episode from the life of Timiryazev, the famous Russian naturalist. The hero of the picture is seventy-five years old. Now what can there be so gripping in a subject about a seventy-five-year-old naturalist? Yet when you can feel the beating of a noble human heart on the screen, when courage, integrity, big-mindedness and love for humanity unfold before your eyes like a beautiful suite, when the eyes of the spectators fill with tears of gratitude to this tall, elderly professor with a youthful heart, you will find *Baltic Deputy* far more thrilling and soul-gripping than films showing hand-to-hand bayonet attacks or the most breath-taking encounters between gangsters and police."

All of us who participated in the making of *Baltic Deputy* were overjoyed at the tribute Soviet spectators—from factory worker to great writer—paid to the picture. We were also happy to hear that the picture had won recognition abroad. The producers of the film, for example, received a brief note of appreciation from Martin Andersen Nexö, who wrote that *Baltic Deputy* was one of the finest pictures he had ever seen—human, straightforward, sincere and deeply stirring. He was certain the film would impress greatly the old world intelligentsia. And Romain Rolland wrote that *Baltic Deputy* carried him away by its technique and psychological and emotional values. "This is one of the first pictures," he wrote, "in which the inner life of the hero is fused with the impetuous actions of the masses. Go on working in the same spirit. Blow up the ground! Penetrate with your soul into the amazing dynamics of Soviet screen art."

A careful study of comment evoked by *Baltic Deputy* helped us to understand what qualities and peculiar traits had made for the success of the film at home and abroad.

I would like to relate a little episode that is not significant in itself, but one that has made a strong impression on me.

It happened ten years after the release of *Baltic Deputy*. With a small group of film people, headed by Grigori Alexandrov, I arrived in Czechoslovakia, where some of the scenes for *Spring,* a picture I was then making, were to be shot. I was motoring in the environs of Prague when my car collided with a lorry. I was injured and had to spend some time in a Prague hospital.

One "visitors' day" a little old lady I had never seen before stuck her head through the half-open door of my ward. "Is Professor Polezhayev here?" she asked, smiling sweetly. I was rather taken aback and did not reply at once. Then I nodded, and she tripped up to my bedside, handing me a nosegay to which a little gingerbread shaped like a heart and wrapped in cellophane was tied. I was deeply touched and understood that the old lady's little gift was not a tribute to my own work only, but to the work of all Soviet film people who are trying to make our screen art the most progressive in the world.

Baltic Deputy gave me the opportunity to meet with larger audiences than I had ever met before. And I made the most of it, giving careful consideration to all that film fans had to say about my acting.

Sometimes an actor gets the chance to speak to the public even before his picture is out, while he is working on his role. That, too, is extremely beneficial. I had such a chance when I played Stasov in *Rimsky-Korsakov,* a Lenfilm production.

In this picture the role of Stasov brought with it different problems from those which faced me in *Moussorgsky.* The film showed the period of the 1905 Revolution and the persecution which Rimsky-Korsakov underwent at the hands of the tsarist officials who had him dismissed from his professor's post at the St. Petersburg Conservatoire. Rimsky-Korsakov's dismissal called forth protests from all progressive-minded people, among them Stasov.

I had to portray the critic in his old age, in an atmosphere charged with revolutionary tension. I had to show his sympathies with the new movement and his belief in a better and brighter future. The well-known words he wrote in a letter to Lev Tolstoi in 1906 expressed his sentiments very well: "The Russian proletariat, as I have come to know it, love and idolize it, is the foremost, the best, the most advanced and the most noble-minded proletariat in all Europe."

I had only a few scenes left to do for the picture, and one of them was to be taken out on location on Kirov Islands in Leningrad.

It was September. We were having warm and sunny weather but still as unreliable as only Leningrad weather can be. In the morning the sun would be dazzlingly bright. But towards noon a thick haze would gather, and though the warm rays would gradually disperse it, still the sun would remain obscured by a milky film. For three days, idly sauntering in the park on the islands in our make-up and costumes, we waited for the sun to reappear.

This waiting gave me the opportunity to keep a promise I had made some time ago to visit one of Leningrad's big print-shops and speak on my work on the stage and screen, and also about my recent trip to

India. I made arrangements at once. And just as I was, in make-up and costume, I got into a car and set out for the print-shop which was quite a long way off.

This was one of the many little conferences I had with my audiences, and it was very lively. I spoke a good deal about Stasov. At first I gave a brief outline of the picture and then dwelt on the episodes in which I still had to play. Among them was one which, though short, was very important in revealing the mental outlook of my character. It dealt with Stasov's reaction to a letter which Rimsky-Korsakov received upon his dismissal from the St. Petersburg Conservatoire. The letter was signed by a group of peasants from Vladimir Gubernia. "It is clear that you have been dismissed because you dared speak the truth," the peasants wrote, "because you refused to join hands with the police. You acted honourably, and we express our greatest sympathy...." Enclosed in the letter was the sum of 2 rubles 17 kopeks, donated by the peasants to the composer.

"I swear to you," Stasov said when he learned of Rimsky-Korsakov's dismissal, "that it is a great honour to suffer persecution from the tsar's dirty dogs! Look what they did to Gorky—locked him up in prison, and to Tolstoi—excommunicated him. And now they've sacked you. You should be proud of it!" After reading the letter from the peasants he added: "There she is, our dear amazing Russia. What gloom and what fire! That's something you must put to music. Make an oratorio of it. Think of Beethoven, Mozart, Liszt—what geniuses they were. Yet they never knew such joy, such triumph, as falls only to us Russians!"

The episode shows that the foremost representatives of Russia's progressive intelligentsia were bone and flesh of the people, always with the people, and that the people felt it, knew it and appreciated it.

The conference that I had at the print-shop, actually with my future audience, was extremely stimulating. It put me into just the mood I needed to complete successfully the scenes I was appearing in.

Like other Soviet actors, I have often spoken to audiences at the motion-picture theatres showing my pictures. At matinées there are often very many children, and I enjoy speaking to juvenile spectators who are particularly responsive, ask the most unexpected questions and create a cheerful and lively atmosphere.

While travelling in the Caucasus one summer I met a large group of Young Pioneers and had a very jolly time with them. The youngsters belonged to a big summer holiday camp and happened to be on the road when my motor car broke down. While the driver was fussing with the engine we took to the fields and chatted, the children asking me all sorts of questions, telling me about their plans for the future and eager to know mine. We rounded out our little talk by singing Paganel's song from *Captain Grant's Children.*

This little encounter set my heart on playing a role which would appeal to a juvenile audience. And some time later I was cast in just such a part. I played Captain Levashov in *Bon Voyage!,* a picture about life in a Soviet naval school. When it was released it brought a deluge of mail from youngsters all over the country to me and other actors who played in it. The children eagerly discussed the many problems raised in the film, one of which was friendship.

"Dear Comrade Cherkasov, I liked *Bon Voyage!* very much," ran a letter I received from a Suvorov cadet. "I have thought a lot about Captain Levashov. How well he managed everything! He discovered who had set off the alarm. He helped to clear Sergei Stolitsin. And he convinced Boris that he must make a clean breast of everything. He is an ideal instructor for training future naval officers and admirals. I think you played Levashov very well. I am not a naval but an army cadet, and I have no great deeds to my credit but I hope some day to become a brave, smart and popular officer like Levashov. We'll be taking our graduation exams soon. I am going to try my very best to make a good showing. I want to take after Sergei. When I feel I'm doing something wrong I think of Sergei and some of the other boys in the picture, and say to myself: 'Sergei would not have acted this way.' I begin to feel ashamed of myself and wonder what Captain Levashov would say. You've made a splendid picture. And I thank you on behalf of all our Suvorov cadets."

Some of the children were so strongly impressed by the picture that they thought Captain Levashov was a real person and even addressed letters to him to the Nakhimov Naval School in Leningrad. This shows how real a screen character may be and is one of the greatest compliments the audience can pay to the actor.

Film-goers will often go out of their way to help an actor in his preparation for a role. For example, when I began working on Popov, I received a letter from which I learned about Popov's taste for music. *Ruslan and Lyudmila*, I was told by my correspondent, was his favourite opera. Little hints of this kind are extremely helpful to the actor in building up his role.

Soon after the première of *Peter I* at the Pushkin Theatre I set out with a group of actors for Kolpino, a place near Leningrad, to perform before the workers of the Izhory Works. When we boarded the train, I attracted attention because of my height. A group of men, among them some elderly workers, moved to give me a seat. They had recognized me and at once began talking about plays and films. One of them remarked that he liked me as Alexei in *Peter I*, and the others echoed him. But when we were discussing my performance as Peter I on the stage, an elderly bewhiskered worker, who had hitherto kept silent, remarked: "It's true Comrade Cherkasov played Alexei well on the screen but I didn't like his acting in the part of Peter I on the stage, particularly in the forge scene. He's neither a smith nor a tsar there."

I learned later that the men I had spoken to in the train were smiths from the Izhory Works. Bits of criticism collected in the manner I have just described are very often to the point, and Soviet actors lose no time in benefiting from them.

So much importance is attached to criticism coming direct from the audience that the Pushkin Theatre has inaugurated weekly discussions of plays (they began in 1952). These discussions are held every Sunday after the matinée.

On these days, before the curtain rises, the public is told that a discussion will be held after the play. Spectators are urged to stay and participate. When the curtain falls on the last act, chairs are arranged in the proscenium for the actors who take their seats as soon as they remove their make-up. The discussion is opened by the régisseur. He dwells briefly on the principal problems of the play. Members of the audience take the floor with stenographers making notes of the speeches. Generally the discussions are lively, with as many as ten or twelve speakers taking the floor. Apart from being beneficial to the actors and the régisseur, they are of great educational value to the public.

Actors often get invitations from workers' clubs and other organizations to make personal appearances, and I gladly accept them. In my programmes which generally contain fragments from plays and recitations, I always allot some time to discussing my future plans and to answering questions. The atmosphere at such evenings is very friendly and helps to bring the actor and his public closer together.

Soviet actors are happy that they serve the people and help to build the new Socialist society. The tribute paid to achievements in the field of art is no less than that paid to successful workers, collective farmers and scientists. Soviet actors may well repeat the words of Mayakovsky, the great poet of the Revolution: "Happy I am that my labours merge with the labours of my Republic."

PLAYING MAYAKOVSKY

The artist in any field day-dreams. These day-dreams are a source of inspiration and vitality.

The actor day-dreams too. He dreams of a part in which he can best express the thoughts that surge in him and in his people, a part that would spur his people to greater achievement in the tasks facing them.

The image of the character the actor longs to play, like the images of other artists, grows out of life, and is nourished by life. But, unlike the painter, writer or composer, the actor cannot always set about materializing his dream. He cannot create alone. He is dependent upon others. So it often happens that his dream to play a certain role to which he has given years of thought meets with obstacles against which he is powerless. The character not existing in dramatic writing at all may be such an obstacle.

Yet the character haunts the actor, sometimes to the point of hallucination. The actor is like one possessed, always thinking about the character, as deep in it as the poet in his rhymes, and, like the poet, going through his tasks of the day mechanically and distractedly.

But the poet, when inspiration comes upon him, writes down his rhymes and works at his poem. Whereas the actor, clearly as he sees the gestures and attitudes of his character, strongly as he feels the character's emotions, remains inarticulate if he has no script to go by, no partner to speak to.

That is what I experienced in relation to Mayakovsky. I dreamed of creating a portrait of this great human being, expressive of the best in our modern age, a great citizen and a man of genius. And that dream grew upon me from day to day.

It all began in 1949 when film directors Zarkhi and Heifetz offered me the role of Mayakovsky. At first I refused. The thought of impersonating Mayakovsky frightened me although I had played the leads in many historical and biographical films. Here one needed more than characterization to fall back upon.

Still I read the first variant of the script and met Vasily Katanyan, the author. He had known Mayakovsky intimately, had made a study of the poet's work and life, and produced a very interesting literary chronicle entitled *Mayakovsky*.

Vasily Katanyan's script dealt mainly with Mayakovsky as a poet and public figure. The writer did well to show the distinguishing features of Mayakovsky's poetry—faith in human nature, ardent patriotism and courage of conviction. I thought the script interesting. It was pervaded by an appealing optimism. Mayakovsky was there—irresistibly charming, clever, witty, big-hearted, a man brimming over with vitality. It promised to be a good picture and roused my enthusiasm.

I was told that the writer himself had expressed the wish to see me in the lead. He saw me for the first time in my everyday clothes and without make-up as Gromov in *Spring* where my own personality fitted in with the part very well. He said: "Here is the actor to do Mayakovsky."

Encouraged by the writer and the directors, I began to study the many-faceted, complex personality of the poet, and became immersed in his life and work.

Mayakovsky—the bard of the October Revolution, from whose pen flowed such poems as "Vladimir Ilyich Lenin" and "Good," the great innovator, himself creating a revolution in many fields of literature, in poetry, in drama, in satire, even in the art of advertisement. The poet-fighter whose words were always on the lips of everyone, from the man in the street to the statesman. The poet-propagandist, and at the same time the great lyric poet, all in all the adored idol of the younger generation.

I felt the time had come to bring to the public a portrait of this most talented poet of the Soviet era. We, who may still be regarded as his contemporaries, were duty-bound to begin this great work. We could get first-hand information about him from his relatives and friends. We could learn details which may escape later generations. But what a great responsibility it was to create a screen portrait of a poet who was a giant among men! I felt dread, joy and great elation.

While I read everything I could get hold of that had to do with Mayakovsky and pondered over the role, the script was going through the usual routine. For one thing, it was being polished up by the writer and the producers. Time went. There were editors and committees setting forth requirements and giving advice, which too often was of a vague and contradictory nature. Finally things came to such a pass that the idea of making the film had to be given up.

But Mayakovsky had become so deeply entrenched in my heart, his image so clearly etched in my imagination that I was determined to create his portrait. My medium was acting, and through it, no matter in what form, I wished to bring Mayakovsky to the public.

I asked Katanyan to write a series of stories about Mayakovsky. I began to read these stories to the public. Although for the most part based on the material of the script, the stories contained many new facts. Particularly moving was the one entitled "Hard Days," which tells of how Mayakovsky, shaken by Lenin's death, was asked by a group of children to read his poem dedicated to the great leader. Another very good story tells of Mayakovsky writing copies of the Russian alphabet and himself distributing them among illiterate men leaving for the Civil War fronts. The story gives deep insight into the poet's character.

Bits of Mayakovsky's poems were inserted in the stories. This presented most difficulty. Only four gramophone records of Mayakovsky's readings of his own poems have remained to our day. From these I was to judge of his recitative style which was marvellous. He recited so that none of the appeal of his poetry was lost, nor the logic of the lines, the force of the underlying idea, the music and poetic quality. I knew I could not learn to recite properly any one of his poems unless I practised reciting many, so as to acquire the right manner and particularly the necessary intonation. And while working on the stories, as an actor I sought to capture the essence of Mayakovsky's personality.

The author of the stories was actually my first director and adviser. I paid attention to every detail, checking results with the help of the tape recorder. I was soon rewarded for my painstaking labour. The first readings of the stories and later broadcasts found an eager and enthusiastic public.

Such were the early stages of my work on the portrayal of Mayakovsky.

I often spoke of my dream to play Mayakovsky at get-togethers with my audiences. The reaction was warm applause, especially from the youth. I gave an interview on the subject, and the result was a stream of mail. There were letters from those to whom Mayakovsky was still a closed book, from others who detested him and his poetry. But these were few and far between, and they did not discourage me. On the contrary, they convinced me of the need for a play which would help to do away with some of the petty prejudices which still surrounded Mayakovsky's name. Most of my correspondents whole-heartedly supported me in my desire to bring Mayakovsky to the stage.

I found many Soviet people eager to help me. Some, like pensioner Y. Urvantsova, shared with me their reminiscences of the poet. Others sent me poems which they thought I may not have read. "I am sending you a magazine clipping of one of Mayakovsky's poems which may have escaped your notice," wrote V. Smirnova, one of my correspondents. "With all my heart I wish you success in your work. I am very glad to hear that you are working on the role of this great man."

The letters I received were indicative of the deep love the poet enjoyed in our country and of the people's eagerness to see him portrayed on the stage.

There was still no play about Mayakovsky when one day the management of the Pushkin Theatre ordered such a play from Vasily Katanyan, author of the film scenario *Mayakovsky*.

This urged me to broaden my knowledge of the poet and his work. I studied his poetry very carefully. I searched everywhere for facts concerning his life. I kept questioning his close friends and acquaintances. I had never seen Mayakovsky myself. Therefore, even the most trifling details relating to his person and life were of value to me.

This is what I learned. Mayakovsky never laughed, only smiled. He was always deep in thought. Familiarity disgusted him. He loved children. Warm-hearted and generous, he was never over-indulgent. He was passionate and venturesome. He was fond of games, played billiards, was a good loser—and even climbed under the billiard table when he lost, if such was the arrangement. Football was one of his favourite outdoor games. And when the youngsters in the yard, after putting their galoshes, schoolbags or caps in a row to mark the goalposts, started kicking the ball about, he would pause to watch the game, would even bet on one of the teams and get quite excited. He was a heavy smoker, a cigarette always dangling from his mouth; he had a habit of shifting his cigarette from one corner of the mouth to the other. He never touched vodka, drank only grape wine.

Mayakovsky was amazingly resourceful and witty in repartee. He was a good listener. Yet he was always deeply lost in the world of his own thoughts even when he carried on a conversation.

He lost his temper easily, even over trifles, but invariably apologized. Most of the day, sometimes as many as eighteen hours, he spent at his desk. He was fond of saying that writing a poem required the sum total of effort needed to put up a big house.

He was not self-conscious about his height and powerful physique. Leaning upon his heavy cane, he would stride along the streets of Moscow, or along the boulevards of Paris, his tall, handsome, manly figure attracting attention.

He always did what he had to do there and then, never putting things off till the next day, and gave earnest attention to minor private matters as well as to important matters of state.

He looked older than his years. He had many friends and enemies. When roused, he fought hard. To keep in constant touch with his reading public was an organic need with him. He went out of his way to meet people in all walks of life—factory workers, students, Red Army men, intellectuals. He did this because he was eager to make his poetry steeped in the Revolution, understandable to the people.

Mayakovsky never went in for "small talk." He had the habit of pronouncing the simplest words pretentiously, as though with the desire to lend greater weight to their meaning. This was especially true when he was in high spirits. He had a habit of drawing out his vowels.

Many were the facts I learned about Mayakovsky. Some of them perhaps are too trifling for the biographer. But to the actor whose business it is not merely to portray his hero, but to *become* him, to assume his personality, even the smallest detail is important. And as the various character traits of my hero, big and small, became stored in my mind, the scattered details gradually fell into place to form a single image of the poet. I was beginning to lose myself in Mayakovsky's personality, acquiring his carriage, his gait, his manner of speaking; I would even catch myself in everyday speech modulating my words in the Mayakovsky manner. Thus I was feeling my way to the second

As Vladimir Mayakovsky reading
"A Soviet Passport." 1954

A scene in the "Poet's Cafe" from *They Knew Mayakovsky.* 1954

Alyosha (Igor Gorbachov) and Mayakovsky (Nikolai Cherkasov) in the "ROSTA" editorial office. 1954

Nikolai Cherkasov in *They Knew Mayakovsky*.

stage in my creation of the Mayakovsky character: I was penetrating into the poet's inner world, I could grasp and experience the sense of restraint peculiar to Mayakovsky and wear the grim smile behind which was concealed a big and tender soul.

In the autumn of 1953 Katanyan brought his play to our theatre.

He gave it a rather vague and non-committal title—*Scenes from the Life of the Twenties*. Later the title was changed to *They Knew Mayakovsky*. The play had neither unified story nor plot. But it had an inner unity, a unity of idea and philosophy. There are plays which may be likened to a symphony or an oratorio. Katanyan's play, in my opinion, was like a symphony suite. It was made up of episodic scenes, yet there was cohesion among them. Endless expressions of form and genre have gone into the making of the drama of socialist realism. And Katanyan's form, it seemed to me, was quite legitimate. Moreover, the literary style was good. On the whole, I was deeply moved by the play and convinced that, written by a man who both knew and loved the poet, it had captured his spirit and would make an interesting and stirring production.

But along with the well-wishers, the play had many enemies who kept harping on its drawbacks, actual and imaginary, and actively opposed the very idea of staging a play about Mayakovsky. To fight these enemies was no easy job.

Finding a suitable director for the play was also a complicated matter. It had to be a man with plenty of experience in staging plays and also one with bold ideas and, what was most important, one who really loved and understood the poet.

The choice fell on Nikolai Petrov, one of the Soviet Union's most prominent régisseurs who had known Mayakovsky personally since before the Revolution. A champion of the modern theme, Petrov produced plays that have made Soviet theatre history, among them Afinogenov's *Fear*, Yanovsky's *Wrath* and Korneichuk's *Truth*. Ever dreaming of great things to be done in the theatre, bristling with ideas, Petrov was just the man for the play. Moreover, he was well familiar with the period which forms the background of the play, for he had then been one of the great enthusiasts of the new Soviet art.

At the time we were hunting for a régisseur to direct the new play, Petrov, in collaboration with directors Yutkevich and Pluchek, was staging Mayakovsky's play *Bath* at the Moscow Theatre of Satire. The performance was a brilliant one, and the directors did justice to Mayakovsky's aesthetic views on the theatre. Their production firmly established Mayakovsky's great comedy on the Soviet stage.

I have known Nikolai Petrov since my youth, that is, since the early twenties. When I told him that we had misgivings about the play because it had many ill-wishers, he exclaimed: "All the better, all the better. It would have been worse if everybody liked the play. All great things are born in the heat of struggle and opposition! And if we are putting on a play about Mayakovsky, struggle and opposition are inevitable. . . ."

We began rehearsals. Nikolai Petrov spoke to us about the poet's views on art and on the theatre, and told us of how he thought the play should be staged. The underlying idea of the production, he said, was briefly: "The poet and the people." It was impossible, of course, not to show Mayakovsky at grips with the enemies of Soviet literature, but that was not to be the principal theme. Mayakovsky's devotion to his people, his great capacity for work and his deep faith in human nature were to be the principal theme of the play. Inseparable from this principal theme was another theme: the poet in the eyes of contemporary youth. Hence the title *They Knew Mayakovsky*.

Reminding us of Mayakovsky's words: "Poetry—all of it—is an excursion into the unknown," Petrov pointed out that every play sets new problems before the theatre and that they must be solved in a new way. When the audience thinks, "Not bad, but we've seen it done before in the same way," the play is a flop.

"Mayakovsky was above all part of life, throbbing life," Lunacharsky had said. And only by bringing to the stage the breath of life, the life of which the poet was so much a part, will we be able to stage a play which can do justice to Mayakovsky.

"The Soviet theatre is now passing through a difficult period," Petrov said. "It is exploring new ways, and a theme like the life of Mayakovsky makes great demands on the theatre—on the acting of the players, on the régisseur's work, on the designer and the composer. Each of the scenes must have the force of dynamite. Our production must not be merely an historical or biographical drama, it must ring modern. It must echo the struggle of today that is being waged for an art serving communist ideals and fighting for peace throughout the world. The hero of our play lives in our midst today and is our loyal comrade in our work."

From the very outset it was clear that it would be impossible to give a full portrait of a character as many-sided as Mayakovsky. Nor did the author of the play set himself such a task. He showed the poet as a fighter for the victory of socialist society; the first scene is laid in the "poet's café" where Mayakovsky reads his famous poem "Left March" in which he makes public his political views. In another scene he is shown doing important work for the new republic, such as putting out the "Windows of ROSTA" posters. There is a scene at the bookseller's doing justice to Mayakovsky's deep concern for the development of Soviet literature.

There was tragedy and grief, too, in Mayakovsky's life, and the play reflects it. It is well known that to the end of his days Mayakovsky suffered from the slanders of philistine elements inside and outside literature and from covert enemies of the Soviet system. He smarted under their poisoned pinpricks and the venom of their constant baiting. But he did not fight his enemies single-handed. He had the Communist Party, the Young Communist League and the great masses of readers behind him. And so after each new attack he plunged with fresh force into his work. The play comes to a climax in the seventh scene in which Mayakovsky is shown crossing swords with the poet Innokenty Khromov, a friend turned enemy. The argument between the two poets forcefully reveals the principal idea of the play.

"Mayakovsky held that the theatre," Petrov reminded us, "should be a lively propagandist and agitator. He championed a progressive militant art, not an art of contemplation, but an art actively building life. Our production must be true to Mayakovsky—it must be militant, dynamic, life-affirming, in short, a battle-cry. And let it come as loud and ringing as the poet's own voice. Let it bring to the stage the spirit of the romantic working youth of the twenties."

The actor builds his role slowly. He tries to grasp the logic of his character's actions by deciding how he himself would behave under similar circumstances. Here he must be careful not to skip intermediate stages in assimilating the role, for confusion may result, and instead of merging with the character, the actor will become a copy of him.

When I began rehearsing Mayakovsky I found myself at a great advantage. I was at home with my character. And therefore at the very first rehearsal I was able to act with the emotional fervour without which it is impossible to show the true Mayakovsky, such as he was and has remained in the hearts of the people.

"Part of throbbing life"—that is what Mayakovsky was, and that is what the cast, and especially I, had to bring home to the audience. There was to be no understatement, no rounding-out of lines, for that would upset the whole idea of the production. Therefore we decided that it would be better to overact at first (even Stanislavsky permits this) and later by restraint to bring the portrait to the desired level.

Every work of art must have a distinct form. I attach great importance to form. And it was just this aspect of the role that presented great difficulty. There were no externals to fall back on, no peculiar gait, no old-fashioned coat, no huge pot-belly and flowing beard, no knight's coat of armour, no geographer's broad-brimmed hat. The colour that made up Mayakovsky's exterior did not invite effects. I knew that he always stood with his feet wide apart, his hands in his pockets or behind his back. He walked with a heavy step. He rarely gestured. He was generally deep in thought, his brain constantly at work. This was felt by everyone who came in contact with him.

To play Mayakovsky I had to change many of my habits. In life I am inclined to stoop a little and have the habit of bending down to those I am speaking to. In the street, in a lobby or hall, I instinctively try to slip by so as not to attract attention to myself. But now concentrating on the bearing and movements of my character, I began to acquire the erect carriage and perfect poise of the poet who seemed to say: "Take me for what I am, and you needn't if you don't wish to, but I shall never bend, never lower myself...."

I began to walk with a firm, steady gait, to take big steps, to stand upright. The least shifting of the weight from one foot to the other, typical of most people, a slightly bent knee, a vague, casual movement—these I knew would at once destroy the image.

Poise and even outer resemblance depended on so minor a thing, for example, as footwear. I asked for heavy, well-fitting boots. And when I got such a pair (soldier boots in the first scene) on thick soles and made of tough leather, it helped me to acquire the steady, ponderous, well-measured steps that were typical of Mayakovsky.

Every actor who plays an historical part does a lot of reading and hunts for paintings, drawings and photographs of his character. I studied very carefully everything I could get hold of. But what helped me most in achieving a striking resemblance so that the audience would know the poet on the stage at once were sculptures of Mayakovsky, particularly Sergei Konenkov's bust. I spent hours looking at it—at the poet's face, austere, intensely dramatic and powerful, his broad shoulders, the jacket flung open and his finger stuck in the vest.

I begged Petrov to watch closely the outward pattern of my portrait and note all the shortcomings. And now and then he would stop rehearsals. "You've got the arm wrong, and the foot's wrong, too, they're out of keeping with the character," he would tell me. I was very grateful to him for pointing these things out to me.

My long experience in acting before the camera has trained me to streamline my poses, to time to a second every turn of the head or glance. I have a well-developed sense of sculptural forms. This, combined with the constant dread of falling out even for a moment with my hero in outer resemblance, made me feel somewhat constrained at first. I felt that I bore myself like a marble statue that had just stepped off the pedestal. But when I became established in the role, I gradually toned down my pattern of the image.

My role required much attention to diction.

The cast was constantly warned against falling into slipshod diction and commonplace tone, as this would be out of keeping with the production, dedicated to a poet who was a great master of language. "Mayakovsky did not chat, he declaimed," I found written and underlined in the margins of my role sheets. Now and then the question arose whether it was necessary to "declaim" when speaking of everyday matters. The director insisted that it was, particularly at the first rehearsals, as this manner of speaking was one of the poet's peculiarities and an expression of his temperament.

The more accustomed I became to "declaiming," the less it jarred on my ear. Yet I tried to use restraint, for I was beginning to scan the words. This was unpleasant both to the ear and to the eye because of the mouth's movements in articulating the sounds. Finally, after working much at my diction, there was only a suggestion left of the declamatory manner. And though the force in Mayakovsky's speech remained, it no longer sounded bombastic or affected.

We worked on the production together with the playwright who attended all the rehearsals and made certain alterations in the play. The action was broken up into episodic scenes with long periods apart. This made things harder for the actors because of the changes in the rhythm and difficulties in showing development of character.

Throughout the play Mayakovsky is portrayed as a man leading a life of strenuous activity and intense drama. My great difficulty in building the role was to show the restraint that was characteristic of Mayakovsky.

In one of the scenes Mayakovsky appears in the big, empty, unheated "ROSTA" editorial office in the early days of the Soviet Republic. Wearing a short coat with a fur collar and heavy army boots, he carries a bundle of posters and a newspaper. He has just read Lenin's speech on the New Economic Policy and is full of enthusiasm. There is an eagerness and purposefulness to all his actions. A poster in response to Lenin's speech must be put out at once. But what is the situation in the office? The chief artist is ill, another is a shirker, and the editor is wasting his time. Mayakovsky with his great energy sets everything into motion. All get busy, even the lad Alyosha, an outsider who happens to be in the office, lights the stove, warms the paints and helps to work on the new poster. Mayakovsky meanwhile writes the clever verses that usually accompanied the "ROSTA" window posters. In this scene Mayakovsky is shown as a man of action and concrete purpose. He does not explain or preach, he acts.

The scene in the "ROSTA" office required a rapid tempo of acting. Here I was to be careful not to "gesture" if I wished to keep in character. Even when Mayakovsky scolded he did so with a mild humour. His tone was never unduly rude though often sarcastic as in the instance when he reproaches the artist Medvedkin for falling down on the job. "If you had died yesterday, and that is your private affair," he says to him, "you should have delivered the poster at the office this morning just the same, even if you had to do it on your way to the cemetery."

In the same scene when he sees everybody on the job and knows the poster will be out, Mayakovsky's spirits mount perceptibly.

In rehearsing my role I tried to show the differences in Mayakovsky's approach to people. Generally he wore a grim smile, as in his dialogue with Victor Malyshev, a young poet. But by the varying tones he used it was easy to tell what went on in his mind when he spoke to a person.

"Why repeat the word NEP to no purpose," he says in a harsh tone to the young poet. "Say: The New Economic Policy of the Soviet Government, that'll be quite plain. You don't object to the policy, do you? Speak up, don't be afraid, I'll report your grievances to the government," he adds in a subdued tone, "if they're worth considering, of course."

The change of tone makes it clear that Mayakovsky is fond of Malyshev, a hungry lad in a padded jacket, doing important work for the government. The lines that follow corroborate this. He tells the young poet not to feel disappointed that there is little time for writing poetry. "Just think of it," he says, "there will come a time when men will have everything, even pigeons' milk. Then you and I will sit down and write some wonderful poetry." Mayakovsky adjusts his young friend's scarf, slaps him on the shoulder and sends him off to work.

For me one of the high lights of the play is his monologue as he steps up to the window and catches sight of Alyosha and Olya standing on the snow-swept pavement. Alyosha and Olya are in love. The lines Mayakovsky speaks have the deep appeal of a lyric poem. "Look at the happiness written on their faces," he says. "They feel good. There is snow everywhere. But round them the snow is thawing. Flowers are budding. Everybody is cold. But Alyosha is not—he is perspiring at his forehead. He plucks a rose and gives it to the girl he loves. It is for them that the boulevards are blooming. And the people follow them with gentle smiles."

In this bit of monologue my problem was to *see* the two lovers, so that when I spoke my lines Marina, the secretary, who was not looking out of the window, could *see* them too, and with her the entire audience. Moreover, I had to cast a poetic spell over the audience. The monologue is recited to the accompaniment of soft music. The music ceases. "They're gone," says Mayakovsky, turning away from the window. "And there's snow again there ... everything's the same." And here for one brief moment there is a pause and Mayakovsky feels a pang of loneliness—there is just a suggestion of this in the play. But he quickly shakes it off, passing to a humorous vein: "Everything's the same ... the janitors are squabbling again."

The scene at the bookseller's was one which required a very careful following of my character's train of thought.

Mayakovsky arrives at the bookseller's after a long cross-country trip. He is eager to know what new books had come out during his absence. In the scene there are a few brief dialogues in which the poet's attitude to different types of people becomes apparent. He speaks now to one person, now to another, the dialogues, like the beads of a necklace, are threaded and put away into the recesses of his mind. Yet all the time he is thinking about his new poem called "A Soviet Passport."

The principal idea behind the scene is to show how deeply concerned Mayakovsky was with the course of the development of Soviet poetry.

In his dialogue with a young working woman who drops in to buy a book and mistakes the poet for a shop assistant, Mayakovsky shows himself as educator and servant of the people. Patiently and with his peculiar gift for reading people's souls he explains to the young woman the essence of real poetry. He picks up a volume of poems which she had rejected and turning the pages says: "This is what I think: let the verses be weak but penned with ardour. They may deal with trifles but lovingly. But the sugarish stuff in that volume can't go to your heart. It mustn't."

He makes the girl feel that she was right in putting the volume aside, and Mayakovsky flings it back on the counter.

Moving away a few steps he speaks his next lines softly and slowly as though trusting her alone with his innermost thoughts. "All this stuff is short-lived. Great poetry is still in the making." And by great poetry he means poetry that will be a strong progressive force in the advancement of society.

Another dialogue at the bookseller's takes place between Mayakovsky and a young poet called Babkin. The latter, red-cheeked, snub-nosed and robust, falling in with one of the literary fads, has written "Lamentative Symphony." Mayakovsky criticizes frankly and severely the trite verses of the poet who had submitted to pessimistic decadent influences.

"You must help to build communism," he says to him. "And do you understand the enormity of that task? People the world over eye us with admiration; some eye us with hatred. And you come here with your drivel, with your whining verses, loosening the screws of our great machine. It is easy enough to whine," Mayakovsky continues with a smile, "to touch the heart-strings, to play on the nerves, so that the public would get out their handkerchiefs. It is pleasant and brings good fees. But I tell you—take this poem away, hide it, and don't show it to anyone, not even to your fiancée."

Convinced that the young poet's pessimism is a mere pose, Mayakovsky parts warmly with him and wishes him success in his future work.

Another scene shows Mayakovsky in the office of a Komsomol newspaper. He arrives there after having read a booklet full of abuse against himself, published by a rabid slanderer. He is boiling inside but does not show it except for a more pronounced heaviness in his walk. Then suddenly the pent-up irritation breaks through his mask of calm. He vents, out his anger on Marina, the secretary, who is a true and dependable friend. He is rude to her as though she were to blame for all his misfortunes. Then he pulls himself together. "Forgive me for being a brute," he says. "It's just the state I'm in. It's overwork. I'm tired and I get no peace from my backbiters." Each of the abrupt sentences required that I read into it a good deal of meaning. I found it extremely difficult to act this scene. My outward manner was to be in sharp contrast to my inner state. To achieve this we wanted it to seem that Mayakovsky was pacing the office and speaking of quite pleasant things. The exterior calm intensifies the impression of the deep injury which he feels. "Everybody's used to seeing mud slung at me. . . . I've got to fight back, snap at my enemies." Mayakovsky speaks his lines straight at the audience. "The public swarms to the halls where I speak. People are curious, eager to know how things will turn out." The atmosphere becomes more and more charged with electricity, and when Mayakovsky, fumbling in his pocket, finds the slanderous booklet the scene becomes explosive. The editor of the newspaper appears, and Mayakovsky again withdraws into himself. But then Marina flings open the cupboard, and out of it come heaps of the hated pamphlet bought up wholesale by her and other friends and loyal supporters of the poet, Mayakovsky feels ashamed of his moment's weakness.

The storm is followed by a lull with a little romantic relief. Mayakovsky speaks kindly and softly to Marina who confesses her love for him. Gently Mayakovsky makes her understand that he cannot reciprocate. But already we feel his spirits soaring, particularly after the arrival of Dolgushin, a lad fresh from Kuznetsk where the first great project of the new Soviet Republic was under construction. All gather to listen to the news he brings and question him eagerly. To Mayakovsky, Dolgushin is one of the millions of new builders of socialism. His meeting with this lad inspires him to write a great poem which he calls "The Story of the Kuznetsk Project and its Builders."

Both the director and myself were up against the greatest difficulties in the seventh scene in which one of Mayakovsky's innumerable public appearances is faithfully reproduced. In this scene, taken from real life, Mayakovsky speaks of his travels abroad to a large audience at a workers' club. He replies to questions and recites some of his poetry. The principal features of the poet's personality are brought into sharp focus in the scene. Mayakovsky is shown as a poet-tribune, always in living contact with his readers. He speaks from a platform amidst the shouts, repartees and applause from an agitated audience.

In such a scene an effective set and well-planned mises-en-scène are of extreme importance. There were various suggestions of how to stage this scene. One of them was to seat supers in the orchestra pit for the audience at the workers' club which would merge with my real audience in the auditorium. This would have given me the opportunity of speaking my lines directly to the audience.

But the director and designer found a different solution—quite bold and unexpected. Alexander Tishler designed a slightly slanting dais for the stage platform of the club, a glimpse of brick wall, an iron door, wings, a grand piano completing the picture. The effect of a stage was intensified by a glare of "prop" footlights on the right side of the dais and above it the blazing of top lights. In between there was darkness, the black gaping hole which represents the auditorium filled with hundreds of imaginary listeners.

The scene opens with a burst of applause and cheers coming from that black hole after Mayakovsky had just recited one of his new poems. The poet approaches the table on the platform. On it is a heap of rolled papers—questions from the audience. He begins to answer them. It is clear that he is not a speaker who has "a way with the audience." He is a hard thinker. He does not speak down to the audience, doesn't meet it half way, but tries to elevate the audience to the level of his own thoughts and images. As he paces up and down the platform he is calm, the master of the situation.

In this scene the director uses a very effective device to draw the spectators into the action on the stage. In answer to the question "What made you travel abroad?" Mayakovsky with his back to the audience walks across the front of the stage and turning to his imaginary hearers speaks his next lines: "What made writers travel abroad before? To see things and marvel at them." Then coming over to the very edge of the dais he goes on: "And that is why I went. But there

I did not marvel, I made others marvel at what we are doing." Then he turns full face to the real audience and leans against the stage portal. Still speaking, he walks across the front of the dais and is caught in the spotlights. Meanwhile the footlights built in the set are extinguished and the whole stage is plunged in darkness. This creates the illusion of the dais turning. At this point I select a few individuals from among the audience to whom I address my lines—one or two spectators in the first row, one or two up in the gallery, in the boxes to the right and left.

In a short while I revert to my old position on the dais. The "prop" footlights are again turned on, and I stand in their glare. My imaginary audience in the black hole is again heard shouting and asking questions. I project my lines above their murmur and again, advancing to the proscenium, speak across the footlights to my real spectators. They include members of the cast who ask some of the questions. Thus I keep dividing my attention between my invisible audience and my real audience seated amidst the red and gold splendour of the Pushkin Theatre.

This scene is a very difficult one because the actor depends on himself alone to hold the attention of the audience. However, the effect produced by the brilliant lines, almost entirely based on Mayakovsky's actual utterances, more than compensates for the strain.

I had to be on the alert all the time. In a scene like this it is very important to get proper cooperation. I was very much dependent on the supers behind the scenes representing the imaginary audience. In explaining to my colleagues how I felt in this particular scene, I compared myself to a tightrope walker and them to the men holding the "safety net" below. A badly timed cue, a wrong response could upset the whole scene. It would make me lose my balance and fall to my "death." The supers, most of them young actors, understood how much the success of the scene depended on them, and I had never had anyone let me down.

This climactic scene presented yet another difficulty. I had to recite some of Mayakovsky's best-known poems. I sought for new colour in my tone and manner but at the same time I knew there were certain rules for reciting poetry which had to be obeyed. It is particularly difficult to recite Mayakovsky because of the peculiar form and rhythm of his verse. As in all poetry, it was important to do justice here both to the substance and to the form, and not to miss the musical quality inherent in the verse. But above all I wanted my audiences to grasp easily and at once the meaning behind the lines. To add force and bring out the colour in the poetry I tried to prolong the natural pauses between the lines. When I read bits from "The Soviet Passport" I tried to bring home to my hearers the deep patriotic sentiments underlying this stirring poem. Here there is sometimes one word to a line but behind that word, uttered staccato, very ringingly and with a well-measured beat, is a wealth of meaning, and subtleties which must be forcefully conveyed to the audience.

After the scene of the meeting there is a brief interlude. The animated public leaving the club-house after Mayakovsky's lecture passes across the proscenium. The curtain rises on the empty club-house with the top-lights extinguished. Fatigued by public appearance, Mayakovsky, with the coat over his arm and holding his cane, walks across the front of the dais, illumined by a single spotlight. Innokenty, an old friend, invites him to have a game of billiards. But before Mayakovsky accepts they get into an argument about poetry. In the heat of the argument it suddenly dawns on Mayakovsky that Innokenty is not a friend but a sworn enemy.

When we play this scene, my partner, Bruno Freindlikh, and I feel the tenseness in the audience which is fully aware that it is witnessing a pitched battle of ideas.

"Don't mind my saying it, Vladimir, but your poetry goes over the heads of the people," Innokenty drops the opening line of this dialogue with an affected casualness. These words from an avowed friend are a great blow to Mayakovsky. It is even difficult for him to grasp the true meaning of the words at first.

I pause here before speaking my lines and the hush in the audience is such that a pin dropped would sound like an avalanche. "If my poetry goes over the heads of the people, I'm the one to blame." I say this in faint, dull tones, as though talking to myself.

"No, you're not to blame for that, you're to blame for going out of your way to make your poetry understandable. That should be no concern of the poet's."

The words stagger Mayakovsky. Innokenty cannot be in earnest, he thinks. He must be jesting, and he replies with a smile, "Yes, poets were never faced with the great problems we face today." Mayakovsky is eager to hear Innokenty recant. He expects him to say: "Come, don't take it seriously, I was jesting, let's go and play billiards." But instead he hears venomous, shameful words that cut him to the quick.

"Great or not great," Innokenty declares with irony, "but I think, Vladimir, it is high time poetry occupied your mind." These strange words again come as a shock to Mayakovsky. The dialogue grows tenser.

"And what do you think occupies my mind?"

"Charity," Innokenty replies coolly.

"What do you mean?" Mayakovsky looks straight at him.

"I mean that you're too concerned about politics, propaganda, public education, the fight for peace and other such highly patriotic stuff."

"And you think all that is no concern of the poet's?" Mayakovsky retorts.

"Yes, that's what I think," Innokenty answers with a drawl. "These things have nothing in common with poetry." It is clear that Innokenty is voicing a highbrow conviction he has long held. A long pause follows Innokenty's lines. I use it to go through a series of movements: I approach the table, put my brief case and cane on it; with a measured step I walk to the grand piano and fling my coat on its cover; then I turn around and look fixedly at Innokenty.

"And these are your views. I dare you to repeat them," says Mayakovsky not wishing to believe that Innokenty is in earnest.

"I'll repeat them any time," Innokenty replies calmly. "These things have nothing in common with poetry," slowly and softly he repeats the words.

"Damn it, if I weren't so tired I'd lose my temper," Mayakovsky exclaims, still hoping that Innokenty would retract. But Innokenty's next line, "That won't change matters. You, Vladimir, are a poet and as a poet..." makes it clear that his hopes are vain. Mayakovsky then begins to hit back.

"Yes, I am a poet. But first of all I am a human being. And with my pen I serve the hour—put that in your pipe and smoke it. I serve present-day reality, life.... And don't you ever forget that!" These lines are spoken with great emphasis.

Freindlikh acts so brilliantly that sometimes we fear his shallow, biting speeches might move the audience to sympathy. I think one of the reasons this has never happened is because of the great admiration Soviet people have for Mayakovsky, which makes audiences eager to see his enemies crushed.

When Mayakovsky asserts that a poet is the mouth-piece of the people, Innokenty tries to preserve his composure but fails. His surging anger makes him stutter. He cries out: "I am not. I speak for myself."

"You're wrong again," says Mayakovsky with perfect calm. "You speak for the vanity and the stupidity of narrow-minded, self-centered individuals, who don't care a fig for society or for their country."

Here Innokenty completely tears off his mask and screams hysterically:

"Ours is an impoverished, semi-literate land, always having to learn from others. It will take it another hundred years to get anywhere near the civilized world——"

"I've heard enough," Mayakovsky cuts him short.

Mayakovsky slowly approaches the proscenium and turns to Innokenty, now seated on the table. He comes up close to him, slightly craning his neck to look into the eyes of the man who had turned out to be a foul creature, and speaks his lines: "I understand what you are." One feels in these words the immeasurable superiority of a giant looking down upon a gnat. His next words are: "Get out!" Mayakovsky then takes a chair, lifts it up high and with a bang brings it down beside himself. He drops heavily into it.

"A game of billiards," he utters sadly. With his head drooping, he chews at a cigarette, completely exhausted by the long meeting and by the strain of the unexpected crossing of swords with a man he had thought of as a friend.

There is a long pause. Innokenty, angrily striking the table with his cane, begins to threaten Mayakovsky. Just then Alyosha makes his appearance. He had stayed after the meeting, hoping for a chance to speak to Mayakovsky, and had witnessed the encounter between the two poets. No longer able to hear the insults hurled at Mayakovsky he shouts at Innokenty: "Get out of here!"

"And who are you to mix in my affairs?" Mayakovsky asks Alyosha gloomily, without recognizing him.

"Your affairs are our affairs, we'll always side with you."

"Who's that 'we'?" asks Mayakovsky.

"The ordinary Soviet people. The argument you were having concerned us as much as you. It's a class struggle, and we're with you."

The emotion that Mayakovsky experiences at these words is a complex one. He is glad to have found support and at the same time is somewhat disconcerted that anyone should imagine him unable to fight his own battles. With a gesture he cuts Alyosha short and asks him for a light. Later, in a weary, sullen voice he says to Alyosha: "Let's go." He picks up his brief case and coat.

"You don't recognize me, do you?" Alyosha asks shyly.

Mayakovsky turns to face him.

"I came to see you once at the 'ROSTA' Office."

Their eyes meet, and Mayakovsky recalls the lad in a soldier's great-coat who had once helped him to heat the office and paint posters. His face slowly breaks into a smile; he nods and says, "Yes, now I remember." They shake hands and look at each other. Mayakovsky realizes that Alyosha is one of the many he can fall back upon, one of the millions building a new society. And putting his arm around the lad he repeats cheerfully, "Let's go!"

Of all the scenes in the play this is my favourite.

We rehearsed this play in an atmosphere of elation. Our director, a man of great vitality and wit, turned our daily rehearsals into virtual holidays of the spirit. With actors of different generations and experience in the cast, he achieved splendid team-work. He helped to give flash and colour to many of the minor roles. An example of this is Freindlikh's performance as Innokenty. The audience is fairly mesmerized by his acting. He appears only in two brief scenes, and in one he drops but a few casual phrases. But the impression that his brilliant acting produces is out of all proportion with the brevity of his part.

Another actor, Kalinis, in the part of Dolgushin, also appears only in two scenes. But he portrays so well Dolgushin's profound faith in communism, his great enthusiasm and integrity, that he at once wins over the audience.

The director also helped by endless suggestions and guidance the actors Solovyov, Osipenko and Gorchakov, who play literary snobs and aesthetes, to put some real salt and pepper satire into their portrayals, and the actor Gorokhov to give a poignant characterization of the lying, slippery, boot-licking literary critic.

Some of the younger members of the company played Soviet youth of the 'twenties. They managed very well to enter into the mental attitudes and feelings of the characters they portrayed. And each of the actors has moulded a charming character of distinct individuality.

The colour that went into the production was varied—from lyric touches to biting sarcasm. But from the very outset the director aimed at blending all the colours and worked to develop a strong feeling of cooperation among the actors.

Just before breaking up for summer vacation each member of the cast received a present from the author and the director—a sealed envelope containing a poem by Mayakovsky which had some bearing on the character the actor played.

In high spirits we went off on our holiday hoping to complete our rehearsals successfully in autumn. While on holiday I kept thinking about my role. To create a character like Mayakovsky, I knew, required long years of preparation. And actually I did spend years in getting ready for this role. I feel, however, that in this role I am still at the foot of the mountain, the summit of which I long so much to reach.

When we returned, we reviewed what we had gone over in spring and gradually passed to stage rehearsals. This is always a difficult moment for the actor for he must now adjust his movements and his tempo to the larger space on the stage.

In the intervals between the scenes we often went upstairs to the designer's studio. Here Tishler would show us his models for the sets. He designed eight complicated interiors that are a credit to his talent. Our stage rehearsals were often watched by other members of the company who wanted to know how we were getting on. And as we went on to full-dress rehearsals the number of spectators grew rapidly. From them we got a good deal of criticism from which I, for one, benefited greatly.

I had never been so nervous in all my life as on this play's first night. I felt that I would be chiefly responsible for the success or failure of the show, particularly as the play had been written because I felt I was equal to the leading part. Just before the first night I received many anonymous letters from people in whose bad books Mayakovsky was and who longed to see the play fail. All through the preparation period I felt certain of its success, but at the première, in the very first scene, when I was reciting "Left March" I was so nervous that my colleagues noticed it.

However, the première went off well. The audience responded warmly, and there was much applause. Most of it, I think, was a tribute to the hero of the play, the poet himself.

After the first night performance our director introduced many changes in the arrangement of the scenes. He also drew our attention to new elements in the acting which he had noticed. At the same time he made a special point of warning against too much stress on historical details and a too pronounced academic spirit.

"Comrades, give the play a contemporary ring!" was his admonition.

Nor was it difficult for the cast to do this, for most of what Mayakovsky says in the play has a deep appeal for the modern audience. I was even often tempted in the middle of the play to cease acting and to cry out to the audience: "Comrades, my lines are the very words once uttered by the poet himself."

I remember speaking one day to a talented and clever fellow-actor and telling him how people tried to talk us out of staging this play.

He replied: "Well, I, too, think it's quite a miracle that it has turned out such a success."

Miracles don't happen. It was simply that the dramatist, the director and the designer were extremely enthusiastic about the production of this play and were great admirers of the poet. Their zeal was an inspiring example to the whole cast and all were eager to pay the highest tribute to so great and beloved a poet.

Soviet spectators were not alone in their deep appreciation of our efforts to bring Mayakovsky to the stage. We had visitors from other countries at our performances. Among them were Indian guests, such as Khwaja Ahmad Abbas, heading a delegation of Indian motion-picture people, Raj Bans, the well-known writer and film director, the poet Ali Sardar Jafri and the playwright Balwant Gargi. We took the guests backstage, and Jafri said to me: "Don't keep Mayakovsky all to yourself. He doesn't belong to you alone but to us as well. We want to see a screen version of this play." There were also screen and theatre people from Cracow, Poland, delegates from the German Democratic Republic and the writers Louis Aragon and Elsa Triolet from France. I was somewhat afraid to act before the French visitors because they had known Mayakovsky personally. They said, however, that they were deeply stirred by the performance. When Elsa Triolet returned to France, she published a favourable review of the play in *Lettres Françaises*.

From Soviet spectators, particularly from students, we keep getting mail. Now and then the letters contain helpful criticism but on the whole the performance has met with approval.

I try constantly to perfect my characterization. Scenes from our production were screened for a television programme devoted to the 25th anniversary of Mayakovsky's death. I got a magnified view of my acting and was able to detect many flaws.

It is not uncommon for the writer when he gets a first copy of a new book to begin turning its pages. and feel that if he only could he would do the book over again and improve it greatly. The film actor often thinks the same, regretting that films, unlike books, do not come out in a second or third edition and that he cannot perfect his performance.

In this respect the stage actor is at an advantage. He *can* improve his performance. I have tried to correct errors and have found audiences extremely responsive to the efforts an actor makes to perfect his characterization.

I always feel greatly elated on the day I play Mayakovsky. I arrive at the theatre long before the beginning, taking my time over my make-up and concentrating upon my role. I like to hear the ringing voices of the very young members of the cast as they ascend the stairs to their dressing-rooms. I feel very happy—happy in the task of bringing the great Soviet poet's life and thoughts to the stage.

CPSIA information can be obtained
at www.ICGtesting.com
Printed in the USA
LVOW03s0012041017

551106LV00002B/377/P